The Palgrave L

Series Editors
Calum Neill
Edinburgh Napier University
Edinburgh, UK

Derek Hook
Duquesne University
Pittsburgh, USA

Jacques Lacan is one of the most important and influential thinkers of the 20th century. The reach of this influence continues to grow as we settle into the 21st century, the resonance of Lacan's thought arguably only beginning now to be properly felt, both in terms of its application to clinical matters and in its application to a range of human activities and interests. The Palgrave Lacan Series is a book series for the best new writing in the Lacanian field, giving voice to the leading writers of a new generation of Lacanian thought. The series will comprise original monographs and thematic, multi-authored collections. The books in the series will explore aspects of Lacan's theory from new perspectives and with original insights. There will be books focused on particular areas of or issues in clinical work. There will be books focused on applying Lacanian theory to areas and issues beyond the clinic, to matters of society, politics, the arts and culture. Each book, whatever its particular concern, will work to expand our understanding of Lacan's theory and its value in the 21st century.

More information about this series at
http://www.palgrave.com/gp/series/15116

Leon S. Brenner

The Autistic Subject

On the Threshold of Language

Leon S. Brenner
Institute for Philosophy
University of Potsdam
Potsdam, Germany

The Palgrave Lacan Series
ISBN 978-3-030-50717-6   ISBN 978-3-030-50715-2   (eBook)
https://doi.org/10.1007/978-3-030-50715-2

This Palgrave Macmillan imprint is published by the registered company Springer Nature Switzerland AG.
The registered company address is: Gewerbestrasse 11, 6330 Cham, Switzerland

Translation Note
All texts strictly published in French have been translated to English by the author.

Foreword

Abstract The foreword, written by Jean-Claude Maleval, introduces the reader to the abundant world of the Lacanian psychoanalysis of autism. Maleval is one of the prominent Lacanian scholars to engage the subject of autism today. In his introduction he provides a vivid description of several unique autistic traits elaborated from within the framework of Lacanian psychoanalysis. Several case studies are presented and provide an initial introduction to Lacanian notions such as the entry into language, the primacy of the sign, and the construction of the rim in autism. Maleval progresses to deliberate the work presented in the scope of this book and provides a general description of the content of each of its chapters.

This book presents a new approach to autism that does not describe it as a pathology but as a *mode of being*. It is rooted in the psychoanalytic elaboration of autism, initially presented by Rosine and Robert Lefort, who introduced the hypothesis of autism being a singular subjective structure in the 1990s; that is, a subjective structure that is distinct from the other subjective structures already elaborated by Sigmund Freud and Jacques Lacan: neurosis, perversion, and psychosis. Being rooted in this hypothesis, this book offers an original development of the conceptual foundations of the contemporary Lacanian clinic of autism.

It was the treatment of Marie-Françoise, a child exhibiting a severe form of autism, that led the Leforts (1998) to conclude that in the transference there is neither a sign for the function of the big Other nor evidence of a proper instatement of drive functionality (pp. 311–320). On top of that, the Leforts also noted that the poverty in Marie-Françoise' babbling seems to imply an interference in her alienation in the signifier.[1] On the other end of the autism spectrum, the Leforts only made use of the notion of the "double" in their attempt to explain the creative richness they identified among high-functioning autistic individuals; a notion that, in hindsight, appears to be insufficient. In order to determine the characteristic of the autistic structure, the development of a few more clinical elements seemed to be necessary. These elements, which the Leforts did not have at their disposal, have since been elaborated by several Lacanian psychoanalysts who contributed greatly to the psychoanalytic understanding of autism today. Many of these elements, like the notion of the autistic rim, the recourse to the sign, and the notion of autistic foreclosure, take center stage in this book. They are meticulously developed beyond their original designation and are presented in a comprehensive fashion in the English language for the first time.

The hypothesis of an autistic structure corroborates the notion of the "autism spectrum disorder" that replaced in the DSM-5 the previous designation of autism under the general category of "pervasive developmental disorders." The constant features that distinguish the autistic structure, despite the plurality of its manifestations, were already accounted for in the mid-twentieth century by both Leo Kanner and Hans Asperger—the pioneers of the field of autism research. Asperger (2008) argued that, from around two years of age, distinct autistic features "remain unmistakable and constant throughout the whole life-span. Naturally, intelligence and personality develop and, in the course of development, certain features predominate or recede, so that the problems presented change considerably. Nevertheless, the essential aspects of the problem remain unchanged" (pp. 67–68). Kanner had noted that out of 96 patients he diagnosed as being autistic at the Johns Hopkins Hospital, 11 had

---

[1] Babblings are speech sounds that a child produces at an early age and are arranged in nonsensical combinations, such as "bababa" and "deedeedee."

successfully adjusted themselves to society. Nevertheless, he emphasized that even they "have not completely shed the fundamental personality structure of early infantile autism" (Kanner, Rodriguez, & Ashenden, 1972, p. 31). This position is validated by Brigitte Harrison, a high-functioning autistic woman, who argues that "even when our autism becomes almost invisible, our structure remains autistic" (Harrisson & Saint-Charles, 2010, p. 29).

There are two opposing hypotheses as to the nature of the constant structural features that distinguish autism from other forms of "developmental disorders." According to the cognitivist approach, it is a unique form of intelligence. According to the psychoanalytic approach, it is a unique mode of subjective functioning. From the vantage point of the cognitivist approach, both these perspectives seem to be incompatible. However, by adhering to the psychoanalytic approach, the hypothesis of the specificity of autistic subjective functioning is able to account for the original way in which autistic subjects accumulate their knowledge and implement it in the development of a unique form of intelligence that characterizes high-functioning autistic individuals.

Today, it is generally agreed upon that two pervasive signs of autism can be detected at a very early age. The first is the avoidance of the gaze, which manifests itself at the age of three months. The second is a lack of joint attention, which starts from about the age of nine months.[2] These two signs are of the same order, as when autistic children avoid the gaze, they do so in order to refrain from communicating with others. These phenomena are not anecdotal; they persist even among high-functioning autistic individuals. However, one must emphasize that it is not only the gaze—the object of the scopic drive according to Lacan—that is problematic for the autistic child; all the drive objects that are mobilized in the first exchanges with the parents are more or less refused or retained by the autistic child—namely, the voice (invocatory drive), the stool (anal drive), and breast (oral drive). Why do we see the retention of the gaze in autism? Some autistic individuals say that it is too disturbing. Why do we see a

---

[2] Joint attention is attention overtly focused by two or more people on the same object, person, or action at the same time, with each being aware of the other's interest. For example, infants of around nine months of age with the capacity for joint attention can follow their parents' gaze and begin to imitate what their parents do (VandenBos, 2007).

general avoidance in all matters that have to do with defecation? One autistic child reports that it is due to a fear that his lungs will explode. Why do autistic individuals enter a state of mutism? Some say that it is due to a fear of emptying their brains. All these phenomena strongly suggest that autism is rooted in a fear of interacting with others; a fear that does not originate in a deficiency in the capacity to understand social relationships but in an irrational anxiety that the subject does not control. This anxiety brings autistic children to refuse to bring drive objects into an exchange. This is what high-functioning autistic individual and writer Donna Williams claims, when she points out that in her childhood everything that revolved "around the act of giving and receiving" remained "totally foreign to her" (Williams & Bartak, 1992, p. 66).

In the Lacanian clinic, we argue that autism originates in a retention of the drive objects (oral, anal, scopic, and invocatory). Because the yielding of the drive objects is the basis for entering into a relationship with the Other, the retention of these objects brings about a disorder of language. Thus, we see, from a very early age, that the cries of autistic babies are monotonous and lack modulation; that autistic babies are either surprisingly calm or constantly scream without stopping. In both cases, parents are not put in a position from where they could interpret these cries as demands. Therefore, we see that, unlike what the Leforts believed, autistic babbling is not utterly absent but is scarce and lacks social orientation (Chericoni et al., 2016).

Autistic children are not initiated into language through their babbling. Their entry into language takes place in solitude, independent of its communicative function, and essentially follows two paths: through echolalia or through the written word. The first path gives rise to what some call a "verbose language" (Lacan, 1989, p. 19) and others a "language of poets" (Williams & Bartak, 1992, p. 157). This form of language is barely utilized in an attempt to communicate with others but is capable of producing vocalizations or soliloquies that provide autistic individuals with a solitary form of satisfaction. The second path can be used in the creation of a "factual language" that, on the one hand, allows one to communicate with others but, on the other hand, is a language that is cut off from one's affects.

Since direct communication is a source of anxiety for autistic individuals, they tend to avoid engaging in the reciprocal exchange of invocatory jouissance. Correspondingly, Williams reports that the material of her echolalic verbose language hardly comes from messages that are addressed to her. She prefers to adopt her words from statements that are separated from their human source: "The development of my own everyday language was essentially based on repeating what I heard in recorded stories and in TV commercials" (p. 300). Thus, we see that anything that detaches the word from invocatory jouissance, whether it is a phone, a radio, a television, or a written medium, is instrumental for autistic learning.

The entry into language through echolalia is not accompanied by its subjectification. Therefore, it is a very different experience from the entry into language through babbling. First, "typical" children that communicate through babbling are in touch with their body. Through their babbling they express hunger, suffering, fatigue, well-being, and so on. For these children, certain vocalizations already appear at around two to three months of age and are used for communication with selected partners. This is not the case for autistic children. Their echolalic appropriation of language is not utilized for expressing their needs to others but for the imitation and reproduction of "sound-objects" that capture their attention. For example, Panayotis Kantzas (1987) argues that "Speaking in ready-made sentences means first and foremost that the use of verbal material does not involve the representation of the speaking subject. It is not deconstructed and reconstructed but simply reproduced as it is" (p. 108). Echolalic speech reflects the outside world without assimilating it. Therefore, it does not endanger the subject, for it does not insert the speaker into an exchange of communication. The fact that autistic echolalic speech is not utilized for communication but only for solitary satisfaction testifies to an interference in the subject's alienation in the signifier. This interference prevents the master signifier (*S1*) from being used in the subject's enunciation (Maleval, 2019, p. 218). Therefore, it takes a long time for some autistic individuals to start to actively use language from a position of enunciation.

Nevertheless, one must note that autistic children, even those presenting the most severe form of autism, are not out of language, nor are they unable to communicate. When they are unable to speak, they usually know how to make themselves understood by using a language composed of gestures. They do so by mimicking the object at stake or the desired action using signs that univocally designate a referent.

The spontaneous use of signs by autistic children was already accounted for a century and a half before Kanner. Already in 1800, French pedagogue Jean Marc Gaspard Itard decided to take a mute child he named Victor de l'Aveyron as a subject in an experiment in which he sought to initiate him into civilization. Itard (1993a) found that Victor understood a "pantomime" language. For example, he recounts that Victor could be sent to fetch water by positioning a vase upside-down, thus demonstrating to him that it is empty. Itard notes:

> The most amazing thing in his disposal to this form of communication is that he needs neither preliminary lessons nor a mutual agreement to be conveyed to him. I became sure of this one day through an incontestable experiment. I chose an object that I knew he has no preconceived sign for from a very long list of objects. This was, for example, the comb that his maid used to comb him with. In order to get him to bring it to me, I stood in front of him after ruffling my hair in all directions and presenting my head to him in such a disorderly manner. He understood me and I soon had what I asked for in my hands. (p. 309)

The fact that Victor did not need any preliminary lesson or agreement in order to understand Itard testifies to his capacity to spontaneously access language. In this case it was a sign language, in which the gesture remains closely related to the designated object; a sign language that he is able to mobilize in order to communicate, even when he is unable to speak.

In order to develop Victor's language and to surpass the obstacle of his mutism, Itard offered him a box with different compartments which contained the different letters of the alphabet. Victor managed to conceive that by assembling these letters together he can construct words that refer to specific objects. However, Itard's pedagogical efforts came up against an unexpected impasse. He (1993b) notes:

It was obvious that my student, far from having conceived a false idea of the value of signs, was simply applying them too rigorously. He had taken my lessons literally and, because I had confined myself to naming the objects in his room, he was convinced that these were the only objects to which these signs applied. Thus, any book that was not in his room was not considered to be a "book." In order to convince Victor to call a book that existed outside of his room by the same name, a perfect resemblance had to be established between the two. Therefore, one can see that, in his use words, Victor was quite different from children who began speaking by giving generic names to specific objects. He confined himself to understanding generic names in the restricted sense of specific objects. (p. 421)

The case of Victor, presented by Itard, underlines a major distinction between the autistic and non-autistic mode of access to language. Signs used by the autistic child adhere to the situation and context in which they were originally learned. In contrast, non-autistic children are initially inclined to over-generalize or hastily generalize. For example, they may call mammals and dinosaurs "dog"; they may use the word "chicken" for all birds and the word "glass" for all containers. This demonstrates that non-autistic children are initially inclined to separate the sign from the designated thing; an inclination that reveals the underlying function of the signifier, which, unlike the sign, enables generalization and abstraction. The autistic child, on the other hand, petrifies the sign to the designated thing and retains a concrete link between them. Because autistic children prefer learning language in solitude, they favor the acquisition of signs at the expense of the acquisition of signifiers. Signs are memorized one by one, object by object, situation by situation; while signifiers, incorporated in the words of the Other, are immediately situated in networks of oppositions that determine their meanings and vary according to context.

Since the acquisition of signs is not dependent on babbling, they do not possess the properties attributed to the signifier; properties that, Lacan argues, make the signifier suitable for ciphering jouissance. Accordingly, the majority of autistic individuals attest to a split between their intellect and their affects. Correspondingly, Asperger notes, as early as 1944, that "these individuals are intelligent automata. Social adaptation has to proceed via the intellect. In fact, they have to learn everything via the intellect. One has to explain and enumerate everything... Autistic children have to learn the simple daily chores just like proper homework, systematically" (Asperger, 2008, p. 58). Furthermore, Williams argues that "Autistic children are secretly trapped in a mutilated affectivity ... [they] have feelings and sensations but these have developed in isolation. They can't verbalize them in a normal way" (Williams & Bartak, 1992, p. 301). To this, Harrison adds: "The brain does not receive messages from the body, even though the brain and the body are doing their work independently" (Harrisson & Saint-Charles, 2010, p. 311). Finally, Temple Grandin, an autistic individual and notable autism advocate, enthusiastically compares her way of thinking to that of a computer (2006, p. 162).

The early refusal to bring the voice into an exchange leads autistic children to a solitary appropriation of language that results in its further development using the written word. Is it possible to incorporate oneself in a language that is cut off from invocatory jouissance? According to Lacan, this is certainly possible. He argues:

> The ordinary experience is that everything the subject receives from the Other in terms of language is received in a vocal form ... [However] The experience of cases that are not so rare, though people always bring up striking cases like that of Helen Keller, show that there are other pathways besides the vocal path by which to receive language. Language is not vocalization. Take a look at the deaf. (SX p. 274; brackets added)

While being deaf, mute, and blind, Helen Keller managed to obtain a university degree in 1904 and subsequently wrote a dozen books. Initially, she gained access to language through tactile sensations. This is how, according to her testimony, the mystery of language was revealed to her:

> Someone was drawing water and my teacher placed my hand under the spout. As the cool stream gushed over one hand, she spelled into the other the word water, first slowly, then rapidly. I stood still; my whole attention fixed upon the motions of her fingers. Suddenly I felt a misty consciousness as of something forgotten—a thrill of returning thought; and somehow the

mystery of language was revealed to me. I knew then that "w-a-t-e-r" meant the wonderful cool something that was flowing over my hand. (Keller & Sullivan, 1905, p. 11)

Such an apprehension of language can be described as "pointillistic" and "intellectual." It is distinguished from the entry into language through babbling. The latter form of language is rich in structured oppositions that already embody the properties of a mother tongue. Accordingly, the babbling of a Japanese baby is different from that of an English or a French baby. Moreover, the babbling of a baby conveys its emotions: joy, suffering, and the call to be heard. Therefore, we see that there is a clear distinction between assuming a language that is already structured and in touch with affects through babbling and assuming language in a pointillistic and intellectual way.

It should be noted that despite her extreme cognitive deficits, Helen Keller was not autistic. She felt the need to communicate and for this she invented a language of gestures. There was no evidence of her ever having eating disorders, or problems with defecation and, above all, she had a strong will to communicate which eventually led her to articulate herself in writting. Accordingly, one must note that, no matter how severe cognitive deficits may be, this does not necessarily mean that a child is autistic. If the child does not refuse entering social exchange and does not retain the objects of the drive, we are most likely not dealing with autism. Correspondingly, we see that, unlike autistic individuals who acquire language in solitude and through imitation, Helen Keller gained access to language through her interactive relationship with her teacher—Miss Sullivan.

Do autistic individuals learn language like the deaf? Laurent Mottron (2004) points out a crucial difference: "the deaf achieve socialization through gestures, while autistic individuals achieve socialization through writing" (p. 149). Many case studies demonstrate that autistic individuals prefer to access language in a way other than through social interactions. Moreover, while definitely preferring a language that is composed of gestures, autistic individuals do not use signs like the deaf-mute do. The former use a language that is composed of sound-forms that are closely linked to images of referents of visual or tactile origin. Thus, a sound-form can be a word, a sentence, a piece of language, a phoneme, a number, and so on. The signs used by autistic individuals oscillate between the iconization of sound-forms—when the subject translates them into images—and the naming of icons—when the sound-form corresponds to an image. Harrison's testimony corroborates this notion: "You take the 'visual' and convert it to a verbal language thus coordinating between the two" (Harrisson & Saint-Charles, 2010, p. 46). This use of signs corresponds with Lacan's definition of the sign provided in 1961: "a sign represents something for someone" (SXI, p. 207).[3] Unlike the signifier, the sign does not erase the trace of the thing, since its image remains; moreover, it does not cipher jouissance and it hardly can be used to signify any form of equivocation.

The signs used by autistic individuals are fundamentally distinct from signifiers on two levels: first—and this is essentially what Grandin describes in her book *Thinking in Pictures* (2006)—they remain attached to their referent—not erasing the trace of the thing represented. Second, they do not function as deposits of jouissance: a phenomenon that autistic individuals testify to by noting the disconnection between language and their affective life. The Leforts (2003) emphasized this point when they argued that "in the autistic structure the signifier fails to be embodied and thus fails to create an affect" (p. 87).

While thinking with signs is not all bad, they do not possess the capacity of signifiers to interchangeably combine together into different formations. Accordingly, their ability to convey abstraction is practically diminished, as they impose a rigid and continuous relationship between unrelated elements. This can result in the stimulation of a child's memory up to a point where the autistic child becomes a mnemonic genius that can sometimes acquire outstanding intellectual and linguistic skills, and even gain access to affects. That is while a typical child becomes a "grammatical genius," around the age of three years, when he or she learns the complexities of grammar without being taught anything about them.

---

[3] In *Television* (Lacan, 1990), Lacan introduced a new definition of the sign. According to Jacques-Alain Miller, this definition was introduced in order to complement the signifier in terms of jouissance. It is not this later definition of the sign that is referred to here.

Signifiers are adopted from a predetermined system that organizes them; whereas signs are initially apprehended by the autistic child one by one. However, they do not remain isolated units, they are not just labels, the subject gradually organizes them in memory in a particular way which allows him or her to compose them into a set of oppositional relationships. When Grandin (2006) uses the icons of "a dove or a pipe" to represent the abstract notion of "peace," she does not only attach these words to an image of a referent; she inserts the image of the dove into an oppositional relationship with other birds, and the image of the pipe with other objects that emit smoke (p. 17).

Not being able to spontaneously learn the grammar of language due to their isolated appropriation of signs, autistic individuals search for rules that organize the relationships between signs. They mainly find these rules in the order they discover in the world. This is why they find the immutability of these rules to be so important. Breaking the immutability of the order of the world damages the fragile organization of signs. The immutable circuits actualize the rules they invent for themselves and the regularities they observe in the world. Accordingly, Williams argues, that she was always "under the rule of a lot of very strict principles." She adds that she is aware that these were "her own rules" and that they were "not compatible with the carefree life of well-adjusted people" (Williams & Bartak, 1992, p. 139).

There is no doubt that high-functioning autistic individuals are capable of learning grammar intellectually. Moreover, they are able to elevate the sign to the level of a concept. They do so by detaching the sign from the situation in which it was originally acquired through the memorization of multiple references. Correspondingly, Grandin (2006) explains that she can attach a multiplicity of particular images to the same sign:

> My concept of dogs is inextricably linked to every dog I've ever known. It's as if I have a card catalogue of dogs I have seen, complete with pictures, which continually grows as I add more examples to my video library. If I think about Great Danes, the first memory that pops into my head is Dansk, the Great Dane owned by the headmaster at my high school. The next Great Dane I visualize is Helga, who was Dansk's replacement. The next is my aunt's dog in Arizona, and my final image comes from an advertisement for Fitwell seat covers that featured that kind of dog. (p. 12)

In addition to learning grammar and constructing concepts, some autistic individuals can also gain access to affects through memorization. For instance, Williams (2015) asks some of her peers to show her how emotions look like in order to memorize them by heart (p. 161). Harrison adds to this that autistic individuals "must first 'import' the meaning of emotions in order to conceptualize them" (Harrisson & Saint-Charles, 2010, p. 333).

The combination of learning grammar, constructing concepts, and memorizing affects leads some high-functioning autistic individuals to engage their bodies in their enunciation as well as to gain access to humor. They develop these capacities up to a level where it is difficult to distinguish their behavior from that of non-autistic people. Nevertheless, they might be distinguished on the basis of the difficulties they have in acquiring these capacities and through the subsistence of the traces of their sign language. On the high-functioning pole of the autism spectrum, the use of signs can develop up to a point where it can be referred to as a language composed of signifiers. That is, a verbose language that seems to allow subjects to express their affects, leading to a transmutation of the linguistic signifier into a psychoanalytic signifier—a sensor of jouissance. However, only few high-functioning autistic individuals reach this level, as even Grandin points out that a clear split persists between her intellect and her affects. On the other hand, this split is less prominent for Daniel Tammet and for Williams. Both have achieved a better apprehension of their emotions and feelings, as their inability to recognize and express them has greatly diminished and they attest to a new feeling of inhabiting their bodies. This feeling is manifest in what Williams (2015) calls the language of "simply being" (p. 285).

Frances Tustin's account of the "protective shell" had led Éric Laurent (1992) to suggest that one of the major characteristics of autistic functioning is the return of jouissance on the rim (p. 156). Three elements usually compose the autistic rim: the autistic object, the double, and specific interests. These will be thoroughly elaborated in this book. Joey's machine, for example, is composed of both an autistic object and a double. Joey cannot separate himself from his machine, which is supposed to provide him with the electricity that animates him. Later on, it becomes the source of his specific interest when he chooses to become an electrician (Bettelheim, 1967, pp. 250–260).

Laurent argues that the return of jouissance on the rim consists in a diversion of an excess of jouissance to the autistic object, which in turn animates the subject. For example, when Joey was plugged into his machine at the Chicago Orthopedic School, he became dependent on its ability to provide him with electricity. With the help of this machine Joey managed to harness the jouissance of the drive, enabling him, for example, to defecate by heating his stools and to regulate his diet when it accompanied him to the toilet. It had a speaker that helped him process his voice and many eye-catching light bulbs with other functions.

By plugging into a machine, or a double, the autistic child treats the feeling of lifelessness, of not having any vital energy, and relieves himself of having to make decisions. Without the elements of the rim, autistic individuals are not capable of interpreting their affects using signs and experience them as surges of anxiety. By plugging into a puppet, for instance, they attempt to regulate their jouissance on the rim. That is why many autistic individuals say that they want to be a machine or a robot—so that they will not feel any affects.

Operating on the basis of the rim, respecting and developing its protective function as well as its capacity to subdue anxiety, to regulate affects, and to provide a point of access to the social bond: these are the principles that guide the Lacanian psychoanalytic approach to autism today.

However, in a recent publication presented by the American Academy of Pediatrics, which concerns the identification, evaluation, and management of autism, psychoanalysis is not mentioned at all, seemingly sealing its fate in all matters that have to do with the clinical work done with autistic children (Hyman, Levy, & Myers, 2020). Admittedly, in the field of autism research, the most fundamental Freudian principles seem to be irrelevant. Nevertheless, the Lacanian approach to autism is not limited to these fundamental principles, as it entails neither the recollection of one's history nor the interpretations of the unconscious. Accordingly, one might even wonder in what way does the Lacanian approach to autism still refer to psychoanalysis. The Lacanian approach to autism is based on the inventions and passions of the child and not on the knowledge of the educator. Accordingly, it can definitely be described as a psychodynamic method. However, the Lacanian approach to autism does owe a lot to the Freudian discovery. We must acknowledge the fact that it was a psychoanalyst, Frances Tustin, who introduced the notion of autistic object. Moreover, the field of study of psychoanalysis begins when one realizes that some of our own actions lie beyond our control. Sometimes we even disapprove of them but cannot help repeating them. Correspondingly, the use of autistic objects, the double and specific interests are part and parcel of the autistic mode of functioning, but they exceed the individual's choice, even if each individual embodies them in his or her own way. Similarly, most autistic individuals have immutable behaviors that aim to create a local coherence in the world and are precursors for their specific interests. They serve the same purpose as the former. All these phenomena are the result of a unique mode of unconscious functioning that is specific to autistic subjects. They appropriate these behaviors in their own way, but their dynamic qualities originate from a source they do not control. This source is unknown to them but determines them much more than they can imagine.

What Lacanian psychoanalysis advocates today with regard to the treatment of autism (when it is necessary and desired) could more or less be described as "nondirective interactive strategies to foster interaction and development of communication in the context of play" (Hyman et al., p. 23). For American pediatricians, such an approach is consistent with methods based on developmental theories. According to these theories, interventions that treat autistic symptoms can fall into two main categories: interventions that are based on the Applied Behavior Analysis (ABA) approach—which seek to change behavior—and interventions that concern a child's development and focus on stimulating interaction dynamics. The Lacanian clinic of autism is similar to the latter, yet it is not based on a developmental framework but on a framework that develops a theory of the subject. It does not trace the steps to be taken in treating autistic subjects; it aims at a finer understanding—that of the autistic modes of defense against anxiety and of strategies aimed to protect oneself from the Other's desire. The latter are consistent: immutable behaviors and the election of the various incarnations of the rim. However, this approach takes into account that the inventions of each autistic subject are different, unavoidably dictating the assumption of a case-by-case approach. This is an approach that psychoanalysis has never ceased to advocate in order to detach itself from the universalizing reductive psychiatric discourses. The psychoanalytic treatment of autistic individuals does not aim at elucidating the past but at the construction of the subject. In it, the interpretations the psychoanalyst provides do not aim to contribute meaning but aim at a lack, as Rosine Lefort argued, in order to temper the excess of jouissance initially attached to the rim (1994, p. 281).

The Lacanian approach is not genealogical in the strict sense of the term. It does not search for the underlying biological cause of a certain mode of subjective structuring. Nevertheless, it does provide an insight into the functional causation of the psyche. Accordingly, it is fundamentally based on a conception of an autistic structure that is determined by three pivots: an initial retention of the objects of the drive, a restricted alienation in language, and an apparatus of jouissance that returns on the rim. In this book, these fundamental pivots of the autistic structure are elaborated in relation to a singular psychic constitutive mechanism the writer terms *autistic foreclosure*. This book comes to elaborate the causal properties of this mechanism on the basis of published clinical case studies but mostly entails meticulous conceptual work that is well versed in both the Freudian and Lacanian edifice. Accordingly, the functioning of autistic foreclosure is elaborated in comparison to other constitutive psychic mechanisms such as repression in neurosis and foreclosure in psychosis. Moreover, the functioning of autistic foreclosure is explicated in terms of its effect on the subject's mode of access to language and the functioning of the drive. By demonstrating that autistic foreclosure is indeed singular and not reducible to the functioning of neurotic repression or psychotic foreclosure, this book emphasizes the singularity of the autistic subjective structure. By doing so, it dictates the adaptation of a singular clinic for autism and progresses an ethical perspective that designates autism as a legitimate *mode of being* rather than a pathology. In the contemporary discourse of autism research, where clinical frameworks that disregard the notion of the subject predominate, this book comes to fill a crucial gap. It introduces—implementing the heuristic richness of the Lacanian approach to autism—a new notion of autistic subjectivity and the clinic of autism that has not yet become very accessible to the English-speaking reader.

*   *   *

This book will be divided into three major parts composed of eight chapters. Part I of this book will establish the perspective through which autism will be elaborated in this book. Chapter 1 will provide a glimpse into the world of autism research. It will begin by presenting a general description of autism in terms borrowed from its elaboration as an object of scientific research. This description will be contrasted with the designation of autism as a *mode of being* progressed by many high-functioning autistic individuals and autism advocates. The perspective through which autism will be designated in this book will then be situated in the intersection between the *realist* scientific approach and *normative* approach. This perspective, rooted in the psychoanalysis of Sigmund Freud and Jacques Lacan, will designate autism as a singular subjective structure that is not reducible to the major structures of subjectivity elaborated in psychoanalysis so far: neurosis, perversion, and psychosis. Chapter 2 will provide conceptual support for the general methodology adopted in this book. It will explicate the conceptual roots of the notion of *constitutive exclusion* developed in relation to neurosis, psychosis, and autism. In this chapter, Freud's account of negation will be associated with the constitutive function of repression and the structure of the subject in psychoanalysis. Relying on Freud's paper "Negation" (1925), this chapter will demonstrate how a psychic mechanism of *constitutive exclusion* is necessarily situated at the origin of all subjective structures accounted for in psychoanalysis. By doing so it will pave the way for the elaboration of a singular autistic mechanism of *constitutive exclusion*—autistic foreclosure.

Part II of this book will go on to elaborate the structure and internal functioning of two major psychic mechanisms of *constitutive exclusion* accounted for by Freud and Lacan—*neurotic repression* and *psychotic foreclosure*. It will do so due to the fact that the elaboration of the mechanism of autistic foreclosure is rooted in the specification of both these mechanisms. This part will be divided into two chapters. Chapter 3 will be devoted to the elaboration of the mechanism of repression according to Freud and Lacan and its role in the constitution of the neurotic subjective structure. It will mostly aim to provide a clear structural distinction between two mechanisms of repression: a primal *constitutive* repression and a secondary repression; that is, repression as *defense*. This distinction will be crucial for the further elaboration of psychotic foreclosure in relation to primal repression in the following chapter. Chapter 4 will be devoted to the elaboration of the mechanism of psychotic foreclosure according to Freud and Lacan and its role in the constitution of the psychotic subjective structure. The similarities and differences in the functioning of neurotic repression and psychotic foreclosure will set the ground for the elaboration of autistic foreclosure in the following chapters.

Part III of this book will present an explicit and thorough account of the structure and internal functioning of autistic foreclosure. This part will be divided into three major chapters. Chapter 5 will account for the functioning of autistic foreclosure on the basis of the model of repression provided by Freud and Lacan. It is through the explication of the different levels internal to the functioning of primal repression that autistic foreclosure will be situated on a level preceding that of the functioning of psychotic foreclosure: in comparison to psychotic foreclosure that is situated in opposition to *Bejahung*, autistic foreclosure will be situated in opposition to *Ausstoßung*. Chapter 6 will present three different frameworks through which the psychic object that is radically excluded in autistic foreclosure can be accounted for. These will include an account of the object of autistic foreclosure as the unary trait, as the hole in the topological figure of the torus, and as the voice—the object of the invocatory drive. In these three sections, an exclusive interpretation as to the nature of the object of autistic foreclosure will be presented as well as provided with further conceptual support, interpretation, and critique. The conclusions reached in Chaps. 5 and 6 will provide the conceptual foundation for the elaboration of the unique mode of linguistic functionality enabled by autistic foreclosure in the next chapter. Chapter 7 will account for the consequences of the functioning of autistic foreclosure on the structuring of autistic linguistic functionality. Firstly, it will account for the lack of access to the symbolic order in autism, described by many contemporary psychoanalysts in terms of the "lack of the Other." Following this section, the chapter will go on to contend that autistic subjects are still considered to be subjects of language but base their linguistic functionality on the logic and laws of the "sign" and not of the "signifier." This exact mode of linguistic functionality will be elaborated and will form the basis for the articulation of a model explicating the varying modalities in the construction of the supplementary rim in autism. This model will be posed as an alternative framework for the development of the clinic of autism. The conclusions reached in this chapter, alongside the conclusions reached in previous chapters, will provide strong support for the designation of autism as a singular subjective structure in Chap. 8. This chapter will summarize all the conclusions reached in the previous chapters and substantiate the hypothesis that autism is a singular subjective structure. It will include a section that highlights the significance of these conclusions in the field of autism research. Finally, it will disclose several prospects for further research in the fields of psychoanalysis as well as empirical psychology.

Rennes, France   Jean-Claude Maleval

* Translated from French by Leon S. Brenner.

Works Cited

Asperger, H. (2008). "Autistic Psychopathy" in Childhood. In U. Frith (Ed.), *Autism and Asperger Syndrome* (pp. 37–92). Cambridge, UK: Cambridge University Press.

Bettelheim, B. (1967). *The Empty Fortress*. New York: The Free Press.

Chericoni, N., de Brito Wanderley, D., Costanzo, V., Diniz-Gonçalves, A., Leitgel Gille, M., Parlato, E., et al. (2016). Pre-linguistic Vocal Trajectories at 6–18 Months of Age as Early Markers of Autism. *Frontiers in Psychology, 7,* 1595.

Grandin, T. (2006). *Thinking in Pictures, Expanded Edition: My Life with Autism*. New York: Vintage.

Harrisson, B., & Saint-Charles, L. (2010). *L'autisme, au-delà des apparences: le fonctionnement interne de la structure de pensée autistique.* Rivière-du-Loup/Québec: Edition Concept Consulted.

Hyman, S. L., Levy, S. E., & Myers, S. M. (2020). Identification, Evaluation, and Management of Children with Autism Spectrum Disorder. *Pediatrics, 145*(1).

Itard, J. M. G. (1993a). De l'éducation d'un homme sauvage et des premiers développements physiques et moraux du jeune sauvage de l'Aveyron. In T. Gineste (Ed.), *Victor de l'Aveyron. Dernier enfant sauvage, premier enfant fou.* Paris: Hachette.

Itard, J. M. G. (1993b). Rapport fait à son Excellence le Ministre de l'Intérieur, sur les nouveaux développements et l'état actuel du sauvage de l'Aveyron. In T. Gineste (Ed.), *Victor de l'Aveyron, Dernier enfant sauvage, premier enfant fou.* Paris: Hachette.

Kanner, L., Rodriguez, A., & Ashenden, B. (1972). How Far Can Autistic Children Go in Matters of Social Adaptation? *Journal of Autism and Childhood Schizophrenia, 2*(1), 9–33.

Kantzas, P. (1987). *Le passe-temps d'un Dieu, Analyse de l'autisme infantile.* Paris: Dialogue.

Keller, H., & Sullivan, A. (1905). *The Story of My Life.* New York: Grosset & Dunlap.

Lacan, J. (1989). Geneva Lecture on the Symptom. *Analysis,* (1), 7–26.

Lacan, J. (1990). *Television.* New York: Norton & Company.

Lacan, J. (2001). In J.-A. Miler (Ed.), *The Seminar, Book XI, The Four Fundamental Concepts of Psychoanalysis (1964).* New York: Norton & Company.

Laurent, E. (1992). Discusion. In *L'Autisme et la Psychanalyse.* Toulouse, France: Presses Universitaires du Mirail.

Lefort, R., & Lefort, R. (1994). *Birth of the Other.* Oxford, UK: University of Illinois Press.

Lefort, R., & Lefort, R. (1998). L'autisme, spécificité. In *Le symptom-charlatan* (pp. 311–320). Paris: Threshold.

Lefort, R., & Lefort, R. (2003). *La Distinction de L'Autisme.* Paris: Seuil.

Maleval, J.-C. (2019). De l'aliénation retenue chez l'autiste. *Ornicar? Revue Du Champ Freudien, 53*, 208–230.

Mottron, L. (2004). *L'autisme: une autre intelligence.* Brussels, Belgium: Mardaga.

VandenBos, G. R. (2007). *APA Dictionary of Psychology.* Washington, DC: American Psychological Association.

Williams, D. (2015). *Somebody Somewhere: Breaking Free from the World of Autism.* Portland, OR: Broadway Books.

Williams, D., & Bartak, L. (1992). *Si on me touche je n'existe plus: le témoignage exceptionnel d'une jeune autiste.* Paris: Robert Laffont.

Acknowledgments

I would like to express my appreciation and gratitude to those who have contributed to this book and made it possible. First, I would like to express my gratitude to Professor Ruth Ronen, my advisor and mentor, for her continuous support, patience, and motivation, all of which enabled the research on which this book is based. Heartfelt thanks go to Professor Jean-Claude Maleval, who inspired a lot of the work presented in this book and had also agreed to write its foreword. Further thanks go to Professors Jan Slaby and Hans-Peter Krüger for supporting my research and making it possible. Deep gratitude goes out to my family and all my friends and loved ones for supporting me spiritually throughout the writing of this book and in my life in general. Finally, special thanks go to Jad Abumrad and Robert Krulwich for producing their terrific podcast Radiolab. It was Radiolab's episode "Juicervose" (2014), disclosing the personal story of Owen, that sparked my curiosity about autism and inspired me to develop a framework through which Owen's growth as an autistic individual could be appreciated and understood.

Cover artwork by Joshua Mößmer

About the Book

This book investigates the notion of autistic subjectivity. It aims to designate autism as a singular *mode of being* that is fundamentally linked to one's identity and basic practices of existence; this designation is posed as an alternative to its general determination as a mental or physical disorder. This alternative perspective on autism finds its origin in the psychoanalytic understanding of the *subject* according to Sigmund Freud and Jacques Lacan. On the basis of this psychoanalytic framework, autism is associated with what Freud defines as a mental structure and Lacan as a subjective structure. Accordingly, the unique features of the autistic subjective structure are investigated and conceptually developed. These features are compared to those of the neurotic and the psychotic subjective structures in order to provide sufficient evidence that attests to the singularity of the autistic subjective structure. This singularization of autism finds its point of departure in the notion of a unique *constitutive exclusion* at the origin of autism. The development of this notion hinges on the psychoanalytic position according to which the defining characteristics of a subjective structure are determined by a constitutive psychic mechanism of exclusion. Accordingly, the lion's share of the work in this book is invested in the structural elaboration of the constitutive psychic mechanism at the origin of autism—*autistic foreclosure*; this elaboration entails its distinction from two constitutive psychic mechanisms at the origin of neurosis and psychosis—repression (*Verdrängung*) and foreclosure (*Verwerfung*), respectively. In order to substantiate the singularity of autistic foreclosure, three decisive factors of its functioning are investigated: (1) its position in the model of repression presented by Freud, (2) the exact nature of its object of exclusion, and (3) the unique mode of linguistic functionality it enables. By distinguishing autistic foreclosure in this way, its singularity as well as that of the autistic subjective structure is substantiated; therefore, autism is designated as a singular subjective structure—irreducible to any of the three major subjective structures elaborated by Freud and Lacan. This warrants the postulation of a new clinical approach to autism offered at the conclusion of this book based on the notion of the "autistic linguistic spectrum."

Contents

Abbreviations

Works frequently cited throughout this study are identified by the following abbreviations:

1. Citations from Freud's papers will be marked by the letters SE (standing for "Standard Edition") followed by a volume number in Roman numerals and a page number:
   Example: (SE XIX, p. 237)
   Sigmund, Freud. "Negation." *The Standard Edition of the Complete Psychological Works of Sigmund Freud, Volume XIX* (1923–1925). Ed. James Strachey. London: Hogarth Press, 1925. p. 237.
2. Citations from Lacan's published seminars will be marked by the letter S (standing for "Seminar") followed by their number in Roman numerals and a page number:
   Example: (SI, p. 125)
   Lacan, Jacques. *The Seminar of Jacques Lacan, Book I: Freud's Papers on Technique* (1953–1954). New York: Norton, 1988. p. 125.
3. Citations from Lacan's unpublished seminars will be marked by the letter S (standing for "Seminar") followed by their number in Roman numerals and the date of the seminar session:
   Example: (SIX, 6.12.61)

Lacan, Jacques. *The Seminar, Book IX. Identification* (1961–1962), Trans. Gallagher, C. Unpublished. 6.12.61.
4. Citations from Lacan's *Écrits.*, Trns. Bruce Fink. New York: Norton & Company, 2006, will be marked by the letter É and a page number: Example: (É, p. 356)

List of Figures

Part I

Subjectivity Negativity

1

Autism as a Mode of Being

Situating Our Perspective in the Field of Autism Research

Autism is commonly defined today as a complex developmental disorder affecting the brain's normal development of social and communication skills and typified by restricted and repetitive patterns of behavior (APA, 2013). Autism is considered to be a pervasive disorder, in which symptoms first appear in early infancy, lasting throughout an individual's lifetime, with poor prognosis in terms of remission (Myers & Johnson, 2007). In its most severe forms, autism may cause an extreme withdrawal from the external world, entailing little or no social interaction as well as persistent repetition of non-adaptive routines and behaviors. In its milder forms, autistic individuals can lead relatively normal lives, primarily struggling with the development of their communication skills as well as having difficulties integrating into society.

Autism was initially designated as a distinct psychological syndrome in the mid-twentieth century by two contemporary psychiatrists: Leo Kanner and Hans Asperger. Until that time, autism was considered to be a unique form of psychosis called "childhood psychosis" due to its early

© The Author(s) 2020
L. S. Brenner, *The Autistic Subject*, The Palgrave Lacan Series,
https://doi.org/10.1007/978-3-030-50715-2_1

onset of symptoms (Potter, 1933; Kanner, 1971). It was Kanner's seminal paper, "Autistic Disturbances of Affective Contact" (Kanner, 1943), that, for the first time, extracted autism from the domain of psychosis and designated it as a distinct syndrome.[1] In this paper, Kanner developed an initiatory account of the singularity of autistic symptomatology. Among the many defining characteristics deduced from the behavior of his autistic patients, Kanner accounted for: late acquisition of linguistic skills; mechanical use of language (mainly focused on the use of nouns and personal pronouns); parrot-like repetition of sounds and words ("delayed echolalia"); general ignorance of the presence of other people; treatment of people like objects; adverse reaction to loud noises and moving objects; poorly coordinated gait; as well as lack of spontaneity and fussiness about food. These unique autistic traits were designated by Kanner under two original meta-psychological categories: "sameness" and "aloneness." Under the first, Kanner designated all those autistic traits having to do with the persistent desire for the maintenance of a static world in which change is not tolerated (Kanner, 1943, p. 245; 1951, p. 106). Under the second, Kanner designated all those characteristics having to do with difficulties in communication and the general disinterest in forming relationships with other people (Kanner, 1943, p. 242). The categories of sameness and aloneness articulated by Kanner can still be found today in a revised or altered manner in some diagnostic manuals.

The most contemporary manual cataloguing the different characteristics meriting a psychiatric diagnosis of autism is the fifth edition of the American Psychiatric Association's *Diagnostic and Statistical Manual of Mental Disorders* (DSM-5). The DSM-5 offers a standardized method for the diagnosis of autism, distributing autistic individuals on a spectrum of "functionality" according to which autism has been re-defined under the scope of the "autism spectrum disorder" (ASD).[2] In the DSM-5, autistic symptoms are divided into two major groups. The first major group includes persistent deficits in social interaction and social communication. Under social interaction deficits the DSM-5 notes: abnormal social

---

[1] It is important to note that Asperger was developing a similar theory at the time in Austria. The work of Kanner and Asperger forms the basis of the modern study of autism.

[2] The following section directly quotes from the DSM-5 (APA, 2013).

approach; difficulties in conversation; reduced sharing of interests, emotions or affects; and a failure to initiate or respond to social interactions. These result in deficits in the development, maintenance, and understanding of relationships at all ages. Under social communication deficits the DSM-5 notes: deficits in verbal and nonverbal communication; abnormalities in eye contact and body language; as well as a difficulty in understanding communicative gestures and facial expressions. The second major group includes repetitive patterns of behavior manifesting as: repetitive motor movements; use of objects or speech (echolalia); inflexibility and adherence to routines or ritualized patterns of verbal or nonverbal behavior; highly restricted and fixated interests; and hyper- or hypo-activity in response to sensory input. According to the DSM-5, the severity of autism is determined by the accumulation of specific symptoms provided in these two major groups. The more symptoms an individual exhibits and the more acute the symptoms are in their behavioral manifestation, the more severe a diagnosis of autism will be, varying on a spectrum between "high-functioning" and the more severe "low-functioning" autism (APA, 2013). Accordingly, we see that the DSM-5 conditions the diagnosis of an individual on the autism spectrum on the quantitative accumulation of autistic behavioral traits.

Regardless of the exact diagnostic framework used to identify autistic symptoms, the prevalence of individuals diagnosed today as being somewhere on the autism spectrum is drastically rising (Blaxill, 2004). The current prevalence of children diagnosed as autistic is estimated to be approximately 1% (Elsabbagh et al., 2012) but has also been reported to be as high as 2.5% (Kim et al. 2011; Xu, Strathearn, Liu, & Bao, 2018). The rising prevalence in cases of autism has made it a popular object of scientific research. Accordingly, while previously the investigation of autism took place solely in the psychologist's or psychoanalyst's clinic, today it can be observed that scientists from a multitude of fields attempt to clarify the underlying causes of autism—explaining its symptomatology using different tools that designate it in behavioral, cognitive, physiological, biological, and genetic terms.

One of the major epistemological presuppositions underlying scientific research is that while scientific knowledge is dynamic and changing, the objects of science are knowledge-independent entities in the world.

Correspondingly, the majority of scientific studies on the subject of autism are rooted in this "realist" approach, addressing autism as a knowledge-independent phenomenon that has been affecting humans even before its discovery and contemporary categorization. Scientists ask: what *kind* of thing is autism? Is it a psychological, physiological, or genetic condition? Scientists also ask what makes autism a singular instance of each of these categories? Which behaviors and conditions distinguish it? They execute meticulously constructed empirical studies in order to clarify these questions and to explain what the essence of autism is (Cushing, 2012, p. 24).

Nevertheless, in spite of the growing amount of publications concerning the subject of autism, the scientific community of the twenty-first century still does not have a clear conception of the essence of autism (pp. 38–39). While the ever-changing behavioral categorization of autism can be found in the DSM-3–5, the multiple attempts to locate its underlying cause in this way have been unsatisfactory up to this day (Grandin, 2006, pp. 35–36; Wing, Gould, & Gillberg, 2011). Various other cognitive theories concerning autism fail to explain the abundance of behavioral conditions presented in different cases (Rajendran & Mitchell, 2007), while other meta-psychological theories are unsuccessful in defining an essential positive category designating autism (Barnbaum, 2008). Biological research suggests results that are either related specifically to a small subset of symptoms or not distinctive to autism alone (Šestan, 2012). Finally, genetic-based research might explain the prevalence of autism in familial groups (Sandin et al., 2014) but has not yet been able to differentiate and pinpoint a specific genetic cause that explains the variance in symptoms and behavior (Cushing, 2012, p. 38; Maleval, 2012, p. 27). When taking this into consideration—as well as the rising prevalence of individuals diagnosed as autistic and the profound impact it has on them and their families—it can be understood why the investigation of autism is still relevant and important for researchers from a multitude of fields and practices.

However, while the work achieved by the scientific community on the subject of autism is vast and crucially important, there remains an acute disparity between, on the one hand, the theoretical and practical frameworks developed in these fields and, on the other hand, the subjective testimonies of "high-functioning" autistic individuals presented in books and popular media. This disparity is not rooted in the use of different terminologies but rather is a manifestation of a qualitative difference between these two descriptive paradigms. While scientists designate autism as a mental or physical disorder to be objectively studied—and as a result to be contained—many autistic individuals attribute autism to their sense of selfhood, defining it as a unique mode of openness to the world that is an immanent aspect of their subjectivity. They describe autism as a *mode of being*, fundamentally linked to their identity and most basic practices of existence. In this sense, they explicitly argue that autism is not a handicap that should be eradicated and state accordingly that they would not wish to rid themselves of their autism even if they had a choice in the matter.[3]

Such testimonies by autistic individuals are plentiful and compose a wide corpus that forwards the notion that autism should be viewed as an accepted *mode of being* as well as questioning the very notion of a "cure" for autism. One of the most renowned autistic individuals and advocates of autistic rights today is Temple Grandin. In her book *Thinking in Pictures* (Grandin, 2006), she explicitly contends: "If I could snap my fingers and be non-autistic, I would not, because then I wouldn't be me. Autism is part of who I am" (p. xviii). Jim Sinclair, an autism-rights movement activist and founder of Autism Network International (ANI), delivers a similar message in a written piece titled "Don't Mourn for Us" (Sinclair, 1993):

Autism isn't something a person has, or a "shell" that a person is trapped inside. There's no normal child hidden behind the autism. Autism is a way of being. It is pervasive; it colors every experience, every sensation, perception, thought, emotion, and encounter—every aspect of existence. It is not

---

[3] This can be contrasted to having type 1 diabetes for instance. Having diabetes from an early age greatly affects one's life, as a child must receive injections, count carbohydrates, and monitor blood sugar on a daily basis. However, while one might be psychologically affected by diabetes, it does not mean that it affects every aspect of one's psychology or understanding of the world. Thus, one may be said to *have* diabetes but not to *be* diabetic. On the other hand, many autistic individuals argue that autism is pervasive and colors every aspect of one's identity, experience, and understanding of the world. This is why, in this book it will be designated as a *mode of being*; that is, something that someone *is* in every respect and not something that someone contingently *has*.

possible to separate the autism from the person—and if it were possible, the person you'd have left would not be the same person you started with.

In a later interview Sinclair adds:

What the rest of the world needs to know about autism is that it's not something that can be separated out from the person, it's part of the person, and so you cannot meaningfully say I love my child but I hate the autism. (Shapiro, 2006)

In the last couple of decades, the moving testimonies of autistic individuals have been cultivated by a growing movement, struggling for the civil rights of all those diagnosed with neurological or neurodevelopmental disorders (Fenton & Krahn, 2007). Initially founded by autistic sociologist Judy Singer, and developed mostly by online groups since the 1990s, this movement is known today as the "neurodiversity movement" (Singer, 1999). The objectives of the neurodiversity movement consist of at least two aspects. The first is based on the idea that neurological differences among human beings, such as autism, should be accepted as natural neurological variations and not described as "disorders" (Griffin & Pollak, 2009). The second aspect moves this discussion into the domain of politics and calls for the equal rights, non-discrimination, recognition, and acceptance of "neurodiverse" individuals (Jaarsma & Welin, 2012). While the movement supports the clinical facilitation of autistic individuals, it opposes the conventional understanding of a "cure" for autism (Ward & Alar, 2000; Ortega, 2009). It does so on the grounds of the psychological harm it might cause autistic individuals (Barnbaum, 2008; Baggs, 2008), the price individuals may pay in terms of the loss of their personal identity (Shapiro, 2006), the loss of autistic talents expressed in the sciences and the arts (Biklen, 2005; Treffert, 2009) as well as the loss of what is today considered to be "autistic culture" and the diversity it produces in the fabric of humanity (Sinclair, 2006).

Taking all of the above into account, we see that while the scientific approach to autism is based on a *realist* theoretical and practical framework—striving to thoroughly categorize *what kind of phenomenon autism is* in scientific terms—the approach adopted by the advocates of the neurodiversity movement is more concerned with the *normative* aspect of such scientific work. It is invested in defining *how autism should be addressed* and is, in fact, rooted in the contention that autism should be addressed as a singular mode of human existence. In this sense, it is critical to the hegemony of the scientific approach to autism and aims to re-establish a *normative* discourse on the essence of autism that exceeds its scientific categorization and objectification.

This book progresses the notion that both the *realist* and the *normative* approaches to autism fall short of designating the singularity of their object and thus, to a greater extent, re-raise the question—*what is the essence of autism?* Accordingly, the general investigative perspective through which autism is addressed in this book will not be limited to one of these approaches but will be situated on the intersection between the *realist* framework and the *normative* framework. On the one hand, it will aim to elaborate the internal functioning and causality underlying autism, addressing autism as a knowledge-independent phenomenon that can be analyzed and elaborated in structural and functionalist terms. On the other hand, it will address autism as a legitimate *mode of being*, fundamentally linked to autistic identity and its most basic practices of existence. While remaining critical to the scientific elaboration of autism, this perspective will also emphasize the inherent subjective facets that are irreducible to the psychiatric categorization of autism as a disorder or pathology.

The conceptual framework through which this perceptive on autism will materialize will be rooted in Sigmund Freud's and Jacques Lacan's psychoanalytic conception of the "subject." According to Freud, the totality of psychic elements composing an individual's sense of reality, as well as the laws governing it, is defined as a *mental structure*. These would include, for instance, being situated in the world on the basis of a sexuated body,[4] subdued to an internal division between consciousness and the unconscious as well as swayed by the demands of the ego, id, or superego. In other words, Freud's meta-psychology strives to

---

[4] "Sexuation" is a term explicitly used by Lacan in order to designate the non-biological, denaturalized subjective positioning of masculinity and femininity. This term is very much distinct from the common use of the term "sex" or "gender."

account for an individual's *mode of being* on the basis of the psychoanalytic terms defining a mental structure.

In the course of his career, Freud attempted to isolate a limited number of general meta-psychological categories that represent the plurality of the *modes of being* available to humanity. These were eventually finalized in a list of three major mental structures prevalent in western society: neurosis, perversion, and psychosis. As will be elaborated in the following chapters, Freud (1911, 1924) did not contend with the phenomenological description of the prevailing behavioral characteristics of each of these mental structures; rather, he contended that it is the elaboration of the *fundamental constitutive psychic mechanisms* underlying their functioning that is the true goal of his meta-psychology (SE XII, p. 59; SE XIX, p. 185). Freud did not provide a finalized list of such mechanisms but did come to elaborate on the mechanism of repression (*Verdrängung*) as the underlying cause for the neurotic mental structure and the mechanism of disavowal (*Verleugnung*) as the underlying cause for the perverse mental structure. It is Lacan, in his seminar devoted to the subject of psychosis (1955–1956), who pointed out that Freud disclosed another fundamental constitutive mechanism underlying the psychotic mental structure— foreclosure (*Verwerfung*).

Lacan continued Freud's work at this point by combining the latter's understanding of an individual's *mental structure* with his structural-linguistic conception of subjectivity. Lacan offers a conceptualization of the human being as a sexuated "speaking being" (*parlêtre*) (SXXIII, p. 27), a being under the sway of the sexual drives (*jouissance*) and the signifier. Accordingly, when addressing Freud's list of *mental structures*, Lacan defines them as "subjective structures" (SI, p. 112; SX, p. 48; SVIII, p. 334). Furthermore, instead of distinguishing the fundamental constitutive mechanisms underlying these three major subjective structures strictly on the basis of the dynamic or functionalist terms borrowed from Freud, Lacan provides a structural-linguistic interpretation of the functioning of these mechanisms. He addresses them as linguistic mechanisms that determine the structure of the subject on the basis of a constructed relationship between jouissance and language. According to Lacan, it is the exact way in which these mechanisms substantiate the mediation between language and jouissance that determines a subjective structure.

Accordingly, based on the aforementioned framework provided by Freud and Lacan, the major goal of this book will be to substantiate the hypothesis that *autism can be accounted for as a singular subjective structure that is not reducible to any of the three major subjective structures elaborated by Freud and Lacan: neurosis, perversion, and psychosis.* This hypothesis is rooted in the basic psychoanalytic assumption that in the formation of subjective structures there is a cultural and historical dimension, and accordingly, as Bruce Fink contends in his book *A Clinical Introduction to Lacanian Psychoanalysis: Theory and Technique* (Fink, 1999), it is conceivable to think that other forms of subjectivity could emerge in culture (p. 77). The elaboration of this hypothesis will entail addressing the unique characteristics of autistic subjectivity in psychoanalytic terms that are both informed of the functioning of the psyche and sensitive to the designation of autism as a *mode of being.*

Autism from a Psychoanalytic Perspective

Autism was initially introduced into the psychoanalytic discourse in 1910, when Swiss psychiatrist Eugen Bleuler borrowed this term from Freud in order to designate a set of unique psychotic symptoms. Derived from the Greek word "autos" (self) and originating in Freud's account of "auto-erotism," this term was used by Bleuler (1950) to designate a unique form of psychotic withdrawal from the outside world:

> The most severe schizophrenics, who have no more contact with the outside world live in a world of their own. They have encased themselves with their desires and wishes… they have cut themselves off as much as possible from any contact with the external world. This detachment from reality with the relative and absolute predominance of the inner life, we term autism. (p. 63)

Freud never endorsed Bleuler's use of the term "autism" and is, in fact, known to explicitly oppose its use as an alternative to his notion of "auto-erotism." According to Ernest Jones (1957)—Freud's official biographer—in a correspondence with Marie Bonaparte, Freud remarked that: "no 'heresies' ever disturbed him so much as feeble concessions to opposition, such as Bleuler's substitution of 'autistic' for 'auto-erotic' so as to avoid the idea of sexuality; it would have been all right, he added jokingly, if Bleuler had inserted a footnote 'by autistic is meant auto-erotic'" (p. 77).

Following Freud's death, several notable psychoanalysts took it upon themselves to investigate the unique form of psychosis described by Bleuler, designating it under the category of "childhood psychosis." Among these one should note Margaret Mahler, a Vienna-based psychoanalyst who integrated Bleuler's account of autism into a theory of child development. Mahler (1967) argued that autism is a mode of defense specifically implemented against an infant's fundamental need for symbiosis with the mother.[5] She situated the onset of autism in a three-leveled developmental model taking place in the first three years of a child's life. Correspondingly, Mahler (1952) described two forms of childhood psychosis: the first, more akin to schizophrenia, originates in a failure in the transition from the second "normal symbiotic phase" to the third "separation-individuation phase" of development (p. 297); the second, identifiable with Kanner's autism, originates in a failure in the transition from the first "normal autistic phase" to the second "normal symbiotic phase" of development (p. 289). Mahler (1967) argued that, by remaining fixated on the autistic stage, children forfeit all emotional ties with their caretakers and also cut themselves from external and internal stimuli that demand affective response. She added that this form of extreme solitude hinders the child's apprehension of reality and causes the collapse of the boundary between self and object and a general disintegration of the ego (p. 756). This unique autistic state of withdrawal, and the fact that it can be located on a specific stage in the subject's structuration, will be a topic of major concern in this book.

---

[5] The active role of the mother in the onset of autism is a well-debated and criticized notion in the field of psychoanalysis. It is important to note that this book develops a rigorous psychoanalytic framework that does not adhere to this motif in any way but concentrates on the subject's relationship with language.

Another notable scholar that came to investigate autism from a psychoanalytic perspective was Bruno Bettelheim. Bettelheim (1967) composed a theory on autism that is based on Freud's psychoanalysis and the school of ego psychology but also on his personal experience as a Jewish intern in the German concentration camps of the Second World War. Corresponding with the brutal and inhumane conditions he experienced in the concentration camps, Bettelheim argued that autistic children withdraw from the world because of an early encounter with extreme conditions of living (p. 63). He called these conditions of "extreme helplessness" that present themselves in a completely unpredictable and life-threatening manner from which there is no escape. Bettelheim argued that when children are exposed to these circumstances in a very early age and lack a proper mitigating environment, they run the risk of conceiving the world as purely evil and, as a result, assume a position of extreme passivity and radical withdrawal from the world (pp. 81–82). *The Empty Fortress*, the title of Bettelheim's famous book on autism, is a metaphor for the emptied out, repetitive, and stereotyped internal world to which the autistic child withdraws. Correspondingly, Bettelheim argued that providing the autistic child with an image of a world that is utterly different from the one he or she initially encountered is a way out of this fortress (p. 93). Bettelheim's work with his autistic patients will be discussed in the course of this book, especially the case of Joey the "mechanical boy," which will exemplify the dependence on autistic ingenuity in the direction of the treatment of autism (Bettelheim, 1967, 1959).

One more psychoanalyst who carried out pioneering work with autistic patients is Frances Tustin. In her book *Autism and Childhood Psychosis* (Tustin, 1972) and many other future publications, Tustin described autism in terms borrowed from the British school of object-relations. Like Bettelheim, she argued that autism originates in an extremely unbearable experience in infancy but added that this experience has to do with the inevitable separation from the mother. Tustin claimed that an extremely traumatic separation from the mother at an early age brings the child to enter a static depressive position that brings affective and cognitive development to a halt. This depressive position is also characterized by a radical isolation from the outside world, where the child wraps itself with a protective shield. Tustin (1992) called this form of radical isolation the protective "autistic shell" and argued that being engulfed by it forces the child to forfeit access to its affects, its sense of selfhood, and all relationships with other people (pp. 191–207). In her work with autistic patients, Tustin (1972) also focused on the unique relationships they form with objects, noting how they surround themselves with hard objects with which they feel equated (pp. 60–68). She emphasized the way autistic children stick objects on their bodies, scarcely using them for their objective functions (p. 115). She argued that they conceive of them as parts of their body and thus gain a sense of self-sufficiency that protects them from the anxiety provoked by their encounters with the precarious outside world. Tustin (1992) argued that "autistic objects" are used in the construction of the autistic shell and, accordingly, are "pathological" and harmful for the child's development (p. 108). She suggested that the treatment of autism should involve the removal of these objects from the child's libidinal economy. In this book, Tustin's account of the autistic shell as well as her description of the autistic object will be a topic of discussion. In this discussion, the notion that autistic objects are fundamentally pathological will be protested and replaced with a more contemporary approach concerning the facilitative use of object in the clinic of autism.[6]

Lacan never addressed the subject of autism explicitly in his seminars or printed papers. Nevertheless, as will be presented in Chaps. 5, 6, and 7, he did deliver two explicit remarks on the subject of autism at two conferences he attended in the year 1975 as well as implicitly addressed autism in his elaboration of two cases of psychosis, which today, in hindsight, are considered to be cases of autism. These are Melanie Klein's (1930) well-known case of "Little Dick," and Rosine Lefort's case of the "Wolf-Child," both deliberated in the course of his *Seminar I: Freud's Papers on Technique (1953–1954)*. Lacan basically argued that, despite their apparent muteness, autistic subjects are in fact subjects of language, just like neurotic, perverse, or psychotic subjects. He stressed their unique relationship with language and started to elaborate on a most rudimentary form of identification warranted by this relationship.

---

[6] Many other notable psychoanalysts such as Donald Meltzer, Melanie Klein, Peter Hobson, Heiman Weiland, and Denys Ribas had worked with autistic patients. All of whom developed approaches to autism that remain sources for its understanding in psychoanalytic terms. Nevertheless, the work of these psychoanalysts will not be included in the scope of this book.

It was Lacan's followers who began explicitly addressing autism as a mental phenomenon independent from the domain of psychosis. This contemporary Lacanian approach to autism is primarily attributed to the work of Rosine and Robert Lefort. Credited with their pioneering conceptualization of the autistic subjective structure, the two came to establish the *École Expérimentale de Bonneuil-sur-Marne* in 1969, where they continued their work with autistic individuals. The work accomplished by the Leforts—as well as their many publications—laid the groundwork that would inspire later Lacanian psychoanalysts to approach this field, further developing their perspective. Among these Lacanian psychoanalysts one should note Éric Laurent and Jean-Claude Maleval, two major scholars whose works will be thoroughly deliberated in this book. With the direction of these prominent figures in the Lacanian field, psychoanalytic notions that are singular to autistic subjectivity started to be developed. As will be elaborated in Chaps. 5, 6, and 7, these were cultivated in the development of the psychoanalytic clinic of autism around the notion of the lack of the Other, the primacy of the sign, the retention of the voice, the development of the rim as well as the notion of the constitutive psychic mechanism of *autistic foreclosure*.

When addressing the unique features of the symptomatic manifestations of autistic subjectivity, Lacanian psychoanalysts describe them on three corresponding levels: autistic linguistic functionality, the autistic mode of access to the body or affect—what Lacanian psychoanalysts refer to as *jouissance*—and autistic identity. Abnormalities in language and speech development are considered to be a defining feature characterizing individuals who are diagnosed today on the autism spectrum. However, in the field of Lacanian psychoanalysis these abnormalities are associated with alterations in the mode of access to the locus of the signifier and the disposition to the use of linguistic signs. As will be disclosed in Chap. 7, the primacy of the sign affects the way autistic individuals experience of the world on a multiplicity of levels and clearly distinguishes their behavior from that of psychotic individuals for example. In Chaps. 6 and 7 the autistic unique mode of access to jouissance will be elaborated in terms of the retention of the object of the invocatory drive (the voice) and the return of jouissance on the rim. These distinct characteristics of the autistic libidinal economy directly affect the capacity of autistic individuals to speak and also warrants a unique mode of satisfaction that finds its focus on the periphery of the body and the surfaces of objects. The singular features in the formation of autistic identity will also be discussed in Chaps. 6 and 7 as well as in the final chapter of this book. These materialize on the level of the formation of the ego and in the relationship between the subject and the body: a relationship that Lacan also directly associates with the coordination of the perceptual system and the capacity to navigate and situate oneself in three-dimensional space (É, p. 77).

All of these unique traits are described in a variety of case studies provided by Lacanian psychoanalysts since the days of Rosine and Robert Lefort and up to this day. These paint a picture of autism that is not determined as an alteration in a "normal" state of development but as a pervasive subjective vantage point that affects every aspect of the internal and external experience of the world from birth—a *mode of being*. Accordingly, in the psychoanalytic clinic of autism, one is not expected to rid him- or herself of his or her autistic traits but to find the means through which these traits can facilitate the development of a unique mode of access to language and the entry into the social bond.

In this book, the elaboration of the autistic *mode of being* will be rooted in the clinical and conceptual framework provided by the aforementioned psychoanalysts. However, instead of accounting for its singularity on the basis of the symptoms and behaviors these psychoanalysts meticulously elaborated in their work, *the singularity of the autistic subjective structure will be accounted for on the basis of the structural elaboration of the constitutive psychic mechanism that is their underlying cause; a mechanism of constitutive exclusion I propose to call autistic foreclosure.* Accordingly, in the course of this book, the psychoanalytic understanding of the autistic *mode of being* will be conceptually developed with a focus on this mechanism's internal functioning. This will lead to an elaboration of the unique mode of autistic linguistic functionality that is enabled by this mechanism and manifests in the distinctive form of autistic jouissance confronted in the clinic of autism. One must stress that due to the fact that autistic foreclosure is associated with Lacan's account of foreclosure in psychosis, as well as the fact that autism has been initially conceived as "childhood psychosis," *another major goal of this book is to specifically differentiate autistic foreclosure from the foreclosure operating in psychosis.*

By adhering to the aforementioned investigative aims, a framework will be provided through which autism can be addressed differently: first, by defining autism as a real knowledge-independent phenomenon, irreducible to its behavioral manifestations or its symptomatic categorization; second, by designating autism as a singular subjective structure—a singular *mode of being*; finally, by attributing the singularity of the autistic subjective structure to the defining characteristic of the constitutive psychic mechanism at its origin. By doing so, this book will provide an alternative to the common determination of autism as a mental or physical disorder, emphasizing the importance of psychoanalytic theorization in the field of autism research.

Works Cited

American Psychiatric Association. (2013). *DSM 5*. *American Journal of Psychiatry* (5th ed.). Washington, DC: American Psychiatric Publishing.

Baggs, A. (2008). The World I Want to Live in. *Autistics.Org – Autism Information Library*. Retrieved from http://archive.autistics.org/library/want.html

Barnbaum, D. R. (2008). *The Ethics of Autism: Among Them, but Not of Them*. Bloomington, IN: Indiana University Press.

Bettelheim, B. (1959). Joey, a 'mechanical boy'. *Scientific American, 200*(3), 116–130.

Bettelheim, B. (1967). *The Empty Fortress*. New York: The Free Press.

Biklen, D. (2005). *Autism and the Myth of the Person Alone*. New York: New York University Press.

Blaxill, M. F. (2004). What's Going on? The Question of Time Trends in Autism. *Public Health Reports, 119*(6), 536–551.

Bleuler, E. (1950). *Dementia Praecox or the Group of Schizophrenias*. Oxford: International Universities Press.

Cushing, S. (2012). Autism: The Very Idea. In J. L. Anderson & S. Cushing (Eds.), *The Philosophy of Autism* (pp. 17–46). Lanham, MD: Rowman & Littlefield Publishers.

Elsabbagh, M., Divan, G., Koh, Y., Kim, Y. S., Kauchali, S., Marcín, C., et al. (2012). Global Prevalence of Autism and Other Pervasive Developmental Disorders. *Autism Research, 5*(3), 160–179.

Fenton, A., & Krahn, T. (2007). Autism, Neurodiversity, and Equality Beyond the "Normal". *Journal of Ethics in Mental Health, 2*(2), 20–30.

Fink, B. (1999). *A Clinical Introduction to Lacanian Psychoanalysis: Theory and Technique.* Cambridge, MA: Harvard University Press.

Freud, Sigmund. (1911). Psycho-Analytic Notes on an Autobiographical Account of a Case of Paranoia (Dementia Paranoides). *The Standard Edition of the Complete Psychological Works of Sigmund Freud, Volume XII (1911–1913): The Case of Schreber, Papers on Technique and Other Works* (pp. 1–82).

Freud, Sigmund. (1924). The Loss of Reality in Neurosis and Psychosis. *The Standard Edition of the Complete Psychological Works of Sigmund Freud, Volume XIX (1923–1925): The Ego and the Id and Other Works* (pp. 181–188).

Grandin, T. (2006). *Thinking in Pictures, Expanded Edition: My Life with Autism.* New York: Vintage.

Griffin, E., & Pollak, D. (2009). Student Experiences of Neurodiversity in Higher Education: Insights from the BRAINHE Project. *Dyslexia, 15*(1), 23–41.

Jaarsma, P., & Welin, S. (2012). Autism as a Natural Human Variation: Reflections on the Claims of the Neurodiversity Movement. *Health Care Analysis, 20*(1), 20–30.

Jones, E. (1957). Sigmund Freud Life and Work, Volume Three: The last Phase 1919–1939. In *Sigmund Freud Life and Work, Volume Three: The Last Phase 1919–1939* (pp. 1–521). London: The Hogarth Press.

Kanner, L. (1943). Autistic Disturbances of Affective Contact. *Nervous Child, 2*(3), 217–250.

Kanner, L. (1951). The Conception of Wholes and Parts in Early Infantile Autism. *American Journal of Psychiatry, 108*(1), 23–26.

Kanner, L. (1971). Childhood Psychosis: A Historical Overview. *Journal of Autism and Childhood Schizophrenia, 1*(1), 14–19.

Kim, Y. S., Leventhal, B. L., Koh, Y.-J., Fombonne, E., Laska, E., Lim, E.-C., et al. (2011). Prevalence of Autism Spectrum Disorders in a Total Population Sample. *American Journal of Psychiatry, 168*(9), 904–912.

Klein, M. (1930). The Importance of Symbol-Formation in the Development of the Ego. *The International Journal of Psycho-Analysis, 11*, 24–39.

Lacan, J. (1988). In J.-A. Miller (Ed.), *The Seminar of Jacques Lacan, Book I, Freud's Papers on Technique (1953–1954).* New York: Norton & Company.

Lacan, J. (1997). In J.-A. Miller (Ed.), *The Seminar of Jacques Lacan, Book III, The Psychoses (1955–1956).* New York: Norton & Company.

Lacan, J. (2006). In B. Fink (Ed.), *Écrits.* New York: Norton & Company.

Lacan, J. (2014a). In J. Miller (Ed.), *The Seminar of Jacques Lacan, Book X, Anxiety (1962–1963)*. Cambridge, UK: Polity.

Lacan, J. (2014b). In J. Miller (Ed.), *The Seminar of Jacques Lacan, Book X, Anxiety (1962–1963)*. Cambridge, UK: Polity.

Lacan, J. (2016). In J.-A. Miller (Ed.), *The Seminar of Jacques Lacan, Book XXIII, The Sinthome (1975–1976)*. Cambridge, UK: Polity.

Lacan, J. (2017). In J.-A. Miller (Ed.), *The Seminar of Jacques Lacan, Book VIII, Transference (1960–1961)*. Cambridge, UK: Polity.

Mahler, M. S. (1952). On Child Psychosis and Schizophrenia: Autistic and Symbiotic Infantile Psychoses. *The Psychoanalytic Study of the Child, 7*(1), 286–305.

Mahler, M. S. (1967). On Psychosis and Schizophrenia in Childhood. Autistic and Symbiotic Psychoses in Early Childhood. *Psyche, 21*(12), 895.

Maleval, J.-C. (2012). Why the Hypothesis of an Autistic Structure? *Psychoanalytical Notebooks, 25*, 27–49.

Myers, S. M., & Johnson, C. P. (2007). Management of Children with Autism Spectrum Disorders. *Pediatrics, 120*(5), 1162–1182.

Ortega, F. (2009). The Cerebral Subject and the Challenge of Neurodiversity. *BioSocieties, 4*(4), 425–445.

Potter, H. W. (1933). Schizophrenia in Children. *American Journal of Psychiatry, 89*(6), 1253–1270.

Rajendran, G., & Mitchell, P. (2007). Cognitive Theories of Autism. *Developmental Review, 27*(2), 224–260.

Sandin, S., Lichtenstein, P., Kuja-Halkola, R., Larsson, H., Hultman, C. M., & Reichenberg, A. (2014). The Familial Risk of Autism. *Jama, 311*(17), 1770–1777.

Šestan, N. (2012). The Emerging Biology of Autism Spectrum Disorders. *Science, 337*(6100), 1301–1303.

Shapiro, J. (2006). Autism Movement Seeks Acceptance, Not Cures. *Disabilityscoop: The Premier Source for Developmental Disability News.* Retrieved from http://www.npr.org/templates/story/story.php

Sinclair, J. (1993). Don't Mourn for Us. Our Voice. *Autism Network International.* Retrieved from http://www.autreat.com/dont_mourn.html.

Sinclair, J. (2006). The Development of a Community and Its Culture. *Autism Network International.* Retrieved from http://www.autreat.com/History_of_ANI.html

Singer, J. (1999). Why Can't You be Normal for Once in Your life? From a Problem with No Name to the Emergence of a New Category of Difference. *Disability Discourse*, 59–70.

Treffert, D. A. (2009). The Savant Syndrome: An Extraordinary Condition. *Philosophical Transactions of the Royal Society of London B: Biological Sciences, 364*(1522), 1351–1357.

Tustin, F. (1972). *Autism and Child Psychosis*. London: Hogarth Press.

Tustin, F. (1992). *The Protective Shell in Children and Adults*. London: Karnac Books.

Ward, M., & Alar, N. (2000). Being Autistic is Part of Who I Am. *Focus on Autism and Other Developmental Disabilities, 15*(4), 232–235.

Wing, L., Gould, J., & Gillberg, C. (2011). Autism Spectrum Disorders in the DSM-V: Better or Worse Than the DSM-IV? *Research in Developmental Disabilities, 32*(2), 768–773.

Xu, G., Strathearn, L., Liu, B., & Bao, W. (2018). Prevalence of Autism Spectrum Disorder Among US Children and Adolescents, 2014–2016. *Jama, 319*(1), 81–82.

2

Exclusion as a Constitutive Feature of the Subject

According to Freud (1914), the elaboration of the unique form of psychic *exclusion* involved in the *constitution* of the subject is "the corner-stone on which the whole structure of psycho-analysis rests" (SE XIV, p. 15). Initially naming it "repression" (*Verdrängung*), Freud (1925) characterized this form of *constitutive exclusion* as a multifaceted psychic mechanism that entails both an *exclusion* and an *affirmation* and takes part in the instatement of the fundamental division between consciousness and the unconscious in the psyche. While being principally *generic*, Freud explicated three distinct modalities of such a *constitutive exclusion*, based on their internal functioning, the object they aim to exclude, and the affirmation they entail in the psyche. These are involved in the constitution of the subject in its three structural modalities commonly known in psychoanalysis as neurosis, perversion, and psychosis.[1] It is through the investigation of the different modalities of this *constitutive exclusion* that Freud is able to provide a certain access to those unique facets of one's *mode of being* associated with the singular "experience" of the subject. As

---

[1] The "subject" in psychoanalysis, as it is accounted for in the course of this book, will be addressed in the neuter—as an "it." This will be done due to the fact that this notion is developed outside the scope of the discourse on gender.

© The Author(s) 2020

L. S. Brenner, *The Autistic Subject*, The Palgrave Lacan Series,
https://doi.org/10.1007/978-3-030-50715-2_2

will shortly be demonstrated, Freud does so by approaching the subject "at the level of its language" (Foucault, 2006, p. 339), in order to distinguish the structural intricacies of the *constitutive exclusion* underlying its different formations. Freud does so by associating the way in which the history of the subject unravels in the clinic through speech with the effects of such a *constitutive exclusion* on the construction of psychic reality.

The following chapter will provide a rudimentary introduction to Freud's analysis of the constitutive function of repression in the structuration of the subject in psychoanalysis. Focusing on Freud's paper "Negation" (Freud, 1925), this chapter will demonstrate how Freud addresses negation (*Verneinung*) as the hallmark of repression (*Verdrängung*); proceeding to demonstrate how negation also functions as the hallmark of the structure of the subject that is constituted through repression. Finally, this chapter will briefly introduce Freud and Lacan's distinction between three modalities of this psychic *constitutive exclusion* (repression, disavowal, and foreclosure) that correspond to the three major subjective structures elaborated in psychoanalysis (neurosis, perversion, and psychosis). The introductory presentation of Freud's explication of these *constitutive exclusions* will pave the way for their meticulous conceptual elaboration in the following two chapters. This will enable the distinction and explication of a fourth singular *constitutive exclusion* at the origin of the autistic subjective structure in Chaps. 5, 6, and 7, therefore making way for the final determination of autism as a singular subjective structure in the final discussion chapter.

Negation as the Hallmark of Repression

In his paper "Negation" (Freud, 1925), Freud attempts to explain the nature of the relationship between a linguistic negation (*Verneinung*) and the mechanism of repression (*Verdrängung*). He begins his paper by providing several examples of the linguistic uses of negations from his patients. In one of the examples, when Freud asks a patient about the identity of a person in his dream, he replies: "You ask who this person in the dream can be. It's not my mother" (SE XIX, p. 235). Freud stresses that, by voluntarily articulating his response in the form of a negation, the patient introduces an explicit opposition to something that was not addressed by the psychoanalyst and could well have been disregarded. As a result, Freud insists that such a negation cannot be exhaustively described as a *denial* of the content of a predicate but should also be characterized as an opposition to the possibility of its *affirmation*. This implies that what is at stake in the patient's negative judgment is a certain opposition to the affirmation of something concerning "mother."

Nevertheless, as the paper progresses, we see that Freud's account of negation is not confined to the notion that a negated predicate such as "it is not my mother" can yield the affirmation of the same predicate, that is, "it is your mother." We see that it is through his account of negation that Freud attempts to convey something of the nature of repression itself and the unconscious. This is rendered explicit when Freud emphasizes that what is at stake in the patient's voluntary use of a negative judgment is not strictly related to the negated predicate but rather hinges on the fact that repression has taken place (p. 236).

The mechanism of repression will be thoroughly elaborated in the following chapter. Therefore, in this chapter, its exact mode of functioning will only be briefly introduced. Briefly stated, Freud (1896) describes repression as a unique psychic mechanism of "defense" (*Abwehr*) by which distressing thoughts or memories are excluded from consciousness and confined to the unconscious (SE III, pp. 162–182). Explicating the functioning of repression, Freud argues that it is a multifaceted mechanism entailing both a specific form of defensive censorship and the persistence of repressed content in consciousness through symptomatic behavior, dreams, slips of the tongue, jokes, and, in our case, negative judgments (p. 177). Accordingly, the mechanism of repression can be said to include the following operations:

1. A specific form of defensive *exclusion* of potentially distressing mental content into the unconscious.
2. The *affirmation* of conscious reality devoid of the repressed content.
3. The *persistence of repressed content* in consciousness through symptomatic behavior.

Correspondingly, these operations can be said to function in relation to the following elements:

a. Repressed content.
b. Psychic reality (conscious discourse).
c. Alterations in psychic reality (unconscious formations).

Freud (1915) argues that in the psychoanalytic clinic, the psychoanalyst listens to the analysand's discourse and sketches out the intricacies of his or her psychic reality. Through the analysis of the alterations in his or her conscious discourse, the psychoanalyst comes to assess the nature of the *constitutive exclusion* that shapes psychic reality. This enables the psychoanalyst to efficiently navigate the analysand in the course of analysis (SE XIV, p. 150). In this sense, the difference between a negative judgment and repression is elucidated further: while a negative judgment is a hallmark of repression and thus helps in the direction of an analysis, repression itself is a multifaceted mechanism that entails: (1) an exclusion, (2) an affirmation, and (3) alterations in psychic reality in the form of symptoms.

As to the matter of repressed content itself, Freud insists that while a negative judgment is the hallmark of repression, the negated predicate in a negative judgment ("not-mother") should not be confused with the repressed content on the basis of which it manifests. According to Freud (1923), repressed content is intrinsically characterized as being inaccessible to consciousness (SE XIX, p. 14). In other words, repressed content is constituted from the start under the mark of repression and thus only registers in consciousness as lacking (Zupančič, 2017, p. 483), that is, in comparison to something that was conscious and forgotten (or denied). This unique ontological status brings Lacan to argue that "the unconscious is manifested to us as something that holds itself in suspense in the area, I would say, of the *unborn*" (SXI, p. 23). This means that repressed content is considered neither as *born* (conscious) nor as *born-and-then-excluded*, but fundamentally *unborn*. In this sense, Lacan argues that repressed unconscious content "may be said to be pre-ontological," or, in other words, that which "does not lend itself to ontology" (p. 39). Put differently, repressed content "exists" only as unconscious and thus cannot be said to ever have existed, per se, in consciousness but only affect consciousness from within by being constituted from without. By explicating the distinction between a negated predicate in a judgment and repressed content, we now have another distinction between negation and repression. While a negation simply entails a negative judgment of a specific predicate in conscious discourse, a repression constitutes its excluded content as unconscious from the start.

If we take into account that (1) repressed content is initially constituted as unconscious, and (2) the conscious formulation of a negative judgment functions as the hallmark of a repression, we infer that the mechanism of repression operates on the threshold of these two domains. Namely, it is fully restricted neither to the domain of consciousness (the negative judgment "not-mother") nor to the domain of the unconscious (the repressed content associated with the negative judgment "not-mother"). In this sense, repression gains a unique ontological status of its own. It is situated in "the impossible space created by their twist and torsion" (Zupančič, 2012). As will be scrupulously demonstrated in the following chapter, this brings Freud to argue that repression *constitutes* the division between consciousness and the unconscious; accordingly, *in the scope of this book, repression will be designated as a constitutive exclusion, for, on the basis of its unique ontological status, it constitutes the division between consciousness and the unconscious in the psyche by excluding an element into the unconscious.*

Negation as the Hallmark of the Subject

In her book *Art Before the Law* (Ronen, 2014), Ruth Ronen attests to the idea that in psychoanalysis a negative judgment is also the hallmark of the subject's unique structure (p. 27). Ronen argues that the psychoanalytic interest in negation is rooted in the assumption that subjective reality cannot be solely identified with what a person consciously says or thinks but is also identified with what he or she denies, refuses, or represses from consciousness (pp. 21–22). In other words, Ronen claims that, in psychoanalysis, negation is rooted in the Freudian notion that conscious discourse is not the sole instance that determines subjective reality. She directs the reader to an intuitive example given by Lacan in his *Seminar XIV: The Logic of Phantasy (1966–1967)*, demonstrating that, with negation, it is not only that an object is affirmed but also the unique structure of the subject in psychoanalysis is revealed:

> *I do not desire*. It is clear that this *I do not desire*, just by itself is designed to make us ask what the negation is brought to bear on. If it is a transitive *I do not desire*, it implies the undesirable (undesirable because of me: there is some particular thing that I do not desire). But, in fact, the negation could mean that it is not *I* (*moi*) who desires, implying that I take no responsibility (*je me decharge*) for desiring, which may also indeed be what carries me while at the same time not being *me*. (SXIV, p. 68)

Ronen (2014) explains how, in this excerpt, Lacan argues that in the negative judgment "I do not desire," the expressed refusal does concern not only the transitive dimension of desire—of the object of desire—but also the exact subjective agency unto which desire is assigned. In this sense, the subject says "not-I-desire," negating the *I* (ego) as the desiring agency, rather than desire itself. By denying the association of desire with the *I* (ego), the subject thus affirms another subjective agency, unto which desire is assigned (p. 27). According to Ronen, divorcing this subjective agency from the domain of the ego entails situating desire where the ego is not. Therefore, she argues that the grammatical structure of negation affirms an additional agency—that of the not-*I* (not-ego) or the "it" (*ça*) (p. 28). Thus we see that with negation the subject is engendered as split between two discursive agencies: the first, the conscious ego or *I*, which articulates the negative judgment; the second, the unconscious or the not-*I*, which is uncovered in negation and is inarticulable in the domain of the ego.[2]

Basing himself on Freud's notion of the *Spaltung*, presented in his paper "Splitting of the Ego in the Process of Defence" (Freud, 1938), Lacan argues that the subject is constituted as fundamentally split between consciousness and the unconscious (SVII, p. 102). This is also

---

[2] It is exactly in this sense that Jean Hyppolite proclaims in his lecture on Freud's paper "Negation" (Freud, 1925) that in psychoanalysis, negation entails "presenting one's being in the mode of *not being*" (É, p. 748).

understood in terms of the split between the *I* and the not-*I* elaborated above, a notion Lacan will later develop in his distinction between the subject of the statement and the subject of enunciation.[3] When addressed as the "split subject" (SXI, pp. 70–185), that is, when not reduced to either of the domains or agencies presented above, the subject is identified by Lacan as nothing but the psychic construct embodying this very split (Fink, 1997, p. 45). Now, if repression is defined as the psychic mechanism constituting the split between consciousness and the unconscious, and the subject is defined as this very split, we see that the subject is constituted as split on the basis of the functioning of the mechanism of repression (Zupančič, 2017, p. 492). This is why, *in the scope of this book, repression is designated not only as a constitutive exclusion but, more specifically, as a psychic mechanism of exclusion that constitutes the structure of the subject as split between consciousness and the unconscious.* Correspondingly, Alenka Zupančič (2012) argues that repression produces not only two things but three: (1) an exclusion that produces an absence of something that is not in psychic reality; (2) an affirmation of psychic reality; and (3) a vantage point or structure, on the basis of which the division between the excluded and the affirmed is established. As I have already stated, this vantage point is neither the *I* nor the not-*I*; it is a psychic construct to which the two rely on in their construction. In this sense, Freud subverts the philosophical notion that views the self-transparent unified self-consciousness as the sole *mode of being* of the subject. Instead of the unitary transcendental subject of modern philosophy, Freud stipulates a subject structurally established as a gap, separating two domains or agencies as well as a knot binding them together and having a direct effect on their materialization and functioning in the construction of psychic reality.

In her paper "Not Mother" (2012), Zupančič associates the structure of the split subject with Lacan's conception of the knot. Lacan borrows the notion of the knot from the field of topology and, more specifically, from knot theory. A knot in topology, just like a shoelace knot, is a figure that is determined by the specific way in which something crosses over or under something else. An interesting aspect of the knot is the fact that,

---

[3] This distinction will be thoroughly elaborated in Chaps. 6 and 7.

on the one hand, it represents a structure that cannot be wholly reduced to the elements it embodies and, on the other hand, it cannot be said to be composed of anything which is more than their summation. Accordingly, Zupančič describes the knot as a structure that is both *constitutive* and *constituted* of the elements from which it is composed. She describes the knot as an underlying structure that marks the relationship between these elements, without being counted as a third element. Repression, as a *constitutive exclusion*, produces this type of knot in the psyche—a certain way in which consciousness and the unconscious twist and tie together, producing a specific subjective structure.

At this point, it is important to stress that repression is described as a *constitutive exclusion* that produces this knot in only *one* of its modalities. More precisely, as will be thoroughly demonstrated in the next chapter, Freud (1896) goes to great lengths to explicate and associate repression with the constitution of the neurotic subjective structure (SE III, p. 166). In the course of his career, Freud will go on to identify three distinct *constitutive exclusions* that correspond to the three major subjective structures elaborated in psychoanalysis. For neurosis, this would be the mechanism of repression (*Verdrängung*); for perversion, the mechanism of disavowal (*Verleugnung*); and for psychosis, the mechanism of foreclosure (*Verwerfung*). These three fundamentally distinct *constitutive exclusions* produce three distinct psychic topologies (knots) that correspond to three distinct subjective structures, which manifest as three singular *modes of being*—none of which is secondary to the others (Zupančič, 2017, p. 487). Accordingly, these *constitutive exclusions* are not only considered to be associated with these subjective structures but are considered to be their cause, functioning as the "condition of the possibility of the existence of a subject" (Fink, 1997, pp. 48, 77). According to Freud (1924), it is the conceptual elaboration of the internal functioning of each of these mechanisms that dictates the singularity of each subjective structure (SE XIX, p. 185). Therefore, this form of elaboration will serve as the method by which the singularity of the neurotic, psychotic, and, most importantly, autistic subjective structure will be accounted for in the following chapters of this book.

A Fourth Constitutive Exclusion

In his book *A Clinical Introduction to Lacanian Psychoanalysis: Theory and Technique* (1999), Bruce Fink explains that the three subjective structures elaborated by Freud and Lacan (neurosis, perversion, psychosis) cover the entire field of subjective structures accounted for by contemporaneous psychoanalytic research. Nevertheless, Fink emphasizes that "it is conceivable that other forms of negation could be found, leading to four or more principal structures" (p. 77).[4] This book starts off at the crossroad paved by this hypothesis. It aims to structurally elaborate a fourth form of *constitutive exclusion* situated at the origin of autism, on the basis of its internal functioning, the psychic object on which it operates and the affirmation it entails in the psyche. By demonstrating that the exclusion at the origin of the autistic subjective structure cannot be structurally reduced to any of the forms of exclusion elaborated by Freud and Lacan, this book will provide support for the hypothesis that autism is a fourth singular subjective structure in line with the three major subjective structures introduced in psychoanalysis.

Now that the general aim and methodological framework have been established, Chaps. 3 and 4 of this book will present a thorough structural analysis of Freud and Lacan's account of the *constitutive exclusions* at the origin of the neurotic and psychotic subjective structures. Based on the conclusions reached in these chapters, Chaps. 5, 6, and 7 will provide an analysis of the *constitutive exclusion* at the origin of autism and compare its structure and functioning with the ones presented in the previous chapters. The conclusions reached in these chapters will be implemented in the discussion chapter, in which the hypothesis of autism being a fourth singular subjective structure will be finally substantiated.

---

[4] Fink uses the term "negation" in order to designate the different forms of constitutive psychic mechanisms underlying the principal subjective structures in psychoanalysis. Due to the distinction that was drawn between "negation" and "exclusion" in this chapter, in this book, this mechanism will be termed *constitutive exclusion*.

Works Cited

Fink, B. (1997). *The Lacanian Subject: Between Language and Jouissance.* Princeton, NJ: Princeton University Press.

Fink, B. (1999). *A Clinical Introduction to Lacanian Psychoanalysis: Theory and Technique.* Cambridge, UK: Harvard University Press.

Foucault, M. (2006). *History of Madness.* London: Routledge.

Freud, Sigmund. (1896). Further Remarks on the Neuro-Psychoses of Defence. *The Standard Edition of the Complete Psychological Works of Sigmund Freud, Volume III (1893–1899): Early Psycho-Analytic Publications* (pp. 157–185).

Freud, Sigmund. (1914). On the History of the Psycho-Analytic Movement. *The Standard Edition of the Complete Psychological Works of Sigmund Freud, Volume XIV (1914–1916): On the History of the Psycho-Analytic Movement, Papers on Metapsychology and Other Works* (pp. 1–66).

Freud, Sigmund. (1915). Repression. *The Standard Edition of the Complete Psychological Works of Sigmund Freud, Volume XIV (1914–1916): On the History of the Psycho-Analytic Movement, Papers on Metapsychology and Other Works* (pp. 141–158).

Freud, S. (1923). The Ego and the Id. *The Standard Edition of the Complete Psychological Works of Sigmund Freud, Volume XIX (1923–1925): The Ego and the Id and Other Works* (pp. 1–66).

Freud, S. (1924). The Loss of Reality in Neurosis and Psychosis. *The Standard Edition of the Complete Psychological Works of Sigmund Freud, Volume XIX (1923–1925): The Ego and the Id and Other Works* (pp. 181–188).

Freud, S. (1925). Negation. *The Standard Edition of the Complete Psychological Works of Sigmund Freud, Volume XIX (1923–1925): The Ego and the Id and Other Works* (pp. 233–240).

Freud, S. (1938). Splitting of the Ego in the Process of Defence. *The Standard Edition of the Complete Psychological Works of Sigmund Freud, Volume XXIII (1937–1939): Moses and Monotheism, An Outline of Psycho-Analysis and Other Works* (pp. 271–278).

Lacan, J. (2006). In B. Fink (Ed.), *Écrits.* New York: Norton & Company.

Lacan, J. (2017). In J.-A. Miller (Ed.), *The Seminar of Jacques Lacan, Book VIII, Transference (1960–1961).* Cambridge, UK: Polity.

Lacan, J. (n.d.). *The Seminar, Book XIV, The Logic of Phantasy (1966–1967).* Trans. Gallagher, C. Unpublished.

Ronen, R. (2014). *Art Before the Law: Aesthetics and Ethics.* Toronto, CA: University of Toronto Press.

Zupančič, A. (2012). Not-Mother: On Freud's Verneinung. *E-Flux, 33.*

Zupančič, A. (2017). Hegel and Freud: Between Aufhebung and Verneinung. *Crisis and Critique, 4*(1), 480–494.

Part II

Neurotic Repression and Psychotic Foreclosure

The contemporary Lacanian approach to autism situates at its origin a unique psychic mechanism of *constitutive exclusion* named *foreclosure*. However, while many contemporary psychoanalysts provide a detailed account of autistic symptomatology resulting from this unique constitutive mechanism, a meticulous attempt to thoroughly distinguish *autistic foreclosure* in structural terms has not yet been fully established. That is due to the fact that psychoanalysts, who address the subject of autism, naturally emphasize its clinical facets more than the structural or conceptual elaboration of its underlying constitutive mechanism.

As will be presented in Part III of this book, psychoanalysts who do conceptually develop the structural characteristics of *autistic foreclosure* in their work do so in direct relation to Lacan's elaboration of the mechanism of psychotic foreclosure. Because Lacan's account of psychotic foreclosure is directly rooted in Freud's rigorous characterization of the mechanism of neurotic repression, it is necessary to identify a transitive thematic relationship between the structural elaboration of neurotic repression, psychotic foreclosure, and autistic foreclosure. This relationship accentuates the importance of the elaboration of neurotic repression for the understanding of psychotic foreclosure and, finally, for distinguishing the singularity of autistic foreclosure in relation to psychotic foreclosure.[1] Hence, one of the contributions of this book would be to address the constitutive mechanism at the origin of the autistic subjective structure in terms borrowed from the elaboration of neurotic repression and psychotic foreclosure. The comparison and distinction of these mechanisms will provide the conceptual foundation for the elaboration of autistic foreclosure in Part III of this book.

Part II of this book will be divided into two chapters. Chapter 3 will address the mechanism of neurotic repression and will be divided into two sections. The first section will be devoted to the Freudian elaboration of repression, starting from its first appearance in Freud's paper *Studies on Hysteria* (1893). The second section will address Lacan's structural linguistic elaboration of repression in the affirmation of the neurotic subjective structure. These two sections will account for the development of the notion of repression in Freud and Lacan's work and will mostly aim to provide a clear structural distinction between two mechanisms of repression—primal and secondary repression. Chapter 4 will address the mechanism of psychotic foreclosure. This chapter will also be divided into two sections. The first section will be devoted to Freud's account of psychosis in three different periods in the development of his work. The second section will directly address Lacan's account of foreclosure in the affirmation of the psychotic subjective structure as it is presented in his *Seminar III: The Psychoses (1955–1956)*. These two sections will also account for the similarities and differences in the functioning of repression and foreclosure and will explicate the unique structural features of psychotic foreclosure.

At this point, the reader might want to keep in mind that the magnitude and depth of the elaboration of the notions presented in these chapters will be determined according to their relevance for the discussion of

---

[1] It is important to note that the mechanism of disavowal (*Verleugnung*), underlying the perverse mental structure, is also considered to be a psychic mechanism of *constitutive exclusion*. Nevertheless, due to the fact that its explication would only have circumstantial value in the inquiry into autism, it is not investigated in this book.

autistic foreclosure in the following chapters. Accordingly, these notions will be presented in a mode of increasing elaborative depth: beginning with repression in general, then focusing on the mechanism of primal repression, and, finally, providing a thorough structural elaboration of the mechanism of psychotic foreclosure.

3

Repression and the Neurotic Subject

Repression in Freud

Repression is one of the most fundamental concepts in psychoanalytic meta-psychology. In fact, in "On the History of the Psycho-Analytic Movement" (1914), Freud explicitly proclaims that "the theory of repression is the corner-stone on which the whole structure of psycho-analysis rests" (SE XIV, p. 15). Correspondingly, the investigation of repression will be the cornerstone of the elaboration of autism in this book. Its preliminary elucidation in this section will provide a framework enabling a clearer and more distinct understanding of the mechanism of foreclosure—first in psychosis and then in autism.

Repression as Neurotic Defense

The first occasion Freud uses the term "repression" (*Verdrängung*) is in his "Preliminary Communications" in *Studies on Hysteria* (1893). Mentioned only once in this paper, Freud (1893) uses this term to describe clinical cases in which patients do not display any apparent reaction to trauma.

© The Author(s) 2020
L. S. Brenner, *The Autistic Subject*, The Palgrave Lacan Series,
https://doi.org/10.1007/978-3-030-50715-2_3

Freud claims that these patients "wished to forget and therefore intentionally repressed" the traumatic memories (SE II, p. 10).

At this early stage in his work, Freud uses the term "repression" solely in order to designate a unique form of psychic "defense" (*Abwehr*) against unwanted memories. Accordingly, in his following paper, "Further Remarks on the Neuro-Psychoses of Defense" (1894), Freud explicitly characterizes repression as a process "opening the door to the *defense* neurosis" (SE III, p. 166; emphasis added), a unique form of "censorship" in which an idea that "had come into distressing opposition with the patient's ego" (p. 162) is excluded from consciousness and is confined to the unconscious (p. 182). Freud adds that the defensive exclusion of an idea from consciousness also affirms the division between consciousness and unconscious, principally claiming that repression is responsible for the constitution of the unconscious. Accordingly, already in this early paper, repression is not only defined as a mechanism of defense but, more specifically, as "the psychical mechanism of (unconscious) defense," affirming and demarcating the confines of the unconscious (p. 162). Because Freud classifies the division between consciousness and the unconscious as an essential quality of the neurotic mental structure, he designates repression as the most fundamental mechanism in neurosis.[1] In this sense, it is considered to be the cause of the neurotic propensity to keep things that do not fit with one's world views or moral principles hidden from others and from the self (Fink, 1999, p. 113). Finally, Freud (1894) adds that neurotic repression does not fully erase repressed content from the psyche. He argues that as a result of repression something necessarily persists in the psyche in various ways (SE III, p. 162). Accordingly, Freud describes repression as a two-faceted mechanism entailing: (1) a specific form of defensive censorship that excludes distressing content from consciousness into the unconscious; as well as (2) the persistence of repressed content in consciousness through

---

[1] While repression is considered to be the constitutive mechanism underlying the neurotic mental structure, it can also lead to a variety of different symptoms and behaviors attesting to the different subcategories attributed to neurosis. Obsession and hysteria, for instance, are considered to be different modes of neurosis and are characterized by a different form of repression entailing a different relationship with language.

symptomatic behavior prevalent in neurosis such as, dreams, slips of the tongue, and jokes.

In his later paper, "Repression" (1915), Freud goes on to provide a further and more detailed account of the mechanism of repression. He elaborates on several aspects of repression such as its "normalizing" function (SE XIV, p. 152) as well as the particular character and magnitude that it takes on in different cases (p. 151). However, most importantly, Freud illustrates a clearer picture of the exact nature of the repressed psychic object and the unique way it persists in consciousness.

Regarding the nature of the repressed object, Freud explains that repression functions in relation to two elements that are generally linked together in the psyche: ideas and affects. According to Freud, in repression, a conflictual idea that exceeds a certain threshold of affective strength is detached from its corresponding "quota of affect" and excluded from consciousness into the unconscious (p. 152). Freud classifies the detachment of an idea from its corresponding affect as an "interference" in consciousness (p. 149). Inherent to this "interference," Freud identifies several corresponding phenomena. Firstly, an idea that is repressed is not fully erased from consciousness but can still be accessible to consciousness without its corresponding affect. Secondly, when an idea is repressed, it gains access to new associations with other repressed ideas in the unconscious. Accordingly, Freud argues that the unconscious consists of these repressed ideas that are detached from their corresponding affects and form among themselves new meaningful relationships. Thirdly, as an idea is detached from an affect and pushed into the unconscious, its corresponding affect can persist in consciousness. This explains the many cases in psychoanalytic literature of neurotic subjects who can consciously attest to a specific affect but have no access to the idea that is the source of this affect; or, on the other hand, cases in which an idea is available to consciousness but is lacking its affective correlate (Fink, 1999, pp. 113–114).

Both the ideas and the detached affects that come under the sway of repression are termed by Freud (1915) as the "derivatives of the repressed" (*Abkömmlinge des Verdrängten*). They are the by-product of repression and shape the reality and the behavior of neurotic subjects. They take part in the formation of new meanings between ideas in the unconscious and are also portrayed in the insistence of isolated affects in consciousness. When doing so, they are considered to be the "indications of a return of the repressed" (SE XIV, p. 154) and manifest themselves in what Freud calls "neurotic symptoms" (p. 150). Freud argues that the psychoanalytic practice revolves around these derivatives. He claims that in analysis these derivatives can be consciously produced in an attempt to pass the censorship of repression: "there must be unconscious thoughts and repressed memories which could be brought into consciousness ... by overcoming a certain resistance" (p. 177). By removing the resistance to repression, Freud argues that one can experience a decrease in the magnitude of the suffering produced by his or her symptoms.

Primal and Secondary Repression

One of Freud's most important characterizations of the mechanism of repression is his distinction between a "primal" and a "secondary" form of repression. The first is a primordial *constitutive mechanism* and the second is a *neurotic defense mechanism*.[2]

Freud introduces the notion of *primal repression* (*Urverdrängung*) by implementing a strict logical rigor when assessing the functioning of repression in general. Freud argues that, logically speaking, secondary repression is primally conditioned by a previously affirmed division between consciousness and the unconscious. Freud insists that only after the instatement of this division can repression function as a defense mechanism and exclude strongly conflictual ideas to the unconscious keeping them away from consciousness:

> Psycho-analytic observation ... leads us to conclude that repression is not a defensive mechanism which is present from the very beginning, and that it cannot arise until a sharp cleavage has occurred between conscious and unconscious mental activity. (SE XIV, p. 147)

---

[2] The latter is also termed by Freud (1894, 1911, 1915) repression as "defense" (*Abwehr*) (SE III, p. 47) as well as "repression proper" or "after-pressure" (SE XII, p. 67). From now on: "secondary repression."

Primal repression is exactly this primordial mechanism that, according to Freud, constitutes the "sharp cleavage" between consciousness and the unconscious and thus precedes and conditions the functioning of secondary repression (pp. 147–148). Freud's most explicit account of the functioning of primal repression is worth quoting at length:

> We have reason to assume that there is a *primal repression*, a first phase of repression, which consists in the psychical (ideational) representative of the instinct [*Repräsentanz des Triebes*] being denied entrance into the conscious. With this a *fixation* is established; the representative in question persists unaltered from then onwards and the instinct [*Trieb*] remains attached to it. (p. 148; brackets added)[3]

This most explicit account of primal repression is compelling on two levels. First of all, in this excerpt Freud (1915) situates primal repression on the level of the functioning of the drive (*Trieb*). In contrast to secondary repression, which functions in relation to consciousness, primal repression functions in relation to a more initial level of drive-stimuli that precedes the construction of the conscious ego.[4] Moreover, Freud discloses the exact nature of the psychic object excluded in primal repression. He claims that, in contrast to secondary repression, in which objects of repression are ideas, in primal repression, the objects of repression are the *representatives of the drive* (*Repräsentanzen des Triebes*). According to Freud, these representatives of drive-stimuli are neither ideas nor instinctual needs (like hunger); they are psychic representations situated in-between ideas and instinctual needs and can be regarded as primordial inscriptions of drive-stimuli in the psyche (pp. 147–148,176). The primal repression of the representatives of the drive is considered to be the first act that affirms the division between consciousness and the

---

[3] Freud uses the term *Trieb* in order to designate the functioning of the drive. When Freud addresses the functioning of the instincts, he explicitly uses the term *Instinkt*. Nevertheless, many English editors—including James Strachey—have not corrected the English translation which does not differentiate between the two. Basing myself on the Lacanian framework, I will from now on address Freud's accounts of the *Trieb* as "drive" and *Instinkt* as "instincts." I will therefore provide the original English translation including this correction in brackets.

[4] See more on the distinction between the level of the drive and consciousness in Freud: SE XIII, pp. 88–89; SE XIV, pp. 76–77.

unconscious (Recalcati & McGlazer, 2012, p. 152). This division allows the subject to begin relating to internal and external stimuli and assign them to different domains of the psyche in secondary repression.

The second compelling aspect of the excerpt presented above has to do with the establishment of a *fixation* in the course of primal repression. Freud does not provide an explicit account of the exact nature of this *fixation* in this paper (1915); nevertheless, he does discuss it in his previous paper, "Psycho-Analytic Notes of an Autobiographical Account of a Case of Paranoia" (1911).[5] In this paper, Freud claims that a *fixation* is instated when a representative of the drive fails to accompany the others in an anticipated path of development. This leads to an inhibition in its development that causes it to persist in an unaltered *fixated* state. Correspondingly, Freud argues that when a representative of the drive is primally repressed, a *fixation* is established and from then onward it functions as a steady anchor point enabling the consistent functioning of the drive (SE XII, pp. 62–68). In this sense, primal repression is considered by Freud to be a two-faceted mechanism that initially (1) *fixates* the development of the drive and then (2) transforms the "passive lagging behind" of a representative of the drive to an anchor point in the unconscious, in relation to which the mechanism of secondary repression can function (p. 67).

Secondary repression is the concrete act of repression presented earlier in this chapter. Following the instatement of the division between consciousness and the unconscious in primal repression, secondary repression functions by detaching a conflictual idea from its corresponding affect and excluding it from consciousness into the unconscious where it can be associated with other repressed ideas. Freud's (1915) distinction between primal and secondary repression provides grounds for better understanding the nature of the repressed idea in secondary repression and its relation to the representatives of the drive:

> The second stage of repression, *repression proper*, affects mental derivatives of the repressed representative [of the drive], or such trains of thought as,

---

[5] The difference between the formula proposed by Freud in "The Psycho-Analytic Notes of an Autobiographical Account of a Case of Paranoia" and "Repression" is outlined by Freud in a letter to Ferenczi of December 6, 1910 (Jones, 1955, p. 499).

originating elsewhere, have come into associative connection with it. On account of this association, these ideas experience the same fate as what was primally repressed. (SE XIV, p. 148; brackets added)

In this excerpt Freud argues that when an idea is repressed in secondary repression it is also associated with repressed representatives of the drive. That is to say that when a conflictual idea is excluded from consciousness, it is necessarily bound together in the unconscious with other mental derivatives branching from the primally repressed representatives of the drive—branching from the primal point of *fixation*. In this sense, Freud classifies primal repression as a mechanism that affirms a point of *fixation* in the unconscious to which all further mental derivatives are bound. That is, compared to secondary repression that functions as an ongoing process in which repressed derivatives establish connections between each other in the unconscious, sequentially compiling a construct that branches from the primally repressed representatives of the drive as its point of origin.[6]

Judgments of Attribution and Judgments of Existence

In his later paper, "Negation" (1925), Freud provides a further account of primal and secondary repression by associating them with two distinct forms of judgments—*judgments of attribution* and *judgments of existence*, respectively (SE XIX, pp. 235–236). Moreover, Freud provides a more detailed analysis of primal repression as a mechanism that functions on the basis of two corresponding structural procedures—*expulsion* (*Ausstoßung*) and *affirmation* (*Bejahung*). These two terms will take center stage in Lacan's account of psychotic foreclosure and therefore will be crucial in the elaboration and distinction of autistic foreclosure in the following chapters.

According to Freud, judgments of attribution play a decisive role in the initial demarcation of the division between consciousness and the unconscious. Functioning on the basis of the "pleasure principle," they

---

[6] See more on this subject in Freud: SE XII, p. 67; SE XIV, p. 151.

do so by differentially attributing a "bad" or "good" "pleasure value" to representatives of drive-stimuli (p. 237). In the most "speculative" part of this paper, Freud associates these two operations of libidinal attribution with two structural procedures internal to the constitution of the subject in primal repression. In the first, *Ausstoßung*, unpleasurable drive-stimuli (representatives of the drives) are determined as "bad" and destined to be excluded. This attribution engenders a prototypical division between an internal "good" and external "bad" psychic space. In the second, *Bejahung*, this division is affirmed as a psychic construct marking a dividing line between an interior and exterior (p. 239). The construct affirmed in *Bejahung* cannot be reduced to the internal or the external alone but is regarded as a structure coinciding with the division between the internal and external itself (Zupančič, 2012).[7]

Just like primal repression, judgments of attribution are considered to solely function at the level of the drive. Accordingly, when Freud (1925) describes them in terms of oral drive-stimuli (*oralen Triebregungen*) they are exemplified in hypothetical sentences such as:

> "I should like to eat this", or "I should like to spit it out"; and, put more generally: "I should like to take this into myself and to keep that out." That is to say: "It shall be inside me" or "it shall be outside me." (SE XIX, p. 237)

By employing *hypothetical terms* such as "should" and "shall" in his exemplification of the judgments of attribution, Freud emphasizes that they are not considered to actually entail a series of ongoing judgments about the *existence* of objects; they only engender a psychic structure that functions as a potential model on the basis of which the succeeding judgments of existence can to do so.

Following the affirmation of a division between an interior and an exterior psychic space in judgments of attribution, judgments of existence materialize the potential of this construct by deciding as to the "reality" of objects represented in consciousness. In other words, they

---

[7] See further discussion on the metaphysical status of the knot in Chap. 2.

determine whether an object is strictly internal to the psyche or also consciously exists in psychic reality:

> It is now no longer a question of whether what has been perceived (a thing) shall be taken into the ego or not, but of whether something which is in the ego as a presentation can be re-discovered in perception (reality) as well. It is, we see, once more a question of *external* and *internal*. What is unreal, merely a presentation and subjective, is only internal; what is real is also there *outside*. (p. 237)

Freud explicitly uses the term "re-discovered" in order to emphasize that "all presentation originate from perceptions and are repetitions of them" (p. 237). In other words, Freud argues that when a representative of the drive is initially encountered and excluded in the judgments of attribution, it is also affirmed as a *trace* (a *fixation*). This trace of libidinal cathexis is then reactivated and pursued in psychic reality. The systematic scrutiny of the judgments of existence—what Freud calls the "reality principle"—is the process in which an object of perception is compared to the *trace* of original drive-stimuli affirmed in judgments of attribution. Put differently, in judgments of existence, it is the relation of the object of perception to the preliminary attribution of the representative of the drive ("it shall be inside/outside me") that enables the determination of its reality. This brings Freud to argue that what is at stake in judgments of existence is "not to find an object in real perception which corresponds to the one presented, but to *re-find* such an object" in reality which corresponds to the *trace* initially affirmed in the judgments of attribution (p. 237).

The fact that judgments of existence can only be realized in relation to an object engendered in the affirmation (*Bejahung*) achieved in judgments of attribution emphasizes the direct dependence of the level of the judgments of existence on the successful execution of the judgments of attribution. It corresponds to the direct dependence of secondary repression on the *fixation* achieved in the course of primal repression presented in the previous section. As will shortly be explained, understanding the nature of this dependence is crucial for the elaboration of the functioning of psychotic foreclosure and the obstruction of secondary repression in psychosis.

Summary

The goal of this section was to structurally assess the functioning of repression as a psychic mechanism of *constitutive exclusion* at the origin of the neurotic subjective structure. So far, this section has established a strictly Freudian account of repression by articulating several defining characteristics of this mechanism presented in his works. Most importantly it has based a distinction between a (1) constitutive primal repression, conditioning the functioning of (2) secondary repression. Both of these entail an exclusion, but this exclusion is achieved on a different psychic element situated on a different level of the functioning of the psyche. Moreover, both of these are divided into two internal aspects—an exclusion and an affirmation. The following section will demonstrate that while secondary repression is singular in the constitution of the neurotic subjective structure alone, primal repression is universal in its functioning in the constitution of all subjective structures. This will make primal repression the main object of investigation in the attempt to elucidate the *constitutive exclusion* at the origin of the psychotic and autistic subjective structures. The conclusions reached so far regarding the model of repression can be summarized in Fig. 3.1:

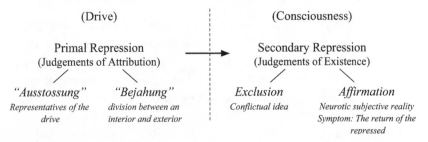

Fig. 3.1 Summary: Freud on primal and secondary repression

Repression in Lacan

In his teaching, Lacan provided several models and interpretations of the Freudian model of repression. The following section will present a comprehensive account of these models, starting with Lacan's early elaboration of repression in linguistic terms, based on *Seminar I: Freud's Papers on Technique (1953–1954)*, *Seminar III: The Psychoses (1955–1956)* as well as Lacan's response to Jean Hyppolite's commentary on Freud's "Negation" (1925) printed in *Écrits* (2006).[8] This section will continue to present several other conceptual innovations offered by Lacan in the later years of his teaching. These convey psychoanalytic notions in mathematical terms. They offer a strict formalization of the psychoanalytic models presented by Freud, explicating the more abstract facets of the functioning of the *constitutive exclusion* at the origin of the structuration of the neurotic subject. The conceptual development of the model of repression is aimed at constructing a sufficient conceptual foundation for the distinction and characterization of *autistic foreclosure* in the following chapters. Therefore, it will revolve around concepts that are useful for the fulfillment of this goal. Accordingly, while the understanding of secondary repression is crucial for the characterization of the neurotic subjective structure, it is the elaboration of the mechanism of primal repression—which is crucial for the characterization of all subjective structure—that will be the main focus of this section.

Primal Repression

Just like Freud, Lacan characterizes the mechanism of repression as having two distinct modalities—primal and secondary repression. These two differ in the level of their functioning, the psychic objects onto which they apply as well as the way in which they shape psychic reality. In each of these modalities Lacan insists there are two logical instances—that of an *expulsion* and an *affirmation*. Correspondingly, internal to the

---

[8] Hyppolite's commentary and Lacan's response were conducted in Lacan's first seminar but were fully accounted for in print in *Écrits* (2006, pp. 308–333, 746–754).

functioning of primal repression, Lacan differentiates between a "primal expulsion" (*Ausstoßung*) (É, p. 324) and a "primordial affirmation" (*Bejahung*) (SIII, pp. 12, 82–84). He relates them both to Freud's (1925) account of the judgments of attribution (SE XIX, pp. 237–239), going to great length in order to exemplify their intricate relationship and their role in the transition from the level of primal repression to that of secondary repression in the affirmation of the neurotic subjective structure.

Primal *Ausstoßung*

Lacan defines *Ausstoßung* as the negative aspect of primal repression. He argues that it functions as a constitutive "expulsion" that initiates the structural basis for the division between consciousness and the unconscious that is later affirmed in *Bejahung* (É, p. 324). Relying on the Freudian (1925) model, Lacan argues that in *Ausstoßung*, a sum of drive-stimuli (jouissance) is initially expelled from the psyche. By defining it as a "primal expulsion," Lacan emphasizes that this sum of drive-stimuli is primordially and structurally expelled, meaning its expulsion precedes its inscription in the psyche and, thus, its only designation in psychic reality is as lost (É, pp. 324–325). In this sense, the primal expulsion achieved in *Ausstoßung* is considered by Lacan to come to pass in a "mythical moment" in the structuration of the subject "rather than a genetic moment" (p. 319).[9] In his commentary on Freud's "Negation" (1925), Jean Hyppolite describes the "mythical moment" in which *Ausstoßung* comes to pass, as that which precedes any distinction between an outside and an inside of the subject. Hyppolite argues that this moment can be associated with a state of pre-Oedipal unity in which there is no division in the subject, where nothing is yet foreign to it and everything is identical to it (p. 751). According to Hyppolite, it is the primordial mechanism of *Ausstoßung* that instates an initiatory gap in this continuity and enables the potential differentiation between what is inside and outside of the subject. This gap is the first designation of a lack introduced in the psyche.

---

[9] The "mythical" status attributed to *Ausstoßung* by Lacan stands in direct homology to Freud's (1925) hypothetical formulation of the functioning of the judgments of attribution on the level of the oral drive presented in the previous section (SE XIX, p. 237).

However, Hyppolite stresses that until it is further affirmed in *Bejahung*, this gap does not yet gain its full symbolic value. Therefore, on the level of *Ausstoßung*, this gap functions only as a marker of a negative expulsion, represented by what he terms as the "symbol of negation" (p. 752–753).[10] Both Lacan and Hyppolite agree that all forms of affirmation in psychic reality, including that of *Bejahung*, are accomplished on the basis of this "gap" or "symbol." Accordingly, *Ausstoßung* is described as the first crucial step in the whole of the dialectical movement in the constitution of the subject (pp. 327, 750–752).

In his response to Hyppolite's commentary, Lacan also elaborates on the function of *Ausstoßung* in terms of the constitutive relationship between the symbolic order and the register of the real.[11] More specifically, he argues that *Ausstoßung* is a mechanism that "constitutes the real insofar as it is the domain of that which subsists outside of symbolization" (p. 324). In this sense, Lacan associates *Ausstoßung* with a primordial expulsion of an initial sum of drive-stimuli (jouissance) that is not yet mediated by the symbolic. By registering this sum of jouissance in the psyche strictly as lost (outside of symbolization), *Ausstoßung* initializes the division between the symbolic and the real by establishing "the real as outside the subject" (p. 324). On the same note, in their paper "Hate as a Passion of Being" (2012), Massimo Recalcati and Ramsey McGlazer further characterize *Ausstoßung* as "an exteriorization of the real itself … the originary process that makes the real exist as exteriority" (p. 154). They add that by marking the real as an exterior domain to the symbolic, *Ausstoßung* serves as the first instance that enables the functioning of the symbolic itself. More precisely, they claim that *Ausstoßung* is "*foundational for the functioning of the symbolic order* … in the sense that it introduces the subject as detached from the exteriority of the [lost] object [of jouissance]" (p. 155; brackets added). Recalcati and McGlazer associate the "exteriority of the object" engendered in *Ausstoßung* with an expelled

---

[10] An analysis of Hyppolite's assessment of the *Ausstoßung* and *Bejahung* will be extensively accounted for in Chap. 5. Especially Hyppolite's unique interpretation of the internal division in *Ausstoßung* and its symbolic product—the "symbol of negation."

[11] Lacan introduces the registers of the imaginary, symbolic, and real, as the three fundamental dimensions of the psyche. These form an outline for a framework that enables the elaboration of various notions in Lacan's interpretation of Freud's meta-psychology.

sum of jouissance. They argue that at the mythical moment preceding *Ausstoßung*, this object is the closest thing to the subject but, through its exteriorization, it becomes its most radical alterity. Accordingly, they claim that by initially excluding a sum of jouissance, *Ausstoßung* engenders the lost object as a symbol of exteriority, thus constituting the most initial relationship with the Other—the symbolic order in which this symbol is inscribed (p. 156).

Primordial *Bejahung*

Lacan's account of primordial *Bejahung* is extensive and takes center stage in his elaboration of psychosis starting from *Seminar III*. Just like Freud (1925), Lacan designates *Bejahung* as the affirmative aspect of primal repression and argues that, in *Bejahung*, the division initialized in *Ausstoßung* is symbolically affirmed as the underlying structure of neurotic psychic reality (É, p. 553).

Lacan's major contribution to the Freudian elaboration of primal repression is rooted in his linguistic interpretation of *Bejahung* as a mechanism that secures the neurotic subject's mode of access to the symbolic order (SIII, p. 12). Under this interpretation, *Bejahung* is designated as a crucial form of symbolic affirmation in the course of the structuration of the subject. It provides the "gap" or "symbol" engendered in *Ausstoßung* with its proper symbolic designation, that is, with a unique form of a *primordial signifier* (p. 156). This signifier functions as a symbolic anchoring point for the divided construct initialized in *Ausstoßung*, bestowing it with a fixed designation in the symbolic order (p. 149). In turn, it renders the symbolic order to be the site for conscious and unconscious registration, the bedrock of subjective reality (p. 156).

When addressing the nature of the primordial signifier affirmed in *Bejahung*, Lacan explicitly bases himself on Freud's (1896) account of the "*Wahrnehmungszeichen* ... the first registration of the perceptions" (SE I, p. 234). Lacan argues that, according to Freud, in order for memory to be organized into conscious subjective history, an initial registration of perception, that is inaccessible to consciousness, has to take place (SIII, p. 181). Addressing this issue in linguistic terms, Lacan analogously claims that in order for the symbolic order to provide a coherent basis for the inscription of subjective reality, an initial instatement of a "primitive" form of "signifying material"—inaccessible from the vantage point of the subject's signified reality—has to be affirmed (p. 156).

Lacan's linguistic account of the "*Wahrnehmungszeichen*" describes the primordial signifier as a "pure signifier," that is, a signifier "distinct from meaning ... characterized by not in itself possessing a literal meaning" (p. 199). According to Lacan, the primordial signifier "doesn't depend on meaning but is the source of meaning" (p. 248). In other words, instead of possessing literal meaning, it designates meaning effects as a whole in the symbolic—the power or potential of symbolization (É, p. 579). In this sense, Lacan describes the primordial signifier as the "point of origin of symbolization" (SIII, p. 46), for he argues that: "Everything radiates out from and is organized around this signifier ... It's the point of convergence that enables everything that happens in this discourse to be situated retroactively and prospectively" (p. 268). Defining the symbolic order as a chain of signifiers, Lacan argues that it is the primordial signifier to which every other signifier inscribed in the symbolic order generically relates to. By doing so, the primordial signifier preserves the consistency in the relationship between the signifier and the signified in the discursive mass and makes it transmissible in the intersubjective domain.[12] This "autonomous" dimension of the primordial signifier (p. 197), subtracted from the order of meaning per se, is related to what Lacan will later term "signifierness" (*signifiance*) (SXX, pp. 18–19). According to Lacan, "signifierness" is embodied in the very existence of all signifiers as a form representing meaning apart from their literal meaning. It marks the fact that a signifier has more than its signifying value (the signified), by denoting the generic quality of having signifying effects (SIII, p. 197; SXX, p. 19).[13]

In his account of the *generic* organizing function of the primordial signifier, Lacan relies on a linguistic framework addressing the formation of semantic networks in language. The basic assumption grounding this

---

[12] Lacan bases his account of the relationship between the signifier and the signified on Ferdinand de Saussure's linguistic theory. This theory will be further elaborated in Chaps. 6 and 7.

[13] For example, when listening to other people speaking a foreign language, we hear the signifiers they use devoid of their meaning: as linguistic units that have signifying effects.

framework is that, in order for a closed semantic network to systematically and coherently convey meaning that is universally attributed to its domain, an element has to be *excluded* from this network and function as its limit point. The exact status of this excluded element is a bit problematic to specify (Fink, 1997, p. 110). On the one hand, it is external to the semantic network, meaning that it does not convey any meaning internal to the domain. On the other hand, it is internal to this network for it has a certain *generic* function relevant for all of the elements in the domain. In order to designate the exact status of this element, Lacan coins the term extimacy (*extimité*) by applying the prefix *ex* from *exterieur* to the word *intimité*. The resulting neologism expresses the way in which the opposition between "inside" and "outside" is structurally affirmed in *Bejahung*, neither as inside nor as outside, but as an "intimate exteriority" (SVII, p. 139).

The *extimate* nature of the primordial signifier gains its first mathematical formulation in Lacan's *Seminar XVIII: On a Discourse That Might Not Be a Semblance (1971)*. In this seminar, Lacan utilizes the notion of the closed-set, borrowed from the domain of set-theory, in order to augment his account of the organizing function of the *extimate* primordial signifier in the symbolic order. Briefly put, a closed-set is defined as a limited domain, constituted on the basis of the exclusion of an element from its confines. In the closed-set, this excluded element functions as an internal limit point. Thus, a closed-set, as a sequential progression of elements, is conditioned by the instatement of an element that, while not being counted as one of its elements, functions as an internal limit point determining all of its elements. Comparatively, Lacan claims that the symbolic order, as the successive chain of signifiers, is constituted on the basis of the primordial exclusion of a signifier from its confines. This signifier, while not conveying meaning by itself, determines the capacity of all other signifiers in the symbolic to coherently convey meaning. Lacan associates the instatement of this primordial signifier as an internal limit point, with its affirmation in *Bejahung* (SXVIII 16.6.71). In this sense, Lacan characterizes primal repression as a *constitutive exclusion* in as much as it determines the initial inscription of the primordial signifier and, thus, stands behind the constitution of the symbolic order.

In *Seminar III*, Lacan complicates this framework by arguing that it is only the neurotic subjective structure that strictly relies on the "undisturbed" functioning of primal repression presented above.[14] Namely, Lacan claims that the proper instatement of the primordial signifier in *Bejahung* is a key feature in the constitution of the neurotic subjective structure and explicitly calls it "the ultimate signifier in neurosis" (SIII, p. 248). In this sense, Lacan strictly attributes the exact mode of linguistic functionality associated with the primordial signifier to the neurotic subject. These neurotic symbolic qualities include "the introduction of an order, of a mathematical order … [to the] signifying structure, which is so essential for finding one's way about the neuroses" (p. 320; brackets added). Moreover, Lacan argues that the primordial signifier introduces something of the neurotic subject's being into the symbolic order. This is what Lacan calls the "quilting point" of the subject in the symbolic (p. 267), an anchoring point through which the first is inserted into the latter as the one acknowledging the reception of meaning (*l'accusé de réception*) (p. 188). In this sense, Lacan argues that the inscription of the primordial signifier in *Bejahung* "subjectivizes" the symbolic order, making it "inhabitable" for the subject (p. 250) as the locus in which its being can be inscribed (Fink, 1999, p. 87). It is this mode of linguistic functionality and the way that it carries the subject's being that makes the inscription of the primordial signifier in *Bejahung* to be the fundamental operation through which neurotic subjective reality is constructed (SIII, p. 322).

The Name-of-the-Father

In *Seminar III*, Lacan offers another major contribution to the structural understanding of primal repression by designating it under the coordinates of the Oedipus complex (pp. 199–202). Particularly, Lacan associates primal repression with the instatement of the "paternal function,"[15] operating within the ternary domain of the child-mother-father (p. 268).

---

[14] As will be elaborated in the next section, according to Lacan, the foreclosure of the primordial signifier prevents the structuration of neurosis and leads to the structuration of psychosis.

[15] Also called "paternal metaphor" (É, p. 463; SV, p. 145).

Following Freud (1925), Lacan claims that the paternal function operates in the Oedipus complex by producing a cut in the hypothesized
unitary state in which there is no division between the child and the
mother (SE XIV, pp. 131–132). In the Oedipal myth, the father keeps
the child at a certain distance from its mother by enacting the prohibition
of incest, thus preventing the total absorption of the child by the mother.
In other words, the paternal function *excludes* an element from the child's
initial libidinal economy, manifests in the unitary relationship with the
mother, and thus introduces into this economy a third term in the form
of a gap (Fink, 1999, pp. 79–80).

It is important to note that Lacan does not view the paternal function
as directly dependent on an actual father figure (p. 79) but uses the
Oedipal vocabulary in order to emphasize an underlying structure in the
constitution of the subject and its relation to the symbolic order (SIII,
pp. 292–293). Correspondingly, Lacan does not consider the paternal
prohibition in terms of the authority of the paternal figure in the family
but in terms of symbolic authority—as an operation that instates the
authority of the law of "signifierness" in the symbolic order (SXX,
pp. 18–19). Accordingly, the primordial signifier, as the marker of "signifierness" in the symbolic order, is transformed by Lacan—in the Oedipal
augmentation of primal repression—into the signifier of the "Name-of-
the-Father" (*Nom-du-Père*). This term plays on the double meaning of the
word *nom* ("name") that marks the authoritative function of the name
and legacy of the father but when spoken also sounds like the word *non*
("no"), evoking the father's prohibition of the child's incestuous urges.

In his paper "On a Question Prior to Any Possible Treatment of
Psychosis," printed in *Écrits* (2006), Lacan presents a developed formula
for the instatement of the paternal function and the "Name-of-the-
Father" in primal repression—see Fig. 3.2:

$$\frac{\text{Name-of-the-Father}}{\text{Mother's Desire}} \cdot \frac{\text{Mother's Desire}}{\text{Signified to the Subject}} \rightarrow \text{Name-of-the-Father} \left[\frac{\text{Other}}{\text{Phallus}} \right]$$

Fig. 3.2 Lacan's formula for the paternal function. (Based on Lacan 2006, p. 465)

In this formula Lacan divides the paternal function into two instances. In the first instance of the paternal function, the Mother's Desire is put under the bar of the signifier of the Name-of-the-Father. This is the instance of the father's *non* subjecting the Mother's Desire to the prohibition of incest. In this instance, a division between the child and the mother is instated and integrated as a gap in the child's libidinal economy. It is here that a sum of jouissance is primally excluded and engendered as lost. In the second instance of the paternal function, the Mother's Desire is further signified for the subject by subjecting it to the symbolic law. By doing so, the initial gap is transformed into the lack that sparks the subject's access to the mediated dimension of its own desire. This is the instance of the father's *nom*, where the signifier of the Name-of-the-Father names the gap in the Mother's Desire for the subject, bringing about a new symbolic access to desire that the child can safely adopt (Vanheule, 2011, p. 61). While the left part of the formula signifies the two instances in the dialectics of the Mother's Desire and the Name-of-the-Father, the right part of the formula (following the arrow) designates its consequence on the structuration of the subject and its relation to the symbolic order. Accordingly, we can see that the outcome of the two instances of the paternal function is the fact that the symbolic Other is completely subjected to the law of signification (phallic logic) (p. 64) and thus functions as the locus of neurotic subjective reality (É, p. 459).[16] This relationship is preserved by the signifier of the Name-of-the-Father.

Similarly, In his book *Clinical Introduction to Lacanian Psychoanalysis: Theory and Technique* (1999), Fink suggests to view the paternal function as entailing two instances: the first includes the act of prohibition that hinders the Mother's Desire from devouring the child (p. 91)—a prohibition of jouissance; the second is the act of symbolization, of situating the father's name in the place of the Mother's Desire in the symbolic. This way, the prohibition of the Mother's Desire is signified as it is named in

---

[16] In other words, the "barred" Other (the symbolic order) functions as the locus of signifiers—the site in which subjective reality is to be constructed in secondary repression.

the paternal function by the signifier of the Name-of-the-Father (pp. 93, 178).[17] We can clearly see how these two instances correspond to the two aspects of primal repression presented so far. The first aspect, *Ausstoßung*, in which a sum of jouissance is excluded and thus engendered as lacking, corresponds to the prohibition of the Mother's Desire. The second aspect, *Bejahung*, in which this exclusion is affirmed and further signified, corresponds to the naming of the Mother's Desire in the inscription of the signifier of the Name-of-the-Father.

Secondary Repression

Lacan adopts the Freudian model of secondary repression from the point in which Freud (1915) characterizes it as an exclusion of an idea from consciousness and its disassociation from its corresponding quota of affect (SE XIV, p. 152). Freud never fully determines the status of the ideas excluded in secondary repression but in some point called them "ideational representatives" (*Vorstellungsrepräsentanzen*) (p. 176).[18] One of Lacan's major contributions to the understanding of secondary repression is his equation of the ideational representatives with his linguistic understanding of signifiers. Unlike the Name-of-the-Father, which is a "pure signifier" that does not possess a literal meaning, Lacan describes the "ideational representatives" as signifiers *suffused with meaning*—signifiers that produce the meaningful content characteristic of the symbolic order (SXI, p. 218). Therefore, according to Lacan, in secondary repression, these meaningful signifiers are repressed and form new meaningful relationships with other repressed signifiers thus composing the chain of signifiers in the unconscious (Fink, 1997, p. 8).

Lacan famously claims that the unconscious is "structured like a language" (SIII, pp. 11, 167). He does so because, just like conscious

---

[17] Fink (1999) suggests that these instances correspond to Lacan's conception of alienation and separation, respectively, as well as Lacan's conception of primal and secondary repression, respectively. Nevertheless, in this book the two instances of the paternal function are attributed to primal repression alone.

[18] These are termed by Lacan the "representatives of representation" (*représentants de la représentation*) (SVII, p. 102).

discourse, the unconscious is composed of a chain of relations between signifiers repressed in secondary repression. Moreover, Lacan adds that the unconscious speaks—"it speaks" (*ca parle*)—beyond what one wants to say (p. 41). In this sense, Lacan argues that the chain of signifiers in the unconscious composes a kind of a foreign discourse that distorts the conscious discourse of the ego (p. 20). According to Lacan, this "chain [of signifiers] nevertheless continues to run on beneath the surface, express its demands, and assert its claims—and this it does through the intermediary of the neurotic symptom" (p. 84; brackets added). The capacity of unconscious signifiers to speak on their own is Lacan's re-adaptation of Freud's notion of the "return of the repressed" (p. 57). It is designated as the affirmative aspect of secondary repression in which repressed signifiers are not simply excluded and forgotten but manifest themselves through dreams, slips of the tongue, jokes, and other various neurotic symptoms. In this sense, according to Lacan, repression and the return of the repressed are one and the same thing (p. 46). They convey the unique structure of the neurotic subject—split between consciousness and the unconscious—through their manifestation in the form of distractions and interruptions of the consistency of conscious discourse (p. 72).

Another interesting contribution that Lacan provides to the Freudian model of secondary repression has to do with the understanding of the role of judgments of existence in the construction of subjective reality. In his linguistic interpretation, Lacan insists that when Freud talks about "reality" he is not strictly addressing what psychiatrists call "external reality," but associates it with the *symbolic* aspect of psychic reality (p. 156): "the reality with which we are concerned [in neurosis] is upheld, woven through, constituted, by a tress of signifiers … that is because we hold that reality implies the subject's integration into a particular play of signifiers" (p. 249; brackets added). Accordingly, Lacan associates the sequential functioning of secondary repression with the construction of the subject's *symbolic reality*—claiming that secondary repression attributes the value of existence (or non-existence) not to real objects but to whatever signifiers denote as objects (p. 150).

Finally, Lacan emphasizes that secondary repression is conditioned by the proper functioning of primal repression. He argues that it is only after the affirmation of the signifier of the Name-of-the-Father in *Bejahung* that signifiers can be repressed in secondary repression and find their anchoring point in the unconscious (É, p. 324). He adds that, in secondary repression, the subject attempts to re-find the lost object instated in primal repression by continuously associating its loss with the *existence* of substitutive signifier (SIII, p. 85). By adhering to this model, Lacan emphasizes the fact that primal repression conditions secondary repression as well as the construction of neurotic subjective reality.

Summary

The integration of the Freudian model of repression in Lacan's teaching offers several new frameworks through which repression can be classified as a psychic mechanism of *constitutive exclusion*. The first is rooted in Lacan's linguistic interpretation of repression. According to this framework, the mechanism of repression is characterized as entailing two distinct linguistic mechanisms—primal and secondary repression. Primal repression entails the primal expulsion (*Ausstoßung*) of a sum of jouissance and the affirmation (*Bejahung*) of the primordial signifier that constitutes and organizes the relationship between the subject and the symbolic order. According to Lacan, it is primal repression that enables the functioning of secondary repression, manifest in the exclusion of signifiers to the unconscious and their return in the guise of symptoms that shape neurotic psychic reality. This framework provides a complex account of primal repression: first, it divides repression into two distinct mechanisms; second, it attributes primal repression with a fundamental constitutive power, to which secondary repression is subordinate; third, it accounts for two modes of functioning internal to primal repression—*Ausstoßung* and *Bejahung*; finally, it explicates the distinct nature of the signifiers that are excluded in primal and secondary repression as well as accounts for the exact organizing effect they have on the mode of linguistic functionality associated with the constitution of the neurotic subjective structure.

The second framework proposed by Lacan re-articulates the functioning of primal repression in terms of the Oedipus complex. Under the scope of this framework, primal repression is understood as the implementation of the paternal function in the ternary domain of the child-mother-father. The paternal function is applied on two levels. The first has to do with the prohibition of the all-encompassing Mother's Desire. On this level, a sum of jouissance is primally excluded and marks the initial gap dividing the child and the mother (*Ausstoßung*). The second level has to do with the affirmation of this gap (*Bejahung*) and the opening up of a space in the child's libidinal economy for his own mediated desire that is succumbed to the father's symbolic authority. By addressing primal repression in Oedipal terms, Lacan provides another angle through which its constitutive function can be addressed, focusing on the function of the primordial signifier of the Name-of-the-Father.

The third framework has to do with Lacan's notion of the three registers of the psyche: the imaginary, symbolic, and the real. Under the scope of this framework, primal repression is classified as a mechanism that initially situates the real as exterior to the symbolic (*Ausstoßung*), later affirming the symbolic as an internal space for the inscription of subjective reality (*Bejahung*). The exact effect primal repression has on the relationship between these three registers adds another level to its characterization and distinction.

In the following chapters, these conceptual frameworks will prove to be crucial for the understanding of the psychic mechanism of *constitutive exclusion* at the origin of psychosis as well as autism. The conclusion reached so far regarding the model of the psychic constitutive mechanism of repression can be summarized in Fig. 3.3:

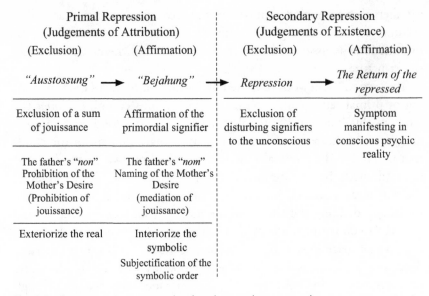

Fig. 3.3 Summary: Lacan on primal and secondary repression

Work Cited

Fink, B. (1997). *The Lacanian Subject: Between Language and Jouissance.* Princeton, NJ: Princeton University Press.

Fink, B. (1999). *A Clinical Introduction to Lacanian Psychoanalysis: Theory and Technique.* Cambridge, UK: Harvard University Press.

Freud, S. (1893). On the Psychical Mechanism of Hysterical Phenomena. *The Standard Edition of the Complete Psychological Works of Sigmund Freud, Volume II (1893–1895): Studies on Hysteria* (pp. 1–17).

Freud, S. (1894). "The Neuro-Psychoses of Defence." *The Standard Edition of the Complete Psychological Works of Sigmund Freud, Volume III (1893–1899): Early Psycho-Analytic Publications* (pp. 41–61).

Freud, S. (1896a). Further Remarks on the Neuro-Psychoses of Defense. *The Standard Edition of the Complete Psychological Works of Sigmund Freud, Volume III (1893–1899): Early Psycho-Analytic Publications* (pp. 157–185).

Freud, S. (1896b). Letter 524 from Extracts from the Fliess Papers. *The Standard Edition of the Complete Psychological Works of Sigmund Freud, Volume I (1886–1899): Pre-Psycho-Analytic Publications and Unpublished Drafts* (pp. 233–239).

Freud, S. (1911). Psycho-Analytic Notes on an Autobiographical Account of a Case of Paranoia (Dementia Paranoides). *The Standard Edition of the Complete Psychological Works of Sigmund Freud, Volume XII (1911–1913): The Case of Schreber, Papers on Technique and Other Works* (pp. 1–82).

Freud, S. (1913). Totem and Taboo. *The Standard Edition of the Complete Psychological Works of Sigmund Freud, Volume XIII (1913–1914): Totem and Taboo and Other Works*, vii–162.

Freud, S. (1914a). On the History of the Psycho-Analytic Movement. *The Standard Edition of the Complete Psychological Works of Sigmund Freud, Volume XIV (1914–1916): On the History of the Psycho-Analytic Movement, Papers on Metapsychology and Other Works* (pp. 1–66).

Freud, S. (1914b). On Narcissism. *The Standard Edition of the Complete Psychological Works of Sigmund Freud, Volume XIV (1914–1916): On the History of the Psycho-Analytic Movement, Papers on Metapsychology and Other Works* (pp. 67–102).

Freud, S. (1915). Repression. *The Standard Edition of the Complete Psychological Works of Sigmund Freud, Volume XIV (1914–1916): On the History of the Psycho-Analytic Movement, Papers on Metapsychology and Other Works* (pp. 141–158).

Freud, S. (1925). Negation. *The Standard Edition of the Complete Psychological Works of Sigmund Freud, Volume XIX (1923–1925): The Ego and the Id and Other Works* (pp. 233–240).

Lacan, J. (1988). In J.-A. Miller (Ed.), *The Seminar of Jacques Lacan, Book I, Freud's Papers on Technique (1953–1954)*. New York: Norton & Company.

Lacan, J. (1992). In J.-A. Miller (Ed.), *The Seminar, Book VII, The Ethics of Psychoanalysis (1959–1960)*. New York: Norton & Company.

Lacan, J. (1997). In J.-A. Miller (Ed.), *The Seminar of Jacques Lacan, Book III, The Psychoses (1955–1956)*. New York: Norton & Company.

Lacan, J. (1998a). *The Seminar of Jacques Lacan, Book XX, Encore: On Feminine Sexuality, the Limits of Love and Knowledge*. New York: Norton.

Lacan, J. (1998b). In J.-A. Miller (Ed.), *The Seminar of Jacques Lacan, Book XX, Encore: On Feminine Sexuality, the Limits of Love and Knowledge (1972–1973), New York*. Norton.

Lacan, J. (2001). In J.-A. Miller (Ed.), *The Seminar, Book XI. The Four Fundamental Concepts of Psychoanalysis (1964)*. New York: Norton & Company.

Lacan, J. (2006). In B. Fink (Ed.), *Écrits*. New York: Norton & Company.

Lacan, J. (2017). In J.-A. Miller (Ed.), *The Seminar of Jacques Lacan, Book VIII, Transference (1960–1961)*. Cambridge, UK: Polity.

Lacan, J. (n.d.). *The Seminar of Jacques Lacan, Book XVIII, On a Discourse that Might Not be a Semblance (1971)*. Trans. Gallagher, C. Unpublished.

Recalcati, M., & McGlazer, R. (2012). Hate as a Passion of Being. *Qui Parle: Critical Humanities and Social Sciences, 20*(2), 151–182.

Vanheule, S. (2011). *The Subject of Psychosis: A Lacanian Perspective.* New York: Springer.

Zupančič, A. (2012). Not-Mother: On Freud's Verneinung. *E-Flux, 33.*

4

Foreclosure and the Psychotic Subject

In autism, there is no clear evidence attesting to the functioning of repression, neither primal nor secondary (Lefort & Lefort, 2003, p. 51; Maleval, 2009, pp. 201, 211, 232; Miller, 2010, p. 28). As a result, autistic subjects are considered to have no access to the level of linguistic functionality these mechanisms enable. Accordingly, in autism we see a radical restriction of the subject's mode of access to the domain of signifiers. This brings several contemporary psychoanalysts in the Lacanian field to suggest that the *constitutive exclusion* at the origin of autism is not a repression but a radical form of *foreclosure* (*Verwerfung*) (Benoist, 2011; Laurent, 2012; Lefort & Lefort, 1994, 2003; Tendlarz, 2003).

The term *Verwerfung* was initially presented by Freud when he described a singular form of *constitutive exclusion* at the origin of the psychotic detachment from reality. Lacan adopted this term from Freud and, in his *Seminar III: The Psychoses (1955–1956)*, reframed it as "foreclosure" (*forclusion*). He argued that, just like repression, foreclosure functions as a psychic mechanism of *constitutive exclusion*. However, unlike repression, it is situated at the origin of the psychotic subjective structure and enables its unique mode of linguistic functionality.

© The Author(s) 2020
L. S. Brenner, *The Autistic Subject*, The Palgrave Lacan Series,
https://doi.org/10.1007/978-3-030-50715-2_4

Contrary to *psychotic foreclosure, autistic foreclosure* has not been exhaustively accounted for in psychoanalytic circles. That is while, even in Lacanian circles, an agreement as to the degree of its divergence from the scope of the clinic of psychosis has not been fully established. Nonetheless, the relevance of the Lacanian elaboration of foreclosure is very much agreed upon and utilized in the clinical work done with autistic subjects today. Therefore, this chapter will investigate the way foreclosure functions in psychosis, in order to elaborate on its functioning in autism in the following chapters.

Foreclosure in Freud

Freud had never provided a fully comprehensive account of the constitutive psychic mechanism at the origin of psychosis. He (1896) did not do so, firstly, due to the scarcity of cases of psychosis at his disposal and secondly, due to his suspicion as to the effectivity of psychoanalytic treatment in cases of psychosis (SE III, p. 175). Nevertheless, several consistent perspectives in the elaboration of this mechanism can be traced in different papers along the progression of his work.

The following section will present three major perspectives through which the *constitutive exclusion* at the origin of psychosis has been elaborated by Freud. The first, presented in his papers "The Neuro-Psychoses of Defense" (1894) and "Further Remarks on the Neurosis-Psychoses of Defense" (1896), presents the mechanism at the origin of psychosis in direct relation to repression and the "neuro-psychoses." Under this framework, psychotic foreclosure gains its first designation in Freud as the "rejection" (*Verwerfung*) of reality. The second, presented in his papers "Psycho-Analytic Notes of an Autobiographical Account of a Case of Paranoia" (1911), "On Narcissism: An Introduction" (1914), and "Repression" (1915), analyzes psychosis in the terms of Freud's theory of the drive and libido. Under this dynamic framework, psychosis is presented as taking form in a regression to an early stage of libidinal development (narcissism) that entails cutting off libidinal ties with the exterior world. The third, presented in Freud's papers "Neurosis and Psychosis" (1924a) and "The Loss of Reality in Neurosis and Psychosis" (1924c), can be considered as a continuation of the first framework, adapted to the terms of Freud's second topology. In these two papers, "rejection" (*Verwerfung*) is reframed under the term "disavowal" (*Verleugnung*), designating a unique psychotic mechanism differentiated from repression. These three frameworks will be of great use in the structural distinction of the mechanism of *autistic foreclosure*. They will firstly lead to the Lacanian elaboration of the mechanism of psychotic foreclosure in the second section of this chapter and only then will be implemented in elaboration of autism in the following chapters.

The Rejection (*Verwerfung*) of Reality

Between the years 1885 and 1899, Freud embarks on an attempt to substantiate his meta-psychological model of a group of disorders he names the "neuro-psychoses." In this group Freud includes hysteria, obsession, and phobias, as well as hallucinatory psychosis and paranoia. In his two papers "The Neuro-Psychoses of Defense" (1894) and "Further Remarks on the Neurosis-Psychoses of Defense" (1896), Freud associates all of the aforementioned neuro-psychoses with a single underlying mechanism that is not spontaneous, deterministic, or hereditary in nature but, rather, entails a voluntary act on behalf of the subject's will (SE III, p. 46). Freud specifically describes the origin of all of these disorders as a moment where the subject is "faced with an experience, an idea or a feeling which aroused such a distressing affect that the subject decided to forget about it because he had no confidence in his power to resolve the contradiction between that incompatible idea and his ego by means of thought-activity" (p. 47). In other words, they all originate from an active repression (pp. 48, 178, 180).

Freud (1894) relates the active repression—utilized in cases of hysteria, obsession, and phobia[1]—to a detachment of a sum of excitation or affect from a disturbing idea with the aim of turning a strongly conflictual idea into a weak one (SE III, pp. 48–49). In all of these cases, Freud claims that "a defense against the incompatible idea was effected by separating it

---

[1] All of these will be later attributed by Freud to the neurotic subjective structure.

from its affect; the idea itself remained in consciousness, even though weakened and isolated" (p. 58). This is what we have associated in the previous chapter with the functioning of secondary repression or repression proper.

In his later paper "Further Remarks on the Neurosis-Psychoses of Defense" (1896), Freud explicitly relates this form of defense to neurosis and psychosis alike: "In each of them [neurosis and psychosis], repression has been shown to be the nucleus of the psychical mechanism, and in each what has been repressed is a sexual experience in childhood" (SE III, p. 183; brackets added). Nevertheless, he argues that in the case of psychosis, we are dealing with "a special method or mechanism of repression which is peculiar to it" (p. 175). This is the exact formula Freud (1894) provides at this time: In the case of psychosis, the subject "rejects [*Verwift*] the incompatible idea together with its affect and behaves as if the idea had never occurred to the ego at all ... *from the moment at which this has been successfully done the subject is in a psychosis*" (SE III, p. 58).

This is the first time Freud employs the term *Verwerfung* to describe a specific form of psychic mechanism of exclusion at the origin of psychosis (Maleval, 2004, p. 39). Translated to English as "rejection," *Verwerfung* is conceived in this paper (1894) as a "much more energetic and successful kind of defense" than is employed in neurotic repression (SE III, p. 58). Unlike neurotic repression, which detaches an idea from its corresponding affect but leaves behind a weakened trace of the idea as well as an isolated affect, psychotic rejection completely abolishes all traces of the conflictual idea as well as its corresponding affect from the psyche.

Freud furthers his account of psychotic rejection by explicitly relating it to a detachment from reality itself. Freud gives an example of an analysand that suffered from the disinterest of a man she felt affection for. He claims that this analysand first attempts to repress the conflictual ideas concerning this man, but these ideas persist in his implied presence in her everyday life, thus rendering the repression ineffective. After a specific event in which the analysand experiences dire disappointment in regard to this man, she progresses into a state of great tension, finally bringing about the rejection of the reality of his absence. According to Freud, at this point the analysand passes into a state of "hallucinatory confusion" in which she occasionally hears his voice calling to her and feels his presence by her side, marking the onset of psychosis (pp. 58–59).

In this example Freud emphasizes two defining characteristics of psychotic rejection. The first is that psychotic rejection is a mechanism of defense superimposed on an ineffective application of a repression. He argues that in cases of repression where the idea—detached from its corresponding affect—is not sufficiently weakened and persists in the subject's reality, a further and "more energetic" attempt of a rejection of this idea, in addition to its corresponding affect, is implemented (p. 58). The second is that the rejection of a conflictual idea and its corresponding affect is achieved alongside any aspect in the subject's reality to which they are related: "The ego breaks away from the incompatible idea; but the latter is inseparably connected with a piece of reality, so that, in so far as the ego achieves this result, it, too, has detached itself wholly or in part from reality" (p. 59).

In his following paper, "Further Remarks on the Neuro-Psychoses of Defense" (1896), Freud goes on to further elaborate on the outcome of psychotic rejection by assessing it in terms of "hallucinatory confusion" and "delusional ideas" that are the symptoms of the "return of the repressed" in the case of psychosis (SE III, pp. 181–182). On the subject of hallucinatory confusion, Freud remarks that, while in neurosis, a repression of an idea would entail its manifestation in obsessive thoughts ("substitution") or somatic symptoms ("conversion"), in psychosis, the rejection of an idea alongside its manifestation in reality entails a state in which the subject's reality is reconstructed around its absence. This would include auditory or visual hallucinations in the form of "images and sensations" that are associated with a rejected memory as well as words "said aloud" associated with rejected "thoughts" (p. 181). On the subject of delusional ideas, Freud argues that, while in neurosis, the repression of an incompatible idea results in its return in the form of symptoms exhibiting self-reproach and distrust inwardly directed at the self (pp. 165, 169–171), psychotic rejection results in the "projection" of feelings of distrust and self-reproach toward other people (pp. 174–175). These feelings commonly manifest in cases of paranoia where subjects view the outside world as persecutory and malevolent. Finally, Freud adds that, due to the fact that psychotic delusions and hallucinations impose themselves on the subject until they are "accepted without contradiction," they also entail an "*alteration of the ego*" (p. 185). This form of "alteration" or "mal-formation" is previously accounted for in "Draft K of the Flies Papers" (1892) as well as later in Freud's "Analysis Terminable and Interminable" (1937). It entails a unique remodeling of the ego in compliance with the subject's delusions and hallucinations (SE I, p. 227) as well as alterations in drive functionality (SE XXIII, p. 224).[2]

Fixation and Regression to the Narcissistic Stage

One of Freud's most elaborate accounts of the constitutive mechanism at the origin of psychosis can be found in his paper "Psycho-Analytic Notes of an Autobiographical Account of a Case of Paranoia" (1911).[3] In this paper, Freud elucidates the functioning of psychosis on the basis of the model of neurotic repression, providing it with a dynamic interpretation rooted in his theory of drive and libidinal development.[4] More specifi-cally, Freud associates the constitutive mechanism at the origin of psy-chosis with a *narcissistic fixation* established in the course of early libidinal development—a hypothesis that will be further developed in his later paper "On Narcissism: An Introduction" (1914).

Freud (1911) hypothesizes that the qualitative variance between the different forms of repression at the origin of the neuro-psychoses is deter-mined by a *fixation* achieved in the course of libidinal development (SE XII, pp. 67–68). In other words, Freud argues that the exact level of libidinal development on which a *fixation* is achieved in early childhood determines the exact mode of functioning of a repression and, as a result, the structuration of the subject and of psychic reality. As will shortly be

---

[2] This point will be further accounted for in Freud's paper "Psycho-Analytic Notes of an Autobiographical Account of a Case of Paranoia" (1911) and later on in his paper "On Narcissism: An Introduction" (1914). It will be elaborated in the following section.

[3] At the time this paper was written, psychosis was divided into several clinical categories such as "paranoia," "dementia praecox," and "schizophrenia." While the term "paranoia" was used in German psychiatry to describe delusions in general, Freud uses the term in this paper in a wider sense, relating it to a combination of these psychopathological experiences.

[4] The difference between the formula proposed by Freud in this paper (1911) and in his paper "Repression" (1915) is outlined by Freud in a letter to Ferenczi, December 6, 1910 (Jones, 1955, p. 499).

disclosed in detail, Freud associates the functioning of what we have so far termed psychotic *rejection* with a *fixation* on the narcissistic stage of libidinal development.

Fixation on the Narcissistic Stage

In his paper "Psycho-Analytic Notes of an Autobiographical Account of a Case of Paranoia" (1911), Freud bases his analysis of psychosis on a single literary case study of the autobiography of Dr. Daniel Paul Schreber, *Memoirs of My Nervous Illness* (1955). Freud finds the book to be a rich source of clinical material, enough to elaborate on the workings of psychosis. He (1911) emphasizes that the distinct quality of psychosis is not to be sought in Schreber's symptoms alone but rather in the unique form of repression that determines his complexes and symptoms:

> The distinctive character of paranoia (or of dementia paranoides) must be sought for … in the particular form assumed by the symptoms; and we shall expect to find that this is determined, not by the nature of the complexes themselves, but by the mechanism by which the symptoms are formed or by which repression is brought about. (SE XII, p. 59)

Freud adds that Schreber's symptoms portray a paranoiac type of psychosis manifest in delusions of persecution (pp. 59, 66) and a general state of megalomania (pp. 48–49). He attributes Schreber's psychosis to a unique type of repression through which he attempts to ward off a re-emerging homosexual wishful phantasy: "We should be inclined to say that what was characteristically paranoic about the illness was the fact that the patient, as a means of warding off a homosexual wishful phantasy, reacted precisely with delusions of persecution of this kind" (p. 59). It is the central role that wishful phantasies of homosexual nature play in the origin of psychosis in Schreber's case that brings Freud to relate the constitutive mechanism at the origin of psychosis to a pathological regression, one which originates in a *fixation* on the narcissistic stage of libidinal development.

Briefly stated, Freud designated three consecutive stages in the course of libidinal development: auto-erotism, narcissism, and object-love (p. 61). In his paper "On Narcissism: An Introduction" (1914), Freud claims that, in the course of this development, the subject progresses from his auto-erotic tendencies in the stage of narcissism, in which the libido is solely invested in the ego ("ego-libido"), to the stage of object-love, in which it is invested in exterior objects as well ("object-libido") (SE XIV, pp. 98–100).

In his earlier paper, Freud (1911) provides another designation to these two modes of libidinal functioning ("ego-libido" and "object-libido") based on the subject's genital affiliation of its object of choice. Freud argues that because in narcissism the libido is invested in the ego itself (ego-libido), a subject situated on this stage will be led "to the choice of an external object with similar genitals—that is, to homosexual object-choice." Correspondingly, Freud claims that in the stage of object-love, the choice of an external object becomes "heterosexual" and the subject forsakes his previous homosexual object-choice: "After the stage of heterosexual object-choice has been reached, the homosexual tendencies are ... deflected from their sexual aim and applied to fresh uses" (SE XII, p. 61).[5]

While the progression from the stage of narcissism to the stage of object-love is achieved by most subjects, Freud claims that some subjects fail to go through this progression and remain *fixated* on the narcissistic stage. Freud argues that these subjects are at the risk of developing pathologies that manifest in the undoing of their libidinal investments in objects, due to a pathological regression of libido:

> People who have not freed themselves completely from the stage of narcissism—who, that is to say, have at that point a fixation which may operate as a disposition to a later illness—are exposed to the danger that some unusually intense wave of libido, finding no other outlet, may lead to a sexualization of their social instincts and so undo the sublimations [of their homosexual tendencies] which they had achieved in the course of their

---

[5] While Freud's account of homosexuality remains questionable today, it is important to note that Freud argues that it is the attempt to ward off homosexual wishful phantasies that brings about the onset of psychosis and not homosexual object choice.

development. This result may be produced by anything that causes the libido to flow backwards (i.e., that causes a "regression"). (p. 62; brackets added)

Freud continues this paragraph and specifically argues that these subjects are at a risk of a pathological regression to the stage of narcissism that might manifest in symptoms of psychosis. From this position, Freud generalizes and explicitly claims: "we can suppose that paranoics have brought along with them *a fixation at the stage of narcissism*, and we can assert that the length of *the step back from sublimated homosexuality to narcissism* is a measure of the amount of regression characteristic of paranoia" (p. 72).[6]

Regression and the Reconstruction of Reality

Freud describes the repercussions of the regression characteristic of psychosis in terms of an "internal catastrophe," a "profound internal change of the world," or the "end of the world" (pp. 68–73). These are Freud's ways of describing the profound changes in the subject's mode of libidinal functioning in psychosis:

> The patient has withdrawn from the people in his environment and from the external world generally the libidinal cathexis which he has hitherto directed on to them. Thus everything has become indifferent and irrelevant to him … The end of the world is the projection of this internal catastrophe; his subjective world has come to an end since his withdrawal of his love from it. (p. 70)

Going back to his account of the course of libidinal development, Freud claims that in the transition from the stage of narcissism to that of object-love, the subject establishes a multiplicity of libidinal investments in objects exterior to the ego. These carry the subject from the secluded world of narcissistic libidinal investment (ego-libido), into the

---

[6] Freud relates this regression to all forms of psychosis noted among his contemporaries, e.g., paranoia, Kraepelin's dementia praecox, and Bleuler's schizophrenia.

intersubjective domain of exterior objects and people (object-libido). Freud argues that, with the onset of psychosis, the subject experiences a regression from the stage of object-love (object-libido) to the stage of narcissism (ego-libido) that entails a devastating detachment of libido from objects and people in the exterior world achieved through the stage of object-love. Accordingly, we see why the loss of libidinal investment in exterior objects entails the dismantling of the world of objects itself—the "end of the world" (p. 72).

Nevertheless, Freud insists that "It cannot be asserted that a paranoic, even at the height of the repression, withdraws his interest from the external world completely" (p. 75). We see this in the continuing interest of the paranoiac in the messages and signs he perceives as being directed to him from the world around him. These manifest especially in cases of megalomania, in which a psychotic individual can develop delusions of persecution, erotomania, and delusions of jealousy (pp. 48, 64–65). Accordingly, Freud (1914) argues that, in the case of psychotic regression, the libido that has been invested in objects in the external world is not totally abandoned but is redirected to the ego. He describes this mode of libidinal investment as a singular form of pathological narcissism. He insists that this form of narcissism is "a secondary one, superimposed upon a primary narcissism that is obscured by a number of different influences" and calls it *secondary narcissism* (SE XIV, p. 75). In this sense, we see that libidinal functioning is not arrested in psychosis but is diverted from the workings of object-libido, solely to the functioning of ego-libido in a secondary pathological form of narcissism.[7]

As for psychotic symptoms, such as delusions or hallucinations, they gain a new designation in Freud's dynamic interpretation of psychotic regression. On the subject of hallucinations, Freud (1911) argues that they cannot be rooted in any form of "projection": "It was incorrect to say that the perception which was suppressed internally is projected outwards; the truth is rather, as we now see, that what was abolished

---

[7] In this paper, Freud (1914) attributes the highest phase of the development of object-libido to the prospect of love, in which the subject abandons all forms of ego-libido in favor of object-cathexis. Contrary to that, Freud compares the psychotic experience of the "end of the world" to the total abandonment of this form of object-cathexis and the complete absorption in ego-libido (SE XIX, p. 76).

internally returns from without" (SE XII, p. 71). In this intriguing passage, Freud brings us closer to his earlier conception of psychotic *rejection* and its distinction from neurotic repression. Freud (1894) had argued that, in psychotic *rejection*, an idea and its corresponding affect are radically excluded, taking with them any aspect in the subject's reality to which they are related (SE III, pp. 58–59). When an idea is radically excluded, it does not exist "internally" and therefore cannot be "projected outward" from the inside. Accordingly, in his dynamic interpretation of psychotic *regression*, Freud argues that a *rejected* drive impulse is not projected from within but returns from without, in the guise of hallucinations perceived in the external world. On the subject of delusions, Freud (1911) still argues that they are rooted in projections aimed in an outward direction. Nevertheless, they are not considered in terms of self-reproach but as the projection of narcissistic libidinal cathexes on to objects, as an attempt to reconstruct the lost investments in objects and people (SE XII, p. 78). Freud claims that this is a double-faceted process that begins by a depletion of libido from exterior objects, followed by an attempt to recover lost object cathexes by reconstructing them through delusions: "The delusional formation, which we take to be the pathological product, is in reality an attempt at recovery, a process of reconstruction" (p. 71).

The Disavowal (*Verleugnung*) of Reality

In two succeeding papers, "Neurosis and Psychosis" (1924a) and "The Loss of Reality in Neurosis and Psychosis" (1924c), Freud provides him most explicit account of the constitutive mechanism at the origin of psychosis. These papers present a systematic integration of Freud's previously fragmented accounts of psychosis in his characterization of "rejection" (1894–1896) and "narcissistic regression" (1911–1915). Utilizing terms borrowed from his second topology, Freud aligns several of the different forms of the neuro-psychoses such as paranoia, schizophrenia, Meynert's amentia, hallucinatory confusion, and paramnesias, under the same underlying psychotic mechanism that he calls "disavowal" (*Verleugnung*).[8] As will shortly be elaborated, Freud provides an initial structural account of this mechanism in comparison to neurotic repression, divides it into two consecutive stages, and attributes its singularity to the first.

The "Simple Formula" of Neurosis and Psychosis

In "Neurosis and Psychosis" (1924a), Freud presents a new "simple formula" that marks out the "genetic difference" between neurosis and psychosis: "neurosis is the result of a conflict between the ego and its id, whereas psychosis is the analogous outcome of a similar disturbance in the relations between the ego and the external world" (SE XIX, p. 149).

In his new formula for neurosis, Freud does not venture too far away from its initial definition in his paper "Repression" (1915) that was presented in the previous chapter. We now (1924a) see that, under the terms of his second topology, the object of repression—the conflictual idea—is now substituted with the term "id" or "id's wishful impulse" (SE XIX, pp. 150–151). Accordingly, Freud explains that in neurosis an impulse in the id that conflicts with the ego is repressed. This repressed impulse then finds a "substitutive representation" in the form of a neurotic symptom, which we have so far called the return of the repressed (pp. 149–150). Freud concludes "Neurosis and Psychosis" (1924a) without further elaborating on the origin of psychosis but calls for a "fresh investigation" of "the mechanism, analogous to repression … by means of which the ego detaches itself from the external world" in psychosis (p. 153).

---

[8] It is important to note that the term "disavowal" (*Verleugnung*) seems to take on itself different meanings in several of Freud's texts. For instance, in Freud's assessment of the mechanism of psychosis in "The Loss of Reality in Neurosis and Psychosis" (1924c), "disavowal" is meant to connote the specific mechanism of *constitutive exclusion* implemented on an undesirable drive-related impulse located in the id (SE XIX, p. 184). In later papers, such as "The Economic Problem of Masochism" (1924b) and "Some Psychical Consequences of the Anatomical Distinction Between the Sexes" (1925), the term is used in relation to the castration complex and psychosis. In his papers "Fetishism" (1927) and "Splitting of the Ego in the Process of Defense" (1938), it is used to connote a denial of a perception of an unacceptable piece of reality and characterizes the functioning of the constitutive mechanism at the origin of perversion.

Two Stages in Neurosis and Psychosis

Freud only truly delves into the investigation of the mechanism at the origin of psychosis in his following paper, "The Loss of Reality in Neurosis and Psychosis" (1924c). In this paper Freud begins by providing a slightly revised version of his "simple formula": "in a neurosis the ego, in its dependence on reality, suppresses a piece of the id (of instinctual life [*Trieblebens*]), whereas in a psychosis, this same ego, in the service of the id, withdraws from a piece of reality" (SE XIX, p. 183).

In the aforementioned revised formula, Freud explicitly clarifies the distinct role "reality" plays in the relationship between the ego and the id in neurosis and psychosis. In the case of neurosis, Freud emphasizes that the ego's strong link to reality determines if an impulse in the id is too conflictual and should be repressed.[9] Nevertheless, Freud remarks that this formula is a bit problematic, for in some cases of neurosis we also see the withdrawal of the ego from reality. Freud explains that this problem can be solved by viewing repression as a mechanism entailing two stages. In the first stage, there is an exclusion of a conflictual impulse. This stage is necessarily followed by "processes which provide a compensation for the portion of the id that has been damaged—that is to say, in the reaction against the repression and in the failure of the repression" (p. 183). The latter is the affirmative aspect of repression, the return of the repressed in the guise of the neurotic symptom. Freud claims that it is only in the second stage of neurotic repression that we see a "loosening of the relation to reality," that is, in the odd symptomatic behavior of the neurotic subject (p. 183).

Freud (1893) provides an example from the case of Elisabeth Von R., in which the analysand, sitting at her sister's deathbed, suddenly is faced with the idea of marrying her newly widowed husband: "Now he is free again and I can be his wife" (SE II, p. 156). Freud (1924c) explains that, in the case of Von R, this conflictual idea is repressed and then affirmed

---

[9] In "Neurosis and Psychosis" (1924a), Freud explicitly associates the subject's strong link to reality with the function of the super-ego which represents commands and influences found in the external world: "It is no contradiction to this that, in undertaking the repression, the ego is at bottom following the commands of its super-ego—commands which, in their turn, originate in influences in the external world that have found representation in the super-ego" (SE XIX, p. 150).

Transference

as it is expressed in her neurotic hysterical symptoms (SE XIX, p. 184). According to Freud, this is the way the neurotic subject attempts to solve a conflict between the ego's sense of reality and the id's wishful impulses: the ego's sense of reality brings about the repression of conflictual impulses that then return as symptoms affecting the subject's psychic reality.

On the other hand, Freud argues that, in the case of psychotic defense, "The psychotic reaction would have been a disavowal [*verleugnen*] of the fact of her sister's death" (p. 184). Namely, a conflictual impulse would have brought about the *disavowal* of that piece of reality that caused the impulse to emerge in the first place.

Accordingly, Freud goes on to distinguish two stages in the functioning of the mechanism of disavowal in psychosis in analogy to repression in neurosis. The first stage entails the withdrawal of the ego from reality—the disavowal of a piece of reality. Freud argues that the subject's reality is composed of the perceptions of the "external world" as well as memories of earlier perceptions that shape the subject's "internal world." Freud claims that the disavowal of reality in psychosis entails both the refusal of new perceptions and the loss of the significance of the previously constructed "internal world" of perceptions. In this sense, Freud associates the disavowal of reality with the "internal catastrophe" described in his earlier papers (1911, 1914). In these papers, psychosis is associated with the dismantling of all libidinal cathexes to external objects and people, the loss of interest in the exterior world and the full investment in ego-libido. Correspondingly, Freud (1924c) argues that the second stage in the functioning of the mechanism of disavowal entails an attempt to reestablish the subject's lost relation to reality. But, instead of renewing the severed libidinal ties to the previously constructed reality, the psychotic embarks on a project of "reparation" manifests in the "creation of a new reality which no longer raises the same objections as the old one that has been given up" (SE XIX, pp. 184–185). Freud characterizes it as the subject's attempt to singlehandedly create "a new external and internal world ... in accordance with the id's wishful impulses" (p. 151). This newly constructed reality takes form through psychotic delusions that are "applied like a patch over the place where originally a rent had appeared in the ego's relation to the external world" (p. 151). In this process, reality is transformed by the alteration of memory-traces, ideas, judgments, and representations, previously derived from the encounter with objects in reality (p. 185). These are altered in order to comply with the conflictual drive impulses that are the cause of disavowal in psychosis. Accordingly, Freud relates psychotic delusions in this paper to "an attempt at a cure or a reconstruction" (p. 151). He adds that they also bring into play new perceptions that correspond to the subject's newly constructed reality— perceptions achieved by means of hallucination (p. 186). Accordingly, the return of the repressed in psychosis is associated in this paper with the delusional alterations of the subject's internal and external reality, accompanied by hallucinated perceptions that comply with these alterations.

Further Comparisons Between Repression and Disavowal

Freud emphasizes a strict homology between the second stages in repression and disavowal. In both cases they are oriented to restore something that has been excluded due to its conflictual nature. In other words, both the return of the repressed in neurosis and the construction of a new reality in psychosis are aimed to preserve the insistence of the id's wishful impulses in the subject's reality. In neurosis, "a piece of reality is avoided by a sort of flight, whereas in psychosis it is remodeled" (p. 185). Freud adds that in psychosis the disavowed piece of reality constantly forces itself upon the mind, just like the repressed impulse does in neurosis. This entails the same consequences—its preservation as a means of a compromise in the form of a symptom. In both cases this compromise is only partially successful in substituting the repressed impulse or remolding the subject's reality (p. 186). In neurosis the conflictual piece of reality is substituted by the "world of phantasy" that is separated from the external world. In psychosis this "world of phantasy" also takes centre stage, as "it is the store-house from which the materials or the pattern for building the new reality are derived" (p. 187).

One of Freud's major contributions in this paper is his explicit designation of the singular nature of disavowal in relation to repression. Freud claims that "Neurosis and psychosis differ from each other far more in their first, introductory, reaction than in the attempt at reparation which follows it" (p. 185). Stated otherwise, Freud argues that the singular nature of the psychotic constitutive mechanism is situated in its initial stage of the exclusion of a piece of the subject's reality, rather than in the subsequent stage of the reconstruction of reality. This argument is intriguing and quite anti-intuitive. For commonly, psychosis is distinguished by the vast delusional world construction as well as its accompanying pervasive elementary phenomena like hallucinations. Nevertheless, Freud implies that while these might be more easily distinguished behaviorally, they are not sufficient in the distinction of psychosis and, in fact, are only secondary to what can truly be characterized as the singular nature of psychosis. According to Freud, what more precisely distinguishes psychosis from neurosis is that the *exclusion* of a piece of reality "is pathological in itself and cannot but lead to illness" (p. 186). Therefore, we see that while, in psychosis, the initial exclusion is necessarily pathological, in neurosis, it can be successful and not cause any form of illness (p. 187).

Summary

In the three frameworks presented in this section, Freud describes the psychic mechanism of *constitutive exclusion* at the origin of psychosis in direct relation to his model of repression. It is my contention that none of these models can be considered to overtake the others in its importance, as they all provide a difference glimpse into Freud's account of psychosis and foreshadow the work Lacan will undertake on the subject of foreclosure in the years to come. We can generally divide them into the first (f1) and third (f3) frameworks, dealing with this mechanism in structural terms, and the second framework (f2) dealing with it in more dynamic terms. When addressing their similarities and differences, we firstly note that in all of these frameworks, the constitutive psychotic mechanism seems to function in relation to a conflictual impulse. In f1 it is simply regarded as a conflictual drive impulse, in f3 this impulse is associated with the id, whereas in f2 it is explicitly regarded as a homosexual narcissistic drive impulse. In this sense, all of the frameworks situate the functioning of the constitutive psychotic mechanism on a level corresponding to primal repression that functions in the domain of the drive and not on a level corresponding to secondary repression functioning in the domain of consciousness. Secondly, all of these frameworks associate a failure in the functioning of repression with the onset of the constitutive psychotic mechanism that is superimposed on this failed repression. In f1 and f3, repression is unsuccessful in keeping a conflictual drive impulse at bay, while in f2 repression entails a pathological *fixation* on the stage of narcissism. Thirdly, in all of these cases, the constitutive psychotic mechanism is considered to be more "energetic" than repression, having a bigger scope and more far-reaching consequences on the construction of psychic reality. In f1 and f3, this mechanism excludes not only a conflictual idea but also its corresponding affect, alongside any aspect in the subject's reality to which they are related. In f2 it excludes all libidinal ties with objects (object-libido) not transitively mediated through the ego (ego-libido). These manifest in what Freud describes as the "rejection of reality," the "internal catastrophe," or the "end of the world" characteristic of psychosis. Finally, in all of these frameworks, the constitutive psychotic mechanism entails a subsequent affirmative aspect in which the reconstruction of psychic reality is attempted by the subject. In f1 and f3 this is the reconstruction of reality in accordance with the excluded drive impulses. In f2 this is the reinvestment of libido in objects through the mediation of the ego (ego-libido)—what Freud calls secondary narcissism. In all of these cases, these attempts include delusional ideas projected onto the world of objects as well as accompanying internal and external perceptions that correspond to the subject's newly constructed reality—hallucinations.

The conclusions reached so far and their comparison to the model of repression can be summarized in Fig. 4.1.

Unfortunately, Freud did not manage to fully explicate the distinctive features of the psychic mechanism of *constitutive exclusion* at the origin of psychosis. Nevertheless, Freud did introduce several concepts such as *Verleugnung*, translated as "denial" or "disavowal," which are linked to his earlier account of *Verwerfung*, initially translated as "rejection" (1894, 1896). It is the formulation of "disavowal" (*Verleugnung*) and "rejection" (*Verwerfung*) as the constitutive mechanisms at the origin of psychosis that will be the main object of interest in the following section. As will be presented shortly, Lacan takes it upon himself to meticulously

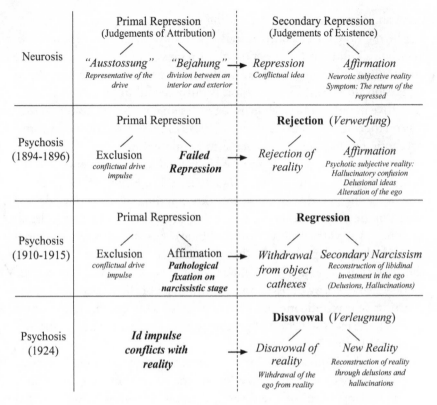

Fig. 4.1 Summary: Freud on the constitutive mechanisms in neurosis and psychosis

differentiate them from the other forms of psychic mechanisms of *constitutive exclusion* in order to account for the singularity of psychosis. At this point, the reader should keep in mind that autism is also considered to be rooted in a foreclosure. Therefore, the elaboration of psychotic foreclosure will be of great value in the elucidation of autism in the following chapters.

Foreclosure in Lacan

Lacan started his career as a psychiatrist and psychoanalyst working with psychotic patients at the Saint Anne's Clinique de Maladies Mentales et de l'Encéphale. The extensive work Lacan achieved at the Saint Anne clinic had first come to fruition in his doctoral dissertation entitled "*De la Psychose Paranoïaque dans ses Rapports avec la Personnalité*" (1981) ("On Paranoiac Psychosis in Its Relations to the Personality"). In this dissertation, Lacan presented his initial account of psychosis that became the source for its later elaboration in his seminars.

Lacan's commentary on the subject of psychosis is vast and delivered at all the stages of his teaching. Nevertheless, it is never provided in a truly systematic fashion and changes as his teaching progresses. Lacan begins his work on psychosis by addressing it using strict Freudian terms, providing these with a linguistic interpretation, later progressing into the domains of mathematics, topology, and set-theory.[10] Lacan presents his early model of psychosis between the years 1953 and 1959 in his *Seminar I: Freud's Papers on Technique (1953–1954)*, in a commentary devoted to Jean Hyppolite remarks on Freud's paper "Negation" (1925), in his *Seminar III* as well as in his paper "On a Question Prior to Any Possible Treatment of Psychosis" printed in *Écrits* (2006). In these years, Lacan collects the many structural insights he deduces from Freud's work (disclosed in the previous section) and articulates them in relation to a constitutive psychic mechanism at the origin of psychosis that he terms "foreclosure" (*forclusion*) (SIII, p. 321).[11] This section will be mostly based on Lacan's work in these years, developing his account of the psychic mechanism of *psychotic foreclosure*.

---

[10] The most fundamental leap in the theorization of psychosis is carried out in *Seminar XXIII: The Sinthome* (1975–1976), in which Lacan introduces the notion of the *sinthome*.

[11] While in his first seminar Lacan proposes the word "excision" (*retranchement*) as a proper translation for Freud's *Verwerfung*, he later establishes its translation as "foreclosure"—a term that will be used in this book. Lacan derives this term from the work of French linguists Jacques Damourette and Édouard Pichon, *Des Mots à la Pensée: Essai de Grammaire de la Langue Française* (1932). Accordingly, "foreclosure" is defined as an utterance which repudiates facts that are treated as either true or merely possible. In other words, a proposition is considered to be foreclosed when it is "expelled from the field of possibility."

Early Distinction Between Neurosis and Psychosis

In his early account of psychosis, Lacan takes it upon himself to meticulously differentiate it from neurosis. Like Freud, Lacan contends that it is by "grappling with the distinction between the neuroses and the psychoses ... by comparing the two, that relationships, symmetries, and contrasts will appear that will enable us to erect an admissible structure for psychosis" (SIII, p. 143). Lacan's earliest distinction between the constitutive mechanism at the origin of neurosis and psychosis can be found in his interpretation of the case of the "Wolf Man" introduced in Freud's paper "From the History of an Infantile Neurosis" (1918). In this paper, Freud presents an explicit distinction between "repression" and his early conception of "rejection" (*Verwerfung*). Freud argues that: "A repression [*Verdrängung*] is something very different from a rejection [*Verwerfung*]" (SE XII, pp. 79–80; brackets added). Specifically, in regard to the case of the Wolf Man, Freud claims that: "He [the Wolf Man] rejected [*verwarf*] castration ... When I speak of his having rejected [*verwarf*] it, the first meaning of the phrase is that he would have nothing to do with it, in the sense of having repressed it [*Verdrängung*]" (p. 84; brackets added). Closely reading these lines, Lacan insists that, in the case of the Wolf Man, "It is not a question ... of repression (*Verdrängung*), for repression cannot be distinguished from the return of the repressed" (É, p. 322). Accordingly, when Freud claims that the Wolf Man did not want to know anything about castration *in the sense of repression* (*Verdrängung*), he in fact implies that the Wolf Man "*did* know something about it" *in the sense of rejection* (*Verwerfung*) (p. 322). Thus, already at this early stage in Lacan's teaching—preceding Lacan's explicit elaboration of the concept of psychotic foreclosure—we can identify a clear distinction between neurosis and psychosis based on the differentiation between *repression* and *rejection*.

The Linguistic Turn

Based on his understanding of repression, in *Seminar III*, Lacan provides his most comprehensive account of psychotic foreclosure in structural linguistic terms. Lacan is quite explicit in claiming that "the emphasis on ... language phenomena in psychosis is for us the most fruitful lesson of all" (SIII, p. 144); further, that it is "the relationship between the subject and the signifier that is distinctive of the very phenomena of psychosis" (p. 157). In this sense, Lacan argues that it is the determination of the unique psychotic mode of access to the language that distinguishes the singular facets of the psychotic subjective structure (p. 321). Accordingly, in *Seminar III*, Lacan is not oriented at deciphering psychotic symptoms in order to deduce the underlying structure of psychosis. He is focused on characterizing the linguistic mechanism that constitutes the psychotic mode of access to language, in order to structurally explain psychosis and its symptoms. In this seminar, Lacan generally characterizes this constitutive linguistic mechanism as diverting the instatement of the relationship between the subject and the symbolic order ordinarily achieved in neurosis. As will be elaborated shortly, Lacan achieves this by situating this mechanism in the model of repression in opposition to the functioning of primal affirmation (*Bejahung*).

Psychotic Foreclosure on the Level of Primal Repression

In congruence with Freud's account of psychosis, in *Seminar III*, Lacan argues that psychotic foreclosure functions on the level of primal repression. According to Lacan, it is this primordial stage—presupposed by Freud in the constitution of all subjective structures—that is "the chosen locus of what for you I am calling *Verwerfung*" (p. 156). Lacan claims that, in the case of psychosis, on this primordial stage "there must have been something there that had not materialized, at a certain moment, in the field of the signifier, that had been *verworfen*" (p. 190).

As was disclosed in the previous chapter, Freud differentiated between two aspects of primal repression—a negative aspect (*Ausstoßung*) and an affirmative aspect (*Bejahung*). This distinction provides Lacan with an even more accurate designation of psychotic foreclosure in the course of primal repression, by situating it in opposition to *Bejahung*: "*Verwerfung* is exactly what opposes the primal *Bejahung*" (É, p. 323). Primordial

Bejahung was previously described as a necessary stage in the structuration of the subject and the coherence of the symbolic order. However, in *Seminar III*, Lacan argues that "within *Bejahung* all sorts of accidents occur" (SIII, p. 83), some of which can cause "a portion of symbolization not to take place" (p. 81). Lacan emphasizes that, resulting from these "accidents," "at the level of this pure, primitive *Bejahung* … an initial dichotomy is established … there is either *Bejahung*, which is the affirmation of what is, or *Verwerfung*" (p. 82). Accordingly, we see that Lacan conceives of *Bejahung* in binary terms—it is either instated, or it is foreclosed (Fink, 1999, p. 82).

As was described in the previous chapter, the affirmative function of *Bejahung* in primal repression is crucial for the further functioning of secondary repression and the construction of neurotic subjective reality. Accordingly, by opposing *Bejahung* and cutting short its affirmative symbolic function, psychotic foreclosure hinders the successive functioning of secondary repression and thus brings about the constitution of the psychotic subjective structure instead of the neurotic one. In this sense, Lacan still maintains Freud's (1894) notion that psychotic foreclosure is a stronger form of *constitutive exclusion* superimposed on a *failed* repression (SE III, pp. 58–59). But, because foreclosure hinders the functioning of secondary repression before it comes into action, we see that he attributes this *failure* to primal repression and specifically to *Bejahung*.

The Foreclosure of the Signifier of the Name-of-the-Father

Lacan specifically argues that foreclosure brings about the constitution of the psychotic subjective structure by radically excluding (foreclosing) the unique primordial signifier affirmed in *Bejahung*:

> What is at issue when I speak of *Verwerfung*? At issue is the rejection of a primordial signifier into the outer shadows, a signifier that will henceforth be missing at this level. Here you have the fundamental mechanism that I posit as being at the basis of paranoia. (SIII, p. 150)

The primordial signifier radically excluded in foreclosure is explicitly designated by Lacan as the signifier of the Name-of-the-Father (pp. 96, 306). Accordingly, when Lacan argues that psychotic foreclosure is considered to oppose *Bejahung,* he means that it radically excludes its affirmative symbolic product—the signifier of the Name-of-the-Father.

It is important to note that Lacan's analysis of psychotic foreclosure necessarily implies that it is a "reactive" mechanism that functions after the fact. For, in order for foreclosure to operate, a psychic object first needs to be evoked in *Bejahung* before it is foreclosed (p. 283). This argument is supported by an important structural point Lacan makes in *Seminar III* in which he explicitly argues that, in the case of psychotic foreclosure, the "subject refuses access to his symbolic world to something that *he has nevertheless experienced*" (p. 12; emphasis added). For the sake of our discussion, this means that in order for psychotic foreclosure to operate, an initial instatement of the Name-of-the-Father has to be "experienced" in *Bejahung* in advance; in other words, only after *Bejahung* has been put into effect, can psychotic foreclosure then radically exclude its affirmative symbolic product—the signifier of the Name-of-the-Father.

The Effects of Foreclosure on Language

As has been elaborated in the previous chapter, the signifier of the Name-of-the-Father has a fundamental role in the determination of the exact mode of linguistic functionality available to the neurotic subject. Accordingly, the foreclosure of the signifier of the Name-of-the-Father has a substantial effect on the structuration of the subject and its relationship with language. In the following section, the foreclosure of the Name-of-the-Father will be elaborated in relation to its effects on the coherence of the symbolic order, on the subject's mode of access to language as well as on the mediation of jouissance in language.

The Symbolic Order as a Discursive Mass

One of the crucial facets of Lacan's elaboration of the foreclosure of the signifier of the Name-of-the-Father is its direct effects on the functioning of the symbolic order. In the previous chapter, the organizing function of the signifier of the Name-of-the-Father has already been disclosed. Briefly restated, the signifier of the Name-of-the-Father is considered to initiate the order in the symbolic by instating the authority of the law of signification and preserving the consistency of the relationship between the signifier and signified. Accordingly, it comes with no surprise when Lacan argues that its foreclosure hinders these organizing functions, putting the coherence of the whole of the symbolic order at risk: "the lack of one signifier necessarily brings the subject to the point of calling the set of signifiers into question" (p. 203). This is not to say that psychotic subjects have no access to the symbolic order or to language. Lacan clearly insists that both the neurotic and the psychotic are subjects of language (p. 120). However, he argues that the neurotic and the psychotic subjects are determined by different modes of access to the symbolic order that entail a different mode of linguistic functionality.

With the foreclosure of the signifier of the Name-of-the-Father the psychotic subject forfeits its authoritative function in the symbolic order. Without the authority of the symbolic law there is nothing that holds the chain of signifiers together and ensures the consistency of signification (pp. 197, 296). There is no excluded primordial signifier that enables the signifying mass to systematically and coherently attribute meaning in its domain. Accordingly, Lacan claims that the psychotic subject is disposed to a symbolic order that functions as a "sentimental mass of the current of discourse, a confused mass in which appear units, islands, an image, an object, a feeling, a cry, an appeal ... a continuum" (p. 261). In this symbolic mass, "the signifier and the signified present themselves in a completely divided form" (p. 268). Therefore, without a fundamental anchoring point, the signified keeps on slipping in the "indefinite sliding of signification," losing its stabilizing effect (É, p. 681).

How can this confused mass of signifiers still maintain certain organizing laws? Lacan argues that, without the internalization of symbolic authority through the instatement of the signifier of the Name-of-the-Father, the psychotic subject can partially assume its organizing function "through a kind of external imitation" (SIII, p. 251). In other words, the psychotic subject is disposed to the fabrication of the symbolic law on the basis of the imitation of behavior and language encountered from without. The fabrication of the symbolic law provides an imaginary supplement that functions as a "fastening point" to the symbolic and intersubjective reality (p. 204).[12] While providing some stabilization, this limited adaptation of the symbolic law renders the consistency and coherence of the symbolic order fragile and apt to collapse at specific junctions in one's life (Vanheule, 2011. p. 50).

The Hole in the Other

Another crucial outcome of psychotic foreclosure is described by Lacan in *Seminar III* as the "hole in the symbolic" (SIII, p. 156). Simply put, Lacan argues that the foreclosure of the signifier of the Name-of-the-Father carves out a "hole" in its place in the symbolic (p. 201). The "hole in the symbolic" is specified by Lacan as a defining feature of psychosis, in the same way that the signifier of the Name-of-the-Father is a defining feature of neurosis (p. 248). Accordingly, this hole does not lack all symbolic value but rather functions as a symbolic unit representing the "minimal relationship to the symbolic" warranted by psychotic foreclosure (Benoist, 2011). At this point in his teaching, Lacan had not yet provided the figure of the hole with a mathematical or topological interpretation but only presented it in abstract descriptive language.[13] Be that as it may, by using this descriptive language, Lacan clearly distinguishes the status of the hole and the lack designated by the signifier of the Name-of-the-Father. As Jacques-Alain Miller argues in his paper "Lacan's Later Teaching" (2001), while a "lack" is considered to be a symbolic designation of an absence, a "hole" implies the disappearance of the symbolic order, representing an effect of the real. This is why, according to Lacan,

---

[12] In this sense, the psychotic subject is disposed to an imaginary mode of identification but lacks access to the symbolic mode of identification (SIII, pp. 93, 176, 212).

[13] A thorough account of the figure of the hole in topological terms will be presented in Chap. 6.

other terms can be inscribed on the backdrop of lack, while the hole allows no such inscription to take place.

Language as a Foreign Entity

According to Lacan, all subjects are born into a language that is foreign, precedes their existence, and which they need to assume for themselves and make their own (Fink, 1999, p. 87). As has been disclosed in the previous chapter, neurotic subjects come to "inhabit" language in this way by "subjectivizing" it (SIII, pp. 188–250). Structurally speaking, the neurotic subject gains its point of insertion into the symbolic order through the signifier of the Name-of-the-Father that functions as a "quilting point"—an anchoring point in the symbolic (p. 267). Accordingly, Lacan argues that by foreclosing this point of insertion in the symbolic, the psychotic subject is unable to "subjectify" language, that is, to make it its own (É, pp. 693–694). In other words, with the foreclosure of the Name-of-the-Father, the psychotic subject loses its own demarcated site in language, a site that is crucial for its subjectification. Therefore, psychotic subjects never internalize language as a thing belonging to them but find themselves being possessed by a thing over which they have no control. Instead of finding language to be a site for their most inner existence, psychotic subjects experience language as an exterior force or entity that in some cases takes on a persecutory nature (Vanheule, 2011, p. 71). That is why Lacan argues that "If the neurotic inhabits language, the psychotic is inhabited, possessed, by language" (SIII, p. 250).

The Mediation of Jouissance

The foreclosure of the Name-of-the-Father also has substantial effects on the capacity of the symbolic order to mediate jouissance. According to Russel Grigg (2009), these effects are rooted in the fact that: "Its [the Name-of-the-Father's] function in the Oedipus complex is to be the vehicle of the law that regulates desire—both the subject's desire and the omnipotent desire of the maternal figure" (p. 9; brackets added). In order to further explicate Grigg's contention, let us take into account Lacan's adaptation of primal repression in Oedipal terms that was presented in the previous chapter. On the basis of this adaptation, we see that psychotic foreclosure does warrant the first instance of the paternal function—the father's "non." Namely, the primordial exclusion of jouissance creating a gap between the Mother's Desire and the child in *Ausstoßung*. However, we see that psychotic foreclosure hinders the functioning of the second instance of the paternal function—the father's "nom." It does so by radically excluding the symbolic unit that names the gap created between the Mother's Desire and the child—the signifier of the Name-of-the-Father—that is affirmed in *Bejahung*. By hindering the second instance of the paternal function, the subject loses the symbolic designation of the site where desire can be safely adopted beyond the Mother's reach (Vanheule, 2011, p. 61). Therefore, we see that, while the psychotic subject does gain its initial separation from the Mother's Desire in *Ausstoßung*, it is deprived of the symbolic means necessary for the regulation and subjectification of desire enabled in *Bejahung*. In this sense, one can argue that in psychosis, "man's desire is [*not*] the desire of the Other" (SXI, p. 235; brackets and emphasis added). That is to say that, because psychotic foreclosure hinders the internalization of the desire of the Other (the Mother's Desire) in the symbolic, it renders desire as alien, as separate from the subject and having a life of its own. This alien desire is perceived as obscure and incomprehensible from the perspective of the subject (Grigg, 2009, p. 10; Ribolsi, Feyaerts, & Vanheule, 2015; Vanheule, 2011, p. 71). Sometimes this desire even takes on itself a persecutory role, embodied by a menacing Other that does not enable or mediate the subject's jouissance but is aimed at fulfilling its own jouissance, even at the expense of the subject itself (Benoist, 2011, p. 3). Lacan describes it as an "unbarred" Other—"an absolute Other, an entirely radical Other, an Other who is neither a place nor a schema, an Other who … is a living being in his own way, and who … is capable, when threatened, of egoism like other living beings" (SIII, p. 274).

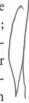

The Onset of Psychosis

Up to this point, the internal functioning of psychotic foreclosure and its effects on the symbolic order have been elaborated. The following section will concern the progression of symptoms prevalent after the onset of psychosis—what is also termed as a *psychotic break*. Because these will not be of major concern in the following chapters, only the main aspects that would be useful in the distinction between psychosis and autism will be briefly introduced.

Structural and Contingent Causality

In the Lacanian clinic, a subject can be structurally diagnosed as psychotic without exhibiting any significant psychotic symptoms. That is because the onset of psychotic symptoms is dependent on two causal factors that must intersect—a *structural causality* and a *contingent causality* (Recalcati, 2005). The *structural causality* is accomplished when the signifier of the Name-of-the-Father engendered in *Bejahung* is foreclosed. The *contingent causality* is accomplished "when the subject, at a certain crossroads of his biographical history, is confronted by this lack that has always existed" (SIII, p. 203). Lacan describes this contingent confrontation as an "encounter" with the lack of the symbolic function of the Name-of-the-Father (pp. 203, 305–306, 320): "For psychosis to be triggered, the Name-of-the-Father—*verworfen*, foreclosed, that is, never having come to the place of the Other—must be summoned to that place in symbolic opposition to the subject" (É, p. 481). In other words, when a subject, at some point in his life, directly addresses the lack of the Name-of-the-Father in the symbolic, there is a risk of suffering from the onset of a psychotic break.

On a more clinical level, Lacan relates this encounter to questions revolving around the paternal function, when, as is apparent in the case of Schreber, the subject is called into action regarding his own power of "virility" or "procreation" (SIII, pp. 292–293). Lacan claims that psychosis is triggered at the moment when these questions are evoked but get no answer, for the paternal function has not been fully instated. He describes it in Oedipal terms by claiming that it is a moment "when the triangular, oedipal relation finds itself to be short-circuited, when reduced to its dual simplification" (p. 305), meaning when it is reduced to the child and the mother or the subject and the Other, with no third term symbolically introduced by the father. Grigg (2009) adds that this moment of "interpellation" takes place when the subject is summoned to make a crucial decision that he must either embrace or repudiate. He suggests that this includes situations where the subject is in a particularly intense relationship involving a strong narcissistic component; when questions of fatherhood arise from an external position; and, in the development of transference in analysis (p. 15).[14]

Symbolic Disintegration

Lacan provides a detailed account of the regression prevalent in the case of the onset of psychosis. Akin to Freud's (1911) account of the "end of the world" or the "internal catastrophe" (SE XII, pp. 68–73), Lacan describes the onset of psychosis as the disintegration of the subject's symbolic reality up to the point where it is relegated to the status of a "confused sentimental mass" as pointed out earlier (SIII, pp. 205, 250, 261).[15]

As was previously stated, the psychotic subject attempts to preserve the consistency of the symbolic order without recourse to the internal law of signification. As was also previously mentioned, Lacan claims that the symbolic order is able to gain a certain measure of consistency in psychosis through imaginary means of imitation. Correspondingly, Lacan argues that the first stage of psychotic regression entails the collapse of these "imaginary crutches which have enabled the subject to compensate [prior to the onset of psychosis] for the absence of the signifier [of the Name-of-the-Father]" (p. 205; brackets added). Thus, the onset of psychosis is

---

[14] See more on this subject in Lacan (É, p. 481; SIII, p. 251).

[15] As had been elaborated in the previous chapter, Lacan relates the notion of reality to that of a "mesh of signifiers" (SIII, p. 199). This "mesh" is constructed on the basis of the affirmation of the signifier of the Name-of-the-Father in primal repression. Accordingly, when Lacan claims that "in psychosis something becomes lacking in the subject's relation to reality" (p. 249), we understand this reality as composed of signifiers. Therefore, the effect of foreclosure on the symbolic should also be understood as affecting psychotic reality.

considered to be "a process whose first stage we have called an imaginary cataclysm, namely that no longer can anything ... which is in itself the relation with the imaginary other, be held on lease" (p. 321). The collapse of the symbolic order's "imaginary crutches" brings about a process of symbolic disintegration—"A great disturbance of the internal discourse" (p. 205)—which in turn brings about: "dissociation, fragmentation, mobilization of the signifier as speech, ejaculatory speech that is insignificant or too significant, laden with non-meaningfulness, the decomposition of internal discourse, which marks the entire structure of psychosis" (p. 321). This process results in what are commonly considered to be significant "negative" and "positive" psychotic symptoms (APA, 2013).

Hallucinations: Reappearance in the Real

According to Lacan, "repression and the return of the repressed are just the two sides of the same coin" (SIII, p. 12). In line with this symmetry, Lacan argues that since a repression functions in the symbolic by excluding a signifier, the return of the repressed is also "expressed in a perfectly articulate manner in symptoms and a host of other phenomena" (p. 12). Stated otherwise, the neurotic subject, having achieved the two stages of repression (primal and secondary), comes to express whatever is repressed in the symbolic, using symbolic means.

In psychotic foreclosure there is a setback in the structuration of the symbolic order and its relation to the subject. Accordingly, Lacan claims that "what falls under the effect of *Verwerfung* has a completely different destiny" than what is repressed (p. 12). In the case of repression, whatever is repressed in the symbolic order returns in the symbolic; while, in the case of foreclosure, Lacan claims that "whatever is refused in the symbolic order, in the sense of *Verwerfung*, reappears in the real" (p. 13). In other words, Lacan argues that whatever is foreclosed from the symbolic is not purely and simply abolished, but, similarly to repression, it returns. Nevertheless, unlike repression, it does not return as a symptom manifested in the symbolic order but reappears from without, in the real. Thus, according to Lacan, psychotic foreclosure unravels radical disturbances in the symbolic order such as the emergence of strange "bits of language"—signifiers that return in the real in the guise of "elementary phenomena" such as thought-echoes, commanding voices, and various other forms of hallucination (Grigg, 2009, p. 10). The persistence of such elementary phenomena demands the permanent alteration of the internal logic of the subject's symbolic reality on the basis of constructed delusions (SIII, p. 86).

Delusions: An Attempt at Stabilization

As presented in the previous section, in his later papers on psychosis, Freud (1911, 1924a, 1924c) argues that delusions play a role in reestablishing the subject's lost relation to reality following its internal catastrophe (SE XII, pp. 71, 77; SE XIX, pp. 184–185). Because Lacan views the subject's reality strictly as symbolic reality, he claims (in accordance with Freud) that delusions convey an attempt at the reconstruction of the symbolic order. This attempt follows the devastating encounter with the hole in the Other that brings about the disintegration of the symbolic order and the intrusion of elementary phenomena such as hallucinations (pp. 6–7, 321). Nevertheless, the psychotic subject's delusions can only support the reconstruction of symbolic reality through imaginary means (Grigg, 2009, p. 16).[16] On these grounds, Lacan is explicitly suspicious of psychoanalysts who view delusions as a cure for psychosis.[17] He carefully employs terms such as "stabilization" (SIII, pp. 69, 86, 140) in order to describe the best possible outcome achieved through the delusional reconstruction of symbolic reality in psychosis[18]:

---

[16] "Imaginary" should be taken in the sense of the register of the *imaginary*.

[17] See for instance: "May we speak of a process of compensation, or even of cure, as some people would not hesitate to do, on the pretext that when his delusion stabilizes the subject presents a calmer state than at its appearance? Is he cured or not? It is a question worth raising, but I think it can only be wrong to speak of a cure here" (SIII, p. 86).

[18] It might be noted that, in a much later seminar, *Seminar XXIII: The Sinthome* (1975–1976), Lacan describes a new form of psychotic stabilization that functions as a substitute for the foreclosed Name-of-the-Father and prevents the onset of psychosis. Lacan names it *sinthome*, and associates it with the work of James Joyce.

It is the lack of the Name-of-the-Father in that place which, by the hole that it opens up in the signified, sets off a cascade of reworkings of the signifier from which the growing disaster of the imaginary proceeds, until the level is reached at which signifier and signified stabilize in a delusional metaphor. (É, p. 481)

As seen in the above excerpt from "On a Question Prior to Any Possible Treatment of Psychosis," Lacan associates stabilizing delusions with "delusional metaphors," relating them to the function of the paternal metaphor. According to Lacan, these can function as building blocks in an imaginary bridge built over the hole in the symbolic. They take form as explanatory theories that have their own internal logic and can some-times be a sufficient substitute for unanswered questions posed on the level of the hole in the symbolic; those are questions that are usually answered on the basis of the signifier of the Name-of-the-Father. They endow psychotic reality with some sense of stability, as through them the psychotic is able to perceive the world from the perspective of a personal organizing law. In this sense, they function as a supplement for the sym-bolic law that has dissolved due to the foreclosure of the Name-of-the-Father.[19]

Summary

In his account of psychosis, Lacan offers an original perspective through which the mechanism of *constitutive exclusion* at the origin of psychosis can be understood. Let us then summarize the different conclusions we have reached in relation to psychotic foreclosure in this section.

In relation to Freud's model of repression, Lacan precisely situates the functioning of psychotic foreclosure in opposition to *Bejahung* in the course of primal repression. Accordingly, foreclosure is described as a mechanism that radically excludes the affirmative symbolic product of

---

[19] In the case of Schreber, Lacan associates the capacity of delusions to instate a certain organizing law in the subject's reality with his intricate descriptions of his relationship with God, his role in His plans for the universe (SIII, pp. 141–162) and with his organizing principles such as "unman-ning" (*Entmannung*) (É, p. 471).

Bejahung, thus deflecting the course of the structuration of neurosis and bringing about the structuration of psychosis. Similarly to Freud's account of psychosis, foreclosure is classified as a mechanism that is superimposed on a failed repression (*Bejahung*). In Lacan's terms, this means that psychotic foreclosure only operates after the initial affirmation of the Name-of-the-Father in *Bejahung.* Namely, only after *Bejahung* has been put into effect, can psychotic foreclosure then radically exclude its affirmative symbolic product—the signifier of the Name-of-the-Father. This logical distinction provides us with another clue as to the way the mechanism of foreclosure operates and will be very useful in the elaboration of autistic foreclosure in the following chapters. Based on this distinction, I suggest that both secondary repression and psychotic foreclosure should be viewed as "reactive" mechanisms sequentially functioning after *Bejahung.* They both are dependent on the affirmative product of *Bejahung* for their functioning (the signifier of the Name-of-the-Father) and, on its basis, bring about the constitution of singular subjective structures. Because secondary repression is conditioned by the successful instatement of the signifier of the Name-of-the-Father, I argue that, by radically excluding this signifier, psychotic foreclosure hinders the application of secondary repression. Therefore, in psychosis we see no secondary repression. Accordingly, I argue that, while primal repression remains a necessary condition for both neurosis and psychosis, secondary repression should be strictly associated with the structuration of neurosis—see Fig. 4.2.

Lacan also furthers Freud's account of the homology between the two aspects of repression and foreclosure presented in the previous section. According to Lacan, in neurotic repression, these are (1) the negative

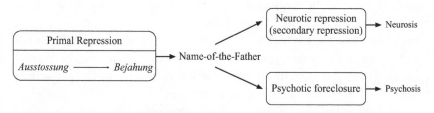

Fig. 4.2 The inscription of the Name-of-the-Father leading to neurotic repression and psychotic foreclosure

aspect that entails the exclusion of a signifier from consciousness and (2) the affirmative aspect that entails the return of the repressed and the construction of symbolic reality. In psychotic foreclosure, these are (1) the negative aspect that entails the radical exclusion of the signifier of the Name-of-the-Father from the symbolic and (2) the affirmative aspect that entails the reappearance of the foreclosed in the real and the reconstruction of symbolic reality.

We have also seen that Lacan provides an explicit account of the exact effects psychotic foreclosure has on the structuration of the symbolic order: first, the symbolic order is rendered as a discursive mass; second, a hole replaces the signifier of the Name-of-the-Father; third, the subject is unable to subjectivize language; lastly, the symbolic mediation of jouissance is compromised. When brought into opposition with these symbolic setbacks, the subject is at risk of experiencing the return of the foreclosed in the real, warranting the onset of psychotic symptoms and the attempted reconstruction of symbolic reality in imaginary means.

Finally, Freud (1924c) explicitly argues that the difference between repression and foreclosure does not lie in the second affirmative aspect of their underlying constitutive mechanisms but only in the first negative aspect (SE XIX, p. 185). That is because in both cases the affirmative aspect comes to substitute or remodel something that has been excluded from the subject's reality. However, it is important to note that Lacan does point out a crucial distinction in the affirmative aspect of the two mechanisms as well. According to Lacan, the affirmative aspect of neurotic repression operates when repressed signifiers symptomatically manifest themselves in the symbolic order (the return of the repressed). On the other hand, in psychotic foreclosure, the foreclosure of the signifier of the Name-of-the-Father causes signifiers to symptomatically manifest themselves in the real (the reappearance in the real). Thus, in psychosis, we see a major shift in weight in subjective reality. While neurotic subjects would be mostly absorbed in the symbolic and imaginary manifestation of their subjective reality, psychotic subjects would be mostly absorbed in the imaginary compensations they establish in relation to the perturbing presence of signifiers that reappear in the real.

The conclusion concerning psychotic foreclosure can be summarized in Fig. 4.3:

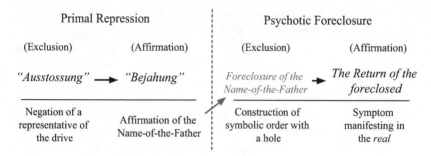

Fig. 4.3 Lacan on psychotic foreclosure

Works Cited

American Psychiatric Association. (2013). *DSM 5. American Journal of Psychiatry* (5th ed.). Washington, DC: American Psychiatric Publishing.

Benoist, V. (2011). L'Autre dans L'Autisme. *International Psychology, Practice and Research*, (2), 1–13.

Damourette, J., & Pichon, E. (1932). *Des Mots à la Pensée: Essai de Grammaire de la Langue Française*. Paris: Bibliothèque du Français Moderne.

Fink, B. (1999). *A Clinical Introduction to Lacanian Psychoanalysis: Theory and Technique*. Cambridge, UK: Harvard University Press.

Freud, S. (1892). Draft K1 The Neuroses of Defence from Extracts from the Flies Papers. In *The Standard Edition of the Complete Psychological Works of Sigmund Freud, Volume I (1886–1899): Pre-Psycho-Analytic Publications and Unpublished Drafts* (pp. 220–229).

Freud, S. (1893). Frälein Elisabeth von R, Case Histories from Studies on Hysteria. In *The Standard Edition of the Complete Psychological Works of Sigmund Freud, Volume II (1893–1895): Studies on Hysteria* (pp. 135–181).

Freud, S. (1894). The Neuro-Psychoses of Defence. In *The Standard Edition of the Complete Psychological Works of Sigmund Freud, Volume III (1893–1899): Early Psycho-Analytic Publications* (pp. 41–61).

Freud, S. (1896). Further Remarks on the Neuro-Psychoses of Defence. In *The Standard Edition of the Complete Psychological Works of Sigmund Freud, Volume III (1893–1899): Early Psycho-Analytic Publications* (pp. 157–185).

Freud, S. (1911). Psycho-Analytic Notes on an Autobiographical Account of a Case of Paranoia (Dementia Paranoides). In *The Standard Edition of the*

Complete Psychological Works of Sigmund Freud, Volume XII (1911–1913): The Case of Schreber, Papers on Technique and Other Works (pp. 1–82).

Freud, S. (1914). On Narcissism. In *The Standard Edition of the Complete Psychological Works of Sigmund Freud, Volume XIV (1914–1916): On the History of the Psycho-Analytic Movement, Papers on Metapsychology and Other Works* (pp. 67–102).

Freud, S. (1915). Repression. In *The Standard Edition of the Complete Psychological Works of Sigmund Freud, Volume XIV (1914–1916): On the History of the Psycho-Analytic Movement, Papers on Metapsychology and Other Works* (pp. 141–158).

Freud, S. (1918). From the History of an Infantile Neurosis. In *The Standard Edition of the Complete Psychological Works of Sigmund Freud, Volume XVII (1917–1919): An Infantile Neurosis and Other Works* (pp. 1–124).

Freud, S. (1924a). Neurosis and Psychosis. *The Standard Edition of the Complete Psychological Works of Sigmund Freud, Volume XIX (1923–1925): The Ego and the Id and Other Works* (pp. 147–154).

Freud, S. (1924b). The Economic Problem of Masochism. In *The Standard Edition of the Complete Psychological Works of Sigmund Freud, Volume XIX (1923–1925): The Ego and the Id and Other Works* (pp. 155–170).

Freud, S. (1924c). The Loss of Reality in Neurosis and Psychosis. In *The Standard Edition of the Complete Psychological Works of Sigmund Freud, Volume XIX (1923–1925): The Ego and the Id and Other Works* (pp. 181–188).

Freud, S. (1925). Some Psychical Consequences of the Anatomical Distinction Between the Sexes. *The Standard Edition of the Complete Psychological Works of Sigmund Freud, Volume XIX (1923–1925): The Ego and the Id and Other Works* (pp. 241–258).

Freud, S. (1927). Fetishism. In *The Standard Edition of the Complete Psychological Works of Sigmund Freud, Volume XXI (1927–1931): The Future of an Illusion, Civilization and Its Discontents, and Other Works* (pp. 147–158).

Freud, S. (1937). Analysis Terminable and Interminable. *The Standard Edition of the Complete Psychological Works of Sigmund Freud, Volume XXIII (1937–1939): Moses and Monotheism, An Outline of Psycho-Analysis and Other Works* (pp. 209–254).

Freud, S. (1938). Splitting of the Ego in the Process of Defence. *The Standard Edition of the Complete Psychological Works of Sigmund Freud, Volume XXIII (1937–1939): Moses and Monotheism, An Outline of Psycho-Analysis and Other Works* (pp. 271–278).

Grigg, R. (2009). Language as Sinthome in Ordinary Psychosis. *Psychoanalytical Notebooks*, (19), 30–40.

Jones, E. (1955). Sigmund Freud Life and Work, Volume Two: Years of Maturity 1901–1919. In *Sigmund Freud Life and Work, Volume Two: Years of Maturity 1901–1919* (pp. 1–507). London: The Hogarth Press.

Lacan, J. (1981). *De la Psychose Paranoïaque dans ses Rapports avec la Personnalité*. Paris: Seuil.

Lacan, J. (1988). In J.-A. Miller (Ed.), *The Seminar of Jacques Lacan, Book I, Freud's Papers on Technique (1953–1954)*. New York: Norton & Company.

Lacan, J. (1997). In J.-A. Miller (Ed.), *The Seminar of Jacques Lacan, Book III, The Psychoses (1955–1956)*. New York: Norton & Company.

Lacan, J. (2001). In J.-A. Miller (Ed.), *The Seminar, Book XI. The Four Fundamental Concepts of Psychoanalysis (1964)*. New York: Norton & Company.

Lacan, J. (2006). In B. Fink (Ed.), *Écrits*. New York: Norton & Company.

Lacan, J. (2016). In J.-A. Miller (Ed.), *The Seminar of Jacques Lacan, Book XXIII, The Sinthome (1975–1976)*. Cambridge, UK: Polity.

Laurent, É. (2012). Autism and Psychosis: Further Dialogue with Robert and Rosine Lefort. *Psychoanalytical Notebooks*, (25), 11–26.

Lefort, R., & Lefort, R. (1994). *Birth of the Other*. Oxfort, UK: University of Illinois Press.

Lefort, R., & Lefort, R. (2003). *La Distinction de L'Autisme*. Paris: Seuil.

Maleval, J.-C. (2004). *La Forclusion du Nom-du-Père. Le Concept et sa Clinique*. Paris: Seuil.

Maleval, J.-C. (2009). *L'Autiste et sa Voix*. Paris: Seuil.

Miller, J. (2010). *L'Avenir de L'Autisme*. Paris: Navarin.

Miller, J.-A. (2001). Lacan's Later Teaching. *Lacanian Ink*, (20), 4–41.

Recalcati, M. (2005). The Empty Subject: Un-Triggered Psychoses in the New Forms of the Symptom. *Lacanian Ink, 26*.

Ribolsi, M., Feyaerts, J., & Vanheule, S. (2015). Metaphor in Psychosis: On the Possible Convergence of Lacanian Theory and Neuro-scientific Research. *Frontiers in Psychology, 6*, 664.

Schreber, D. P. (1955). *Memoirs of My Nervous Illness*. New York: New York Review of Books.

Tendlarz, S. E. (2003). *Childhood Psychosis: A Lacanian Perspective*. London: Karnac Books.

Vanheule, S. (2011). *The Subject of Psychosis: A Lacanian Perspective*. New York: Springer.

Part III

The Autistic Subject

Lacan never provided a comprehensive account of autism in his teaching. As a matter of fact, he delivered only two explicit remarks on the subject at two conferences he attended in the year 1975 at Geneva and Columbia University. In these two short instances, very late in his career, Lacan presented his audience with more of an ethical imperative than an analysis of autistic subjectivity, basically claiming that autistic subjects, just like neurotic, perverse, or psychotic subjects, are subjects of language.

In addition to these two instances, in the course of *Seminar I: Freud's Papers on Technique (1953–1954)*, Lacan addressed Melanie Klein's well-known case of "Little Dick," and Rosine Lefort's case of the "Wolf Child." Although, at the time they were presented, none of the children in these cases were strictly diagnosed as autistic, these cases are now considered as early accounts of autism. Accordingly, they provide a glimpse into Lacan's early intuitions about autism.

The contemporary Lacanian approach to autism is primarily attributed to the work of Rosine and Robert Lefort. Credited with the first presentation of a case of autism in Lacan's seminars, the two came to establish the *École Expérimentale de Bonneuil-sur-Marne* in 1969, where they continued their work with autistic subjects. The Leforts published four books on the subject of autism: *Les structures de la Psychose: L'Enfant au Loup et le Président* (1988), *The Birth of the Other* (1994), *Maryse*

Devient une petite Fille: Psychanalyse d'une Enfant de 26 Mois (1998), and *La Distinction de L'Autisme* (2003). In these books, the Leforts provided a vast clinical account of autism, focused on notions such as the mechanism of foreclosure, the circuit of the partial drives, and the function of the double in autism.

The Leforts laid the groundwork that would inspire later Lacanian psychoanalysts to approach this field, further developing the Leforts' perspective. Part III of this book will focus on the writings of two such Lacanian psychoanalysts: Éric Laurent, who wrote various papers on the subject as well as a book, *La Bataille de l'Autisme* (2012), and Jean-Claude Maleval, who has published a book on the subject, entitled *L'Autiste et sa Voix* (2009), and has also been an author and collaborator in several other publications in French and English.

While the elaboration of the clinic of autism provided by these psychoanalysts is extensive and rich, the main focus of this book is the structural analysis of the constitutive psychic mechanism called *autistic foreclosure.* Accordingly, Part III of this book will go on to distinguish the functioning of autistic foreclosure. In Chap. 5, autistic foreclosure will be distinguished on the basis of its position in the model of repression developed by Freud and Lacan. In comparison to psychotic foreclosure that is situated in opposition to *Bejahung* (É, p. 323), autistic foreclosure will be indicated as being situated in opposition to *Ausstoßung*. This will be accomplished by investigating the functioning of *Ausstoßung*, dividing it into two internal operations—negative and affirmative—and finally, arguing that autistic foreclosure is sequentially situated after the affirmative aspect of *Ausstoßung*, taking its affirmative symbolic product as an object of exclusion. In Chap. 6, autistic foreclosure will be determined on the basis of the exact nature of the psychic object that is excluded in its scope. This will be achieved by developing three different frameworks through which the psychic object excluded in autistic foreclosure can be accounted for. These will include an account of the object of autistic foreclosure as the unary trait, as the hole in the topological figure of the torus, and as the object of the invocatory drive. In these three sections, an exclusive interpretation as to the nature of the object of autistic foreclosure will be presented as well as provided with further conceptual support, interpretations, and critique. The conclusions reached in these two chapters will supply the conceptual foundation for the elaboration of the exact mode of linguistic functionality enabled by autistic foreclosure in the Chap. 7. This is a mode of access to language that is rooted in the primacy of the sign and goes hand in hand with the construction of what will be called the autistic rim. The combination of the different conclusions presented in these chapters will provide sufficient grounds for the designation of autism as a singular subjective structure in the last chapter of this book.

5

Autistic Foreclosure in the Model of Repression

In the previous chapters, the two constitutive psychic mechanisms at the origin of neurosis and psychosis have been determined under the coordinates of the model of repression presented by Freud. Neurotic repression has been situated as sequentially following the full instatement of primal repression and, in more exact Freudian terms, following the successful affirmation of a construct marking a distinction between consciousness and the unconscious achieved in *Bejahung*. In Lacanian terms, neurotic repression was situated as sequentially following the successful affirmation of the signifier of the Name-of-the-Father. Based on Lacan's *Seminar III: The Psychoses (1955–1956)*, psychotic foreclosure has been situated in opposition to *Bejahung*, in the sense that it radically excludes its affirmative symbolic product—the signifier of the Name-of-the-Father. By foreclosing this primordial signifier, psychotic foreclosure has been said to hinder the structuration of neurosis and brings about the structuration of psychosis.

Autism, as a distinct mental phenomenon, has been systematically formulated in relation to psychosis ever since the days of Kanner and Asperger. Accordingly, up until today, Lacanian psychoanalysts still characterize autism using conceptual coordinates borrowed from the clinic of

© The Author(s) 2020
L. S. Brenner, *The Autistic Subject*, The Palgrave Lacan Series,
https://doi.org/10.1007/978-3-030-50715-2_5

psychosis. One of the major structural features autism shares with psychosis, according to Lacanian psychoanalysis, is the constitutive mechanism that lies at its origin—the foreclosure of the Name-of-the-Father. The first classification of autism in terms of the foreclosure of the Name-of-the-Father can be found in the Leforts' book *The Birth of the Other* (1994).[1] In a chapter addressing the case of Marie François, an autistic child analyzed by Rosine Lefort, the Leforts declare that, in autism, the relationship with the signifier of the Name-of-the-Father is "radically missing or dissolved" (p. 341). In another of their books, *La Distinction de L'Autisme* (2003), the Leforts go on to explicitly assert that "There certainly is a foreclosure in autism" (p. 51), eventually stating: "Can we speak of a foreclosure of the Name-of-the-Father in this [autistic] structure? Certainly yes" (pp. 61–62; brackets added).

These inaugural formulations made by the Leforts have become integrated into the Lacan's teaching ever since. Accordingly, among the majority of contemporary psychoanalysts working with autistic subjects, there is a general consensus that, in autism, we are dealing with a mechanism of foreclosure—an *autistic foreclosure* that entails the structuring effects of the foreclosure of the signifier of the Name-of-the-Father in psychosis (Benoist, 2011; Borgnis-Desbordes, 2009, p. 103; Esteban, 2002; Laurent, 2012a, pp. 66–69; Lefort & Lefort, 1994, p. 341; 2003, pp. 26, 61; Maleval, 2009, 2012, p. 34; Tendlarz, 2003, pp. 12, 23).

Nevertheless, several contemporary Lacanian psychoanalysts seem to believe that psychotic foreclosure does not exhaustively characterize the functioning of autistic foreclosure (Benoist, 2011; Laurent, 2012a, 2012b; Lefort & Lefort, 2003). These scholars argue that, while autistic foreclosure encompasses the structuring effects of the foreclosure of the Name-of-the-Father, it exceeds it in its scope and so cannot be fully reduced to the break with the paternal metaphor that Lacan identifies in *Seminar III*. Just as Freud (1894) described psychotic foreclosure as a more "energetic" form of defense than neurotic repression (SE III, p. 58), these scholars classify autistic foreclosure as a more "radical form of psychotic foreclosure" (Laurent, 2012b, p. 17)—a foreclosure that has a

---

[1] The original French version, *Naissance de L'Autre*, was printed in 1980.

more comprehensive effect on the structuration of the symbolic order and its relation to the subject.

Before delving into the elaboration of the exact structuring effects autistic foreclosure has on the symbolic order and its relation to the subject in Chap. 7, this chapter will first attempt to characterize the exact level on which autistic foreclosure functions in the model of repression. By pinpointing its coordinates in this model, autistic foreclosure will be understood in terms of its functionality and structure, attesting to its singularity in comparison to psychotic foreclosure.

Minimal Signification

In his paper *L'Autre dans L'Autisme* (2011), Lacanian psychoanalyst Vincent Benoist suggests that the main distinction between autistic and psychotic foreclosure lies in the exact level of symbolic signification that conditions their functioning:

> The specificity of autism demonstrates that it is a different structure from the structure of psychosis as it is indicated to us in Lacan's first account of the foreclosure of the Name-of-the-Father … It seems that the concept of foreclosure, whether of the Name-of-the-Father or of S1, is not an apt one to describe this subjective position because the Lacanian foreclosure is a foreclosure of a signifier and thus indicates a minimal relationship with the symbolic that does not exist in autism. (Benoist, 2011)

In the previous chapters, both neurotic repression and psychotic foreclosure were described as mechanisms that are dependent on the instatement of the signifier of the Name-of-the-Father in *Bejahung*. In the paragraph quoted above, Benoist associates the instatement of the signifier of the Name-of-the-Father with a most "minimal relationship" with the symbolic order. He adds that while the functioning of psychotic foreclosure is preliminarily conditioned by the initial instatement of the signifier of the Name-of-the-Father in *Bejahung*, this "minimal" relationship is never instated in autism. Accordingly, what Benoist implies is that in autism, *Bejahung* does not come to function at all; in other words, in autism, the signifier of the Name-of-the-Father is not engendered prior to the functioning of autistic foreclosure—not even engendered only to be foreclosed, as is the case of psychotic foreclosure.

The fundamental lack of a minimal relationship with the symbolic order is a characteristic that many psychoanalysts associate with autism. As will be elaborated in Chap. 7, this has been attested to since the days of the earliest practitioners dealing with autism, such as Kanner, and has been a major point of agreement between contemporary Lacanian psychoanalysts. Briefly stated, according to the Leforts, the autistic subject is deprived of the most fundamental relationship to the symbolic order (Lefort & Lefort, 2003, p. 66). They describe it as the lack of the alienation in the Other (p. 27), or a "lack of castration" (p. 52). Conditioned by this lack, the Leforts claim that "the subject remains … far away from any phallic signification" (p. 52).

While the majority of contemporary Lacanian psychoanalysts comply with these characterizations of autism, they attribute them to the structuring effects of autistic foreclosure. What is so compelling about Benoist's argument is that *he associates this "lack" with the level of signification preceding and conditioning the functioning of autistic foreclosure and not with its structuring consequences.* In other words, Benoist claims that the most minimal relationship with the signifier of the Name-of-the-Father is not instated even before autistic foreclosure comes to operate. He claims that this lack—preceding the functioning of autistic foreclosure—prohibits us from assuming that autistic foreclosure functions (similarly to psychotic foreclosure) by the radical exclusion of the signifier of the Name-of-the-Father. Accordingly, *I argue that autistic foreclosure is situated prior to Bejahung in the model of repression and is thus conditioned by a more elementary level of symbolic signification than that of the Name-of-the-Father.*[2] By hypothesizing that autistic foreclosure functions on a level prior to the affirmative aspect of primal repression (*Bejahung*), we are

---

[2] Another way to comply with Benoist's argument is by claiming that autistic foreclosure comes to operate after the foreclosure of the Name-of-the-Father in psychotic foreclosure. Accordingly, autism is characterized as a more extreme form of psychosis. This line of argumentation suggests that a subject is first psychotic and only then autistic in structure. I do not adopt this line of argumentation in this book.

compelled to speculate that it functions on either one of the following levels:

1. On the level of the negative aspect of primal repression (*Ausstoßung*) preceding and conditioning the affirmative aspect of primal repression (*Bejahung*).
2. On a level prior to primal repression altogether—prior to *Ausstoßung*.

There are several reasons to oppose the second option presented above. The elaboration of a structure is conditioned by the determination of a defined domain—space, for instance—in which it can be accounted for. In Lacanian terms this domain is the symbolic order in which subjective reality is structured (SIII, p. 156). In this sense, even at its most minimal manifestation, subjective reality materializes in one way or another in language. Or, stated otherwise, without any relationship with language, one cannot account for any structured subjective reality (p. 148; SIX, 13.12.61). As was demonstrated in the previous chapters, primal repression is the most initial aspect in the constitution of the subject and its relation to the language (É, p. 324). Accordingly, we infer that the only way to account for the structuration of subjective reality is by grounding it in a certain level of signification accomplished in the course of primal repression.

Freud (1905) does discuss an auto-erotic libidinal state that precedes even the most primordial mechanism of primal repression (SE VII, pp. 181–184, 222); this he (1915) later calls as the "original-reality ego" (SE XIV, pp. 134–136). Nevertheless, Lacan insists that Freud does not go on to give this state more than a hypothetical consistency but only considers it as a logical presupposition (SIII, pp. 146–147). He remarks that we can indeed find, in the theory of Melanie Klein, a continuation of the discussion of a repression that exists even before primal repression. Nevertheless, he deems it as "fantasmatic,"[3] and explicitly claims that there is no way to account for a pre-Oedipal form of repression without recourse to the symbolic order engendered in primal repression (pp. 41, 146–147).

---

[3] This term is implemented by Lacan in *Seminar III* in his discussion of hallucination.

Because primal repression is a necessary and most initial aspect in the structuration of the symbolic order; and because we cannot account for a structuration of subjective reality that precedes this most initial form of symbolic signification; it is my contention that, *in order to truly account for its effects on the structuration of subjective reality, autistic foreclosure cannot be designated on a level prior to that of primal repression but can only be accounted for in its horizon. Accordingly, because autistic foreclosure is situated prior to Bejahung, I contend that it is situated on the level of Ausstoßung.* The following sections will provide conceptual support for this hypothesis based on texts provided by the Leforts (2003), Jean Hyppolite (2006) as well as Jean Laplanche and Serge Leclaire (1972).

Two Levels of Foreclosure

In *La Distinction de L'Autisme* (2003), Rosine and Robert Lefort argue that the mechanism of foreclosure functions on two levels. The first level is that of the "judgements of attribution" related to the mechanism of *Bejahung* and primal repression. The second level is that of the "judgments of existence" related to the mechanism secondary repression.[4] The Leforts claim that the first type of foreclosure is associated with the origin of autism, whereas the second type is associated with the origin of psychosis (p. 52). According to this distinction, we can specify an autistic *attributional foreclosure* functioning in relation to primal repression and *Bejahung*, and a psychotic *existential foreclosure* functioning in relation to secondary repression respectively:

- Attributional foreclosure (*Bejahung*) ⇒ autism
- Existential foreclosure (secondary repression) ⇒ psychosis

Nevertheless, it is important to give this distinction a further clarification, for we know that Lacan explicitly associated psychotic foreclosure with "what opposes the primal *Bejahung*" (É, p. 323) and neurotic repression with secondary repression. How can it be then that the Leforts now

---

[4] See discussion on judgments of attribution and existence in Chap. 3.

attribute a foreclosure associated with the level of *Bejahung* to autism and a foreclosure associated with the level of secondary repression to psychosis?

In the previous chapter, I have suggested that foreclosure should be described as a "reactive" mechanism, sequentially functioning after *Bejahung*. In other words, I have argued that the signifier of the Name-of-the-Father has to first be engendered in *Bejahung* in order for it to function as the object radically excluded in psychotic foreclosure. Viewed in this way, psychotic foreclosure is not designated as a mechanism that prohibits the functioning of *Bejahung* altogether but rather as a mechanism that sequentially follows its functioning while, at the same time, radically excluding its affirmative symbolic product. This classifies the mechanism of psychotic foreclosure in relation to its object of exclusion. It is said to oppose the level of *Bejahung* for it radically excludes the signifier affirmed as its symbolic product.

Correspondingly, we can also classify the mechanism of psychotic foreclosure in relation to its consequential effect on the mechanism of secondary repression. Because the signifier of the Name-of-the-Father is a necessary precondition for the functioning of secondary repression, its foreclosure in psychotic foreclosure hinders its functioning altogether. Viewed in this way, psychotic foreclosure is characterized as a mechanism that opposes secondary repression for, by foreclosing the signifier of the Name-of-the-Father, it impedes its application even before it is set in motion.

Taking this into acount, it is my contention that the attributional and the existential forms of foreclosure are designated by the Leforts on the basis of the exact mechanisms that they *precede* and cancel out. In other words, it is psychotic existential foreclosure that hinders secondary repression by radically excluding the symbolic unit that precedes and conditions its functioning—the signifier of the Name-of-the-Father, while, respectively, it is autistic attributional foreclosure that hinders *Bejahung* by radically excluding the symbolic unit that precedes and conditions its functioning. According to the Leforts (2003), while a foreclosure that hinders secondary repression leads to the constitution of a psychotic structure, in the case of a foreclosure that hinders *Bejahung* we are dealing with the "most radical foreclosure" that leads to the constitution of an autistic structure (p. 54).

- *Ausstoßung* ⇒ Attributional foreclosure ⇒ ~~*Bejahung*~~ ⇒ autism
- *Bejahung* ⇒ Existential foreclosure ⇒ ~~Secondary Repression~~ ⇒ psychosis

Following the structural argumentation presented so far, I adopt the Lefort's distinction presented above and suggest that autism is based on a more "archaic" form of foreclosure than that of the Name-of-the-Father, one that includes its structuring effects in its scope. It does so by functioning on a level that hinders *Bejahung* by radically excluding the symbolic affirmative product preceding and conditioning its functioning.

In Chap. 3, I have demonstrated that, in primal repression, the functioning of *Bejahung* is preceded and conditioned by the functioning of *Ausstoßung*. I have also characterized *Ausstoßung* as a mechanism that sanctions the most initial instatement of the subject's relation to the symbolic (É, pp. 752–753). Consequently, *I contend that autistic foreclosure is situated on the level of Ausstoßung and, more precisely, is a mechanism that radically excludes the affirmative symbolic product engendered in Ausstoßung.* It is in this sense that it hinders the functioning of *Bejahung* altogether in the course of primal repression. The following section will provide a more detailed account of the functioning of *Ausstoßung*, situate the mechanism of autistic foreclosure within its scope, and initially specify the particular form of symbolic affirmation it produces.

Ausstoßung as an Affirmative Mechanism

In psychoanalysis, psychic mechanisms of *constitutive exclusion* such as repression and foreclosure entail a negative and affirmative aspect. Moreover, the *exclusion* of an element from a psychic domain gives rise to the affirmation of an organizing psychic construct that supports the structuration of the subject. It is my contention that *Ausstoßung* is a psychic mechanism of *constitutive exclusion* that excludes an element from the psychic domain but also affirms a psychic construct that enables the functioning of *Bejahung*.[5] Accordingly, *I propose to distinguish two aspects internal to Ausstoßung: the primordial operation of "expulsion" elaborated on so far, as well as an affirmative signifying function.*

This section will provide support for the hypothesis of an internal division in *Ausstoßung* based on Hyppolite's interpretation of Freud's "Negation" (1925). Moreover, it will provide further support for the attribution of an affirmative signifying function to *Ausstoßung* based on Jean Laplanche's and Serge Leclaire's account of the constitution of the unconscious (1972). At this point the reader should take in mind that this chapter concerns the level on which autistic foreclosure functions in the model of repression and thus will only briefly account for the signifying unit that is engendered in *Ausstoßung* and radically excluded in autistic foreclosure. This issue will be thoroughly deliberated in the next chapter.

Internal Division in *Ausstoßung*

Jean Hyppolite, a Hegelian philosopher in training, provides a philosophical interpretation of Freud's paper "Negation" (1925) in one of the sessions of Lacan's *Seminar I: Freud's Papers on Technique (1953–1954)*. According to Hyppolite, when reading Freud's paper, one should first differentiate, on the one hand, between what Freud relates to as a form of *constitutive exclusion* and, on the other hand, the general attitude of negativity expressed in speech. Hyppolite claims that while the latter is the original point of departure of Freud's paper, it is the former that carries its "philosophical density" (É, p. 747).

Hyppolite associates the constitutive type of exclusion with the concept of "ideal negation" discussed in Georg Wilhelm Friedrich Hegel's account of *Aufhebung* (Hegel, 1977, §113). Analogous to the crucial role "ideal negation" plays in Hegel's dialectics in *Phenomenology of the Spirit*

---

[5] A problematic might arise with this exact line of reasoning. If we assume that every mechanism of *constitutive exclusion* entails both a negative and an affirmative aspect, we are compelled to assume that its internal negative aspect also entails two such aspects, and so forth ad infinitum. On the other hand, this is just a logical necessity, in relation to constitutive mechanisms in the psyche, we are free to assume such internal division only up to the level of *Ausstoßung*.

(1977), Hyppolite claims that *constitutive exclusions* play an essential role in the origin of thought (É, pp. 747–748). Further explicating this role in psychoanalytic terms, he associates it with the function of primal repression in the constitution of the symbolic order and its relation to the subject (p. 750).[6]

Hyppolite identifies, in accordance with Freud, two non-symmetrical *tendencies* internal to primal repression. The first is characterized by a "destructive tendency" and corresponds to the function of *Ausstoßung*. The second is characterized by a "unifying tendency" and corresponds to the function of *Bejahung*. Parallel to this distinction, Hyppolite describes two *operations* interior to primal repression. The first is an "operation of expulsion," in which a drive-stimulus is attributed as non-pleasurable and thus externalized. The second is an "operation of introjection," in which a drive-stimulus is attributed as pleasurable and thus internalized. Hyppolite claims that in the "operation of expulsion" a division between the interior and exterior of the subject is initially instated, later to be substantiated in the "operation of introjection." It is only after the demarcation of such a division is achieved through both of these operations that secondary repression (judgments of existence) can operate and decide as to the relationship between representations and perception (p. 751). Up to this point, Hyppolite only substantiates the model of repression presented in Chap. 3. Hyppolite merely uses new terms to describe the constitutive "expulsion" (*Ausstoßung*) at the basis of primal repression that conditions the constitutive "affirmation" (*Bejahung*) of a division between consciousness and the unconscious, finally enabling secondary repression to operate in neurosis.

Nevertheless, in a compelling passage, Hyppolite suggests that while the affirmative aspect of primal repression (*Bejahung*) strictly involves an affirmative union (*Vereinigung*), the negative aspect of primal repression (*Ausstoßung*) includes both an expulsion and an affirmation of a unique "symbol":

---

[6] Primal repression is addressed in Hyppolite's commentary as "judgements of attribution" (É, pp. 750–752). See the correspondence between judgments of attribution and primal repression as well as the correspondence between judgments of existence and secondary repression in Chap. 3.

What is there behind affirmation [*Bejahung*]? There is *Vereinigung*, which is Eros. And what is there behind negation (careful—intellectual negation will be something more)? The appearance here of a fundamental, dissymmetrical symbol. Primordial affirmation is nothing more than affirming: but to negate is more than to wish to destroy. (p. 750)

In this excerpt Hyppolite emphasizes that while *Bejahung* ("primordial affirmation") is limited to its affirmative function, *Ausstoßung* cannot be reduced to the function of a destructive expulsion alone but also functions in the affirmation of a "dissymmetrical symbol." According to Hyppolite, the "dissymmetrical symbol" affirmed in *Ausstoßung* is the most fundamental symbolic manifestation in the course of the structuration of the subject in relation to language. It precedes the level of the signifier as well as the level of the primordial signifier of the Name-of-the-Father. Hyppolite claims that it embodies "the fundamental attitude of symbolicity rendered explicit" (p. 752). It stands for the most initial symbolic representation of difference—a distinction between an inside and an outside—"linked to the concrete attitude of negation" (p. 753). Therefore, it symbolically affirms the most initial division in the subject and, thus, "alone makes possible something like the use of the unconscious" through its distinction from consciousness (p. 753). Without providing a comprehensive account of its exact nature, Hyppolite terms this symbol the "explicit symbol of negation" (p. 753).[7]

In summary, we see that Hyppolite's account of Freud's "Negation" (1925) supports the internal division I have proposed in *Ausstoßung*. He too differentiates between the operation of expulsion (*Ausstoßung*) and introjection (*Bejahung*) internal to primal repression but emphasizes that inside the operation of expulsion (*Ausstoßung*) we also find two non-symmetrical tendencies—a destructive expulsion as well as an affirmation of the explicit symbol of negation. Accordingly, we can characterize the internal progression in the Freudian model of repression as originating in a destructive expulsion followed by a symbolic affirmation, both internal to *Ausstoßung*. This affirmation conditions the functioning of *Bejahung* that enables the functioning of secondary repression and the

---

[7] A comprehensive account of the nature of the "symbol of negation" will be provided in Chap. 6.

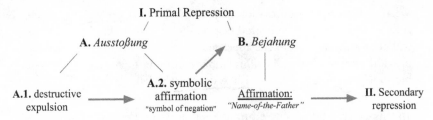

Fig. 5.1 Primal repression, including negative and affirmative aspects of *Ausstoßung*

structuration of neurotic subjective reality. These conclusions are summarized in Fig. 5.1.

Affirmation of the Signifier of Pure Difference

In a compelling passage in their paper "The Unconscious: A Psychoanalytic Study" (1972), Jean Laplanche and Serge Leclaire give further support to the idea that both *Ausstoßung* and *Bejahung* introduce the subject into two different levels of symbolic affirmation. Explicitly addressing primal repression as "the process that introduces the subject into a symbolic universe" (p. 161), they provide the following explanation, which is worth quoting at length:

> One could describe, abstractly, two stages in this process. At a first level of symbolization, the network or web of significant oppositions is cast onto the subjective universe; but no particular signified is caught in any *single* mesh. What is simply introduced, along with this system coextensive to experience, is pure difference, scansion, the bar: in the "Fort-da" gesture, the edge of the bed … The second level of symbolization is that which, following Freud, we called primal repression and, following Lacan, [the paternal] metaphor. It is this which really creates the unconscious … and which is lacking—to a greater or a lesser extent—in the symbolic world of the schizophrenic … To borrow a term used by Merleau-Ponty in relation

to perception, this second stage is one of an *anchoring* (*ancrage*) in the symbolic world. (pp. 161–162; brackets added)[8]

First Level of Symbolization

Let us slowly delve into this dense passage that distinguishes a "first" and a "second" level of symbolization in the introduction of the subject into the symbolic universe. According to Laplanche and Leclaire, the "first level of symbolization" is achieved when the subject is initially introduced to the symbolic order as large network of oppositions. This network is not yet capable of signifying meaning but introduces the structure through which symbolic meaning is achieved in the opposition between signifiers. Laplanche and Leclaire relate this level of symbolization to the function of "pure difference," which is to say, a "scansion" or a dividing "bar." These all represent a fundamental level of linguistic functioning that does not signify anything more than a distinction between two terms, without attributing anything to the terms themselves other than their separation.[9]

Laplanche and Leclaire also relate the first level of symbolization to the "experience" presented in Freud's (1920) account of the *Fort-da* game ("gone-there" in German). In this game the symbolic opposition between two arbitrary terms substantiates the child's relation to objects in the world (SE XVIII, pp. 14–17). According to Laplanche and Leclaire (1972), following the hypothesized undivided state preceding the first level of symbolization, the *Fort-da* game introduces into the child's universe the symbolic opposition between the presence of the object and its absence when it is dropped under the bed. Laplanche and Leclaire emphasize that this division is initially signified in the *Fort-da* game by the figure of the "edge of the bed," designating a dividing line in relation to which the child's whole symbolic universe is established (p. 153).

---

[8] Laplanche and Leclaire's association of primal repression with the paternal metaphor is a point of disagreement between the two. A footnote presented in the same paper (1972) discloses that Laplanche associates it with both instances of the paternal metaphor, while Leclaire associates it only with the first (p. 162).

[9] The exact signifying nature of "pure difference" will be further elaborated in Chap. 6.

Laplanche and Leclaire's argument corresponds to Lacan's reformulation of the *Fort-da* game in his paper "The Function and Field of Speech and Language in Psychoanalysis" printed in *Écrits* (2006). In this paper Lacan associates the *Fort-da* game with the moment "at which the child is born into language" (É, p. 262). He argues that, in this moment, a "symbol" eclipses the real absence of the object by being introduced in its place. Lacan describes this as an act that "gives birth to the symbol" (p. 262)— that which Hyppolite terms the symbol of negation.

Finally, Laplanche and Leclaire (1972) relate the first level of symbolization to the initial inscription of the drive in psychic reality (pp. 159, 166, 171, 174). Namely, they relate it to a *fixation* of a drive-stimulus and its manifestation as a mental representative of the drive in the psyche. Accordingly, Laplanche and Leclaire describe the first level of symbolization as "a process by which, and by which alone, the drive is introduced into and present in the unconscious" (p. 159). The introduction of the drive into the unconscious enables its further introjection in *Bejahung* that, in its turn, affirms the distinction between consciousness and the unconscious (p. 161).

Laplanche and Leclaire's interpretation of the "first level of signification" complies with Freud and Lacan's account of *Ausstoßung* on several levels: firstly, in their definition of this level as preceding and conditioning the functioning of *Bejahung* in primal repression; secondly, in its association with the level of the drive and, more specifically, with the function of the representatives of the drive in judgments of attribution; finally, in its association with the prototypical instatement of a gap that initiates the division between consciousness and the unconscious.

Second Level of Symbolization

The "second level of symbolization" is simply designated by Laplanche and Leclaire, in accordance with Lacan, as the level of the "paternal metaphor" (p. 160). It is the level in which the initial division achieved in *Ausstoßung* is affirmed by its further designation under the primordial signifier. This is the level of *Bejahung*, in which the Name-of-the-Father is inscribed, providing an anchoring point for the subject in the symbolic and instating the symbolic law. In accordance with the account presented in the previous chapters, Laplanche and Leclaire emphasize that this level of signification is exemplary in neurosis but is lacking in the case of psychosis (p. 162).

Laplanche and Leclaire's adaptation of primal repression into a framework entailing a "first" and a "second" "level of symbolization" complies with the model of the two instances of the paternal metaphor presented in Chap. 3. Accordingly, the "first level of symbolization" corresponds to the instance of the father's *non*, in which the paternal function engenders a gap in the child's libidinal economy. The "second level of symbolization" corresponds to the instance of the father's *nom*, in which this gap is affirmed by the signifier of the Name-of-the-Father.

What is most compelling in Laplanche and Leclaire's interpretation of the division internal to primal repression is their insistence on an affirmative signifying function inherent to both of its levels. In the first one, *Ausstoßung*, the subject is initially introduced to the symbolic order through a symbolic figure representing "pure difference." This corresponds to what Hyppolite associates with the affirmative aspect of *Ausstoßung* and the symbol of negation (É, p. 753). In the second one, *Bejahung*, the paternal metaphor is instated, inscribing the signifier of the Name-of-the-Father and properly anchoring the subject in the symbolic domain.

Conclusion: Autistic Foreclosure Opposes *Ausstoßung*

So far, with the help of Hyppolite (2006), this chapter has asserted an internal division within *Ausstoßung*, dividing it into a negative and affirmative aspect. Moreover, on the basis of Laplanche and Leclaire (1972), it has attributed an affirmative symbolic product to both *Ausstoßung* and *Bejahung*. As a result, it has provided grounds for a revised three-leveled model of primal repression presented in Fig. 5.2.

Based on this model, we can now associate Benoist's "minimal relationship with the symbolic" (Benoist, 2011) with the "second level of

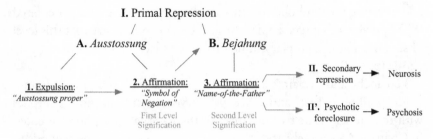

Fig. 5.2 Primal repression, including levels of signification and structuration of neurosis and psychosis

symbolization" presented by Laplanche and Leclaire (Laplanche & Leclaire, 1972, pp. 161–162). This level of symbolization precedes and conditions the functioning of neurotic repression and psychotic foreclosure but is not engendered at all prior to autistic foreclosure.

With the combined assistance of the Leforts (2003), Benoist (2011), Hyppolite (2006), and Laplanche and Leclaire (1972), we can now situate the functioning of autistic foreclosure in this newly derived model. Let us summarize the relevant conclusions produced in this chapter in an argumentative form:

1. Autistic foreclosure is situated on a level preceding and conditioning the functioning of *Bejahung* (Benoist).
2. Autistic foreclosure is internal to primal repression.
3. *Ausstoßung* precedes and conditions the functioning of *Bejahung*, as well as is internal to primal repression (Freud, Lacan).
   Intermediary conclusion: Autistic foreclosure is situated on the level of *Ausstoßung.*
4. *Ausstoßung* can be internally divided into a negative and an affirmative aspect (Hyppolite).
5. In the affirmative aspect of *Ausstoßung*, a signifying unit conditioning the functioning of *Bejahung* is inscribed in the symbolic (Laplanche and Leclaire, Hyppolite).

Conclusion: Autistic foreclosure functions on the level that sequentially follows the affirmative aspect of Ausstoßung and takes as its object of exclusion the signifying unit it produces—what Hyppolite has termed the "symbol of negation" (É, p. 753) and Laplanche and Leclaire have termed "pure difference, scansion, the bar" (Laplanche & Leclaire, 1972, p. 161).

The foreclosure of the signifying unit produced in the affirmative aspect of *Ausstoßung* hinders the functioning of *Bejahung*. It thus prevents the instatement of a minimal level of signification necessary for the structuration of both the neurotic subjective structure in secondary repression and the psychotic subjective structure in psychotic foreclosure. Viewed in this way, autistic foreclosure encompasses the foreclosure of the signifier of the Name-of-the-Father, not because it forecloses this signifier directly, but through a relationship of cause and effect. That is, because it forecloses the symbol of negation and thus wards off the possibility of the inscription of the signifier of the Name-of-the-Father before it even happens. Or, stated otherwise, without the father's *non* established in *Ausstoßung*, the father's *nom* can never be inscribed in *Bejahung*.

Consequently, we can now argue that, in the same way that psychotic foreclosure opposes *Bejahung* (É, p. 323), *autistic foreclosure opposes Ausstoßung*. Both forms of foreclosure entail different levels of functioning in the model of repression, revolve around different objects of exclusion, and, as a result, produce different effects on the structuration of the symbolic order and its relation to the subject.

Taking these conclusions and integrating them with the conclusions reached in the previous chapters, we can now see that the revised three-leveled model of repression entails the level of functioning of three distinct psychic mechanisms of *constitutive exclusion* at the origin of the neurotic, psychotic, and autistic structures. While both neurotic repression and psychotic foreclosure function on the basis of the instatement of the signifier of the Name-of-the-Father in *Bejahung*, autistic foreclosure functions on the basis to the instatement of the symbol of negation in

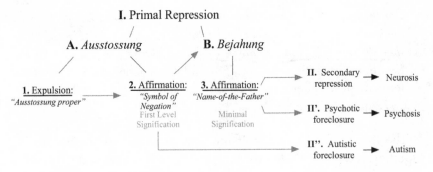

Fig. 5.3 Primal repression and the structuration of neurosis, psychosis, and autism

Ausstoßung and precedes and hinders the instatement of the signifier of the Name-of-the-Father. These conclusions are summarized in Fig. 5.3.

Works Cited

Benoist, V. (2011). L'Autre dans L'Autisme. *International Psychology, Practice and Research*, (2), 1–13.

Borgnis-Desbordes, E. (2009). Autisme, Transfert et Inventions Subjectives: Deux Cas. In J.-C. Maleval (Ed.), *L'autist, son double et ses objets* (pp. 101–114). Rennes: Presses Universitaires de Rennes.

Esteban, M. (2002). Autism: Divergent Positions in Psychoanalysis. *Mental ONLINE*, (11), 57–67.

Freud, S. (1894). The Neuro-Psychoses of Defence. *The Standard Edition of the Complete Psychological Works of Sigmund Freud, Volume III (1893–1899): Early Psycho-Analytic Publications* (pp. 41–61).

Freud, S. (1905). Three Essays on the Theory of Sexuality. *The Standard Edition of the Complete Psychological Works of Sigmund Freud, Volume VII (1901–1905): A Case of Hysteria, Three Essays on Sexuality and Other Works* (pp. 123–246).

Freud, S. (1915). Instincts and Their Vicissitudes. *The Standard Edition of the Complete Psychological Works of Sigmund Freud, Volume XIV (1914–1916): On the History of the Psycho-Analytic Movement, Papers on Metapsychology and Other Works* (pp. 109–140).

Freud, S. (1920). Beyond the Pleasure Principle. *The Standard Edition of the Complete Psychological Works of Sigmund Freud, Volume XVIII (1920–1922): Beyond the Pleasure Principle, Group Psychology and Other Works* (pp. 1–64).

Freud, S. (1925). Negation. *The Standard Edition of the Complete Psychological Works of Sigmund Freud, Volume XIX (1923–1925): The Ego and the Id and Other Works* (pp. 233–240).

Hegel, G. W. F. (1977). *Phenomenology of Spirit.* Oxford, UK: Oxford University Press.

Hyppolite, J. (2006). A Spoken Commentary on Freud's Verneinung. In *Écrits* (pp. 746–754). New York: Norton & Company.

Kanner, L. (1943). Autistic Disturbances of Affective Contact. *Nervous Child, 2*(3), 217–250.

Lacan, J. (1988). In J.-A. Miller (Ed.), *The Seminar of Jacques Lacan, Book I, Freud's Papers on Technique (1953–1954).* New York: Norton & Company.

Lacan, J. (1997). In J.-A. Miller (Ed.), *The Seminar of Jacques Lacan, Book III, The Psychoses (1955–1956).* New York: Norton & Company.

Lacan, J. (2006). In B. Fink (Ed.), *Écrits.* New York: Norton & Company.

Lacan, J. (n.d.). *The Seminar of Jacques Lacan, Book IX, Identification (1961–1962).* Trans. Gallagher, C. Unpublished.

Laplanche, J., & Leclaire, S. (1972). The Unconscious: A Psychoanalytic Study. *Yale French Studies,* (48), 118–175.

Laurent, É. (2012a). *La Bataille de l'Autisme.* Paris: Navarin.

Laurent, É. (2012b). Autism and Psychosis: Further Dialogue with Robert and Rosine Lefort. *Psychoanalytical Notebooks, 25,* 11–26.

Lefort, R., & Lefort, R. (1994). *Birth of the Other.* Oxford, UK: University of Illinois Press.

Lefort, R., & Lefort, R. (2003). *La Distinction de L'Autisme.* Paris: Seuil.

Maleval, J.-C. (2009). *L'Autiste et sa Voix.* Paris: Seuil.

Maleval, J.-C. (2012). Why the Hypothesis of an Autistic Structure? *Psychoanalytical Notebooks, 25,* 27–49.

Tendlarz, S. E. (2003). *Childhood Psychosis: A Lacanian Perspective.* London: Karnac Books.

6

The Object of Autistic Foreclosure

Freud argues that psychic mechanisms of *constitutive exclusion* are implemented on psychic "representatives" that are associated with different faculties in the psyche. In Chap. 3 I have demonstrated that, in the case of primal repression, these are the representatives of the drive and, in the case of secondary repression, the ideational representatives. In Lacanian terms, the objects excluded by such constitutive mechanisms are unique signifying units that play a crucial role in the organization and construction of different psychic registers. Accordingly, Lacan argues that in neurotic repression, signifiers are repressed and come to form the consecutive chain of signifiers in the unconscious. In *Seminar III: The Psychoses (1955–1956)*, Lacan adds to the Freudian list another type of constitutive mechanism—psychotic foreclosure. According to Lacan, this mechanism is situated "in opposition" to *Bejahung* and radically excludes the signifier of the Name-of-the-Father (É, p. 323). By doing so, psychotic foreclosure hinders the functioning of secondary repression as well as the structuration of the neurotic subjective structure and brings about the structuration of the psychotic subjective structure.[1]

---

[1] See Chap. 4.

© The Author(s) 2020
L. S. Brenner, *The Autistic Subject*, The Palgrave Lacan Series,
https://doi.org/10.1007/978-3-030-50715-2_6

In the previous chapter another constitutive mechanism has been added to this list—autistic foreclosure. This mechanism was described as opposing *Ausstoßung* in the model of repression. More specifically, it has been classified as a mechanism that radically excludes the signifying unit produced in *Ausstoßung*. Hyppolite termed this signifying unit the "symbol of negation" (É, p. 753) and Laplanche and Leclaire associated it with the function of "pure difference" (Laplanche & Leclaire, 1972, p. 161). Although they have named this symbolic unit, neither Hyppolite nor Laplanche nor Leclaire provided us with an explicit and rigorous analysis of its nature.

In contemporary psychoanalytic literature, the object of autistic foreclosure has not been explicitly elaborated, other than by implication. The two most compelling elaborations of the object of autistic foreclosure are presented by Laurent (2012a), in his account of the "foreclosure of the hole" and by Maleval (2009), in his account of the retention of the object of the invocatory drive. Nevertheless, these cases have not been conceptually developed in association with the functioning of autistic foreclosure in the model of repression. Accordingly, this chapter will present a detailed conceptual analysis of the nature of the object of autistic foreclosure. Namely, it will provide three possible frameworks through which the nature of the object of autistic foreclosure can be addressed. Each section will develop an exclusive interpretation of the object of autistic foreclosure based on Lacan's teaching, strengthening it conceptually as well as providing points of critique. In the first section, the object of autistic foreclosure will be associated with the "unary trait" based on Lacan's *Seminar IX: Identification (1961–1962)*. This section will attempt to pinpoint the nature of the object of autistic foreclosure in Lacan's corpus itself but will also be supported by several notions derived from contemporary psychoanalysts developing the Lacanian clinic of autism. The following two sections will go on to explore the two prominent contemporary approaches to autism developed by Éric Laurent and Jean-Claude Maleval. The second section will present Laurent's notion of the hole as the object of autistic foreclosure. Based on Lacan's topological account of the function of the hole in the figure of the torus in *Seminar IX*, it will develop Laurent's notion of the "foreclosure of the hole." The third and final section will present Maleval's account of the autistic retention of the object of the invocatory drive. Based on Lacan's *Seminar X: Anxiety (1962–1963)* and *Seminar XI: The Four Fundamental Concepts of Psychoanalysis* (1964), this section will clarify Maleval's account of the voice and its function in the circuit of the drive. Above all it will provide its reformulation under the terms of the mechanism of foreclosure, finally introducing its further development in contemporary Lacanian models of drive dynamism. The accumulation of the conclusions provided in this chapter, in addition to the conclusions achieved in the previous chapter, will enable the elaboration of the unique autistic mode of linguistic functionality enabled by autistic foreclosure in the following chapter. The accumulated conclusions derived from these three chapters will provide evidence of the singularity of autistic foreclosure and, as a result, of the singularity of the autistic subjective structure in the final chapter of this book.

The Unary Trait as the Object of Autistic Foreclosure

The [unary] trait has a function on the threshold of the symbolic: it is a mark for the subject that conditions its anchoring in the field of the Other and thus conditions its being a speaking subject. (Borgnis-Desbordes, 2009, p. 103; brackets added)

This is the major difficulty that the autistic subject has to confront. Not possessing the function of the unary signifier that links jouissance to language and enables the representation of being in the symbolic. (Maleval, 2009, p. 120)

This failure is situated at the level of what Lacan calls the unary trait—the first symbolic mark for a subject … through which the subject is represented in its entirety before being introduced to alterity; this unary trait, the autistic subject rejects it. (Borgnis-Desbordes, 2009, p. 102)

The term "unary trait" (*trait unaire*) is an original translation, provided by Lacan, that is rooted in Freud's distinction between his notions of identification and object-choice in his paper "Group Psychology and the Analysis of the Ego" (1921). In this paper, Freud presents two cases in which the analysand's "object-choice has regressed to identification" as they both take on themselves a distinct characteristic from their object (SE XVIII, p. 107).[2] The term "single trait" (*einen einzigen Zug*) is used by Freud to emphasize that "in both cases the identification is a partial and extremely limited one and only borrows a *single trait* from the person who is its object" (p. 107; emphasis added).

The German term *einen einzigen Zug* is translated by Lacan to French as *trait unaire* and is used to connote a primordial level of identification. More specifically, Lacan emphasizes the crucial role the unary trait plays in engendering pure difference in the symbolic order, a level of signification that is fundamental for the constitution of the symbolic order and its relation to the subject. Based on Lacan's *Seminar IX*, this section will explicate the crucial role the unary trait plays in engendering pure difference in the symbolic order. Moreover, it will provide a structural elaboration of the function of the unary trait in the course of primal repression. Furthermore, it will designate the unary trait as the affirmative symbolic product of *Ausstoßung* and present compelling evidence that attests to its designation as the object radically excluded in autistic foreclosure. Lastly, it will provide further clinical support for this hypothesis based on psychoanalytic case studies.

Pure Difference

According to Aristotle, any conceptualization of difference is necessarily representational (May, 1997, pp. 192–193), meaning that difference can only be determined in thought in accordance with a supposed relation of contrariety or identity between intelligible categories (Aristotle, 1995, *Topics*, VI, 6–8). This is demonstrated by Aristotle in his definition of "specific differences" as entailing a relation of contrariety between two species subordinated to the same generic category. Thus, in the generic category of "plants," a specific differentiation between an "edible" and a "poisonous" plant can be achieved. The specific difference between these two species is represented by a predicate that also defines them: for instance, "edibility by humans." Aristotle adds that, among generic

---

[2] In both cases, the second being the famous case of Dora, the analysands assume the cough of one of their caretakers.

categories, difference becomes weaker but can still be determined in relation to a supposed analogy between two categories. Accordingly, we see that Aristotle suggests that both a relation of contrariety between species and a relation of analogy between genres can only be determined in thought on the basis of shared and accepted empirical knowledge of relationships and concepts (Deleuze, 1994, p. 160). In more linguistic terms, the Aristotelian account of difference is utterly dependent on one's preliminary assimilation of the symbolic values of the differentiated terms that comply with their relation of contrariety or analogy.

In his account of the crucial role that difference plays in the materialization of symbolic meaning, Lacan can be said to adopt the Aristotelian representationalist framework but, at the same time, to turn it on its head. Accordingly, it is not the preliminary assimilation of symbolic values that conditions our conception of difference, but rather it is the differentiation between signifiers that conditions symbolic meaning itself. In other words, Lacan argues that signifiers are constructs that convey meaning in language on the basis of their differentiation from other signifiers: "What distinguishes the signifier, is simply being what the others are not; that which, in the signifier, implies this function of the unit, is precisely to be simply different" (SIX, 29.11.61). In saying so, Lacan relies on a framework provided by Swiss linguist Ferdinand de Saussure, in which meaning can only be engendered in language through difference:

> In language there are only differences without positive terms. Whether we take the signified or the signifier, language has neither ideas nor sounds that existed before the linguistic system, but only conceptual and phonic differences that have issued from the system ... A linguistic system is a series of differences of sound combined with a series of differences of ideas; but the pairing of a certain number of acoustical signs with as many cuts made from the mass thought engenders a system of values. (de Saussure, 1959, p. 70)

In this excerpt, de Saussure offers an unconventional interpretation of the production of meaning in language. He argues that meaning does not arise from a direct relationship between a signifier and a signified but through the differentiation between one signifier and another. In other words, for de Saussure, language is a system of functional differences and oppositions between signifiers (p. 121); moreover, it is a system that is initiated by an opposition between two signifiers (Sturrock, 1979, p. 10). Accordingly, de Saussure (1959) claims that "concepts are purely differential and defined not by their positive content but negatively by their relations with other terms of the system. Their most precise characteristic is in being what the others are not" (p. 117). Lacan's argument presented above resonates with these lines from de Saussure. Both fundamentally agree that, in a linguistic system, difference is prior to meaning, and signification is conditioned by a preliminary introduction of difference into the system.

Lacan diverges from de Saussure's framework when he identifies the symbolic dimension of difference as inherent to the structure of the signifier itself and not as dependent on the relationship between signifiers in a linguistic system. While de Saussure's account of the function of difference dictates that the signifier itself is empty, Lacan distinguishes between the differential relationships between signifiers that produce meaning in a linguistic system and the fundamental differential structure inherent to every signifier. While the first describes difference as a function in the production of meaning, the latter designates difference as the "pure materiality" of the signifier independent of its corresponding significations:

> When I speak about the pure materiality of the signifier I am designating here the opposed couple of two elements ... The essential is that the articulation of these two traits which are, at the extreme, pure materiality, totally stripped of signification. (SXII, 31.3.65)

Lacan associates the manifestation of difference in "the pure materiality of the signifier" with "pure difference" (31.3.65).[3] This "pure" dimension of difference takes form as an actual structure that is inherently imprinted in every signifier, even the first signifier instated in the

---

[3] In this passage Lacan also associates the term "pure difference" with the "the signifier ... as pure connotation of antinomy" (SXII, 31.3.65).

symbolic order.[4] Stated otherwise, it is a generic structure internal to all signifiers in the symbolic order that precedes and conditions their capacity to convey meaning.[5]

Lacan takes a further step away from de Saussure's original framework when he argues that pure difference is instated in the symbolic order through the inscription of a particular signifying unit—the unary trait. Accordingly, in the next section, based on Lacan's *Seminar IX*, the unary trait will be presented as central in the integration of the dimension of pure difference in the symbolic order. As a result, based on the association of pure difference with autistic foreclosure in the previous chapter, the unary trait will be designated as the object radically excluded in autistic foreclosure.

The Stroke of the Primitive Hunter

In *Seminar IX*, Lacan provides the most comprehensive account of his conception of the unary trait. Firstly, commenting on the role of the "single trait" in Freud's (1921) account of identification (SE XVIII, p. 107), Lacan describes the unary trait as a "most simple structural trait, of the unique trait, absolutely depersonalized … not alone of all subjective content, but even of all variation which goes beyond this single trait" (SIX, 22.11.61). Diverging from Freud, Lacan goes on to characterize the unary trait as a unique symbolic unit that is utterly devoid of any content or variation. Contrasting it to his notion of the signifier, Lacan relates the unary trait to a single "stroke" (*bâton*) or marking of a line { | } about which he remarks "has always been sufficient for minimal notation" (29.11.61).

Lacan provides an intriguing example in order to clarify the nature of the unary trait and its relation to pure difference. This example concerns a "primitive hunter" who repetitively marks strokes on a bone instrument

---

[4] On the level of the first signifier, difference cannot be accounted for through a relationship with another signifier but only through a relationship between the same signifier and itself.

[5] The idea of pure difference as the generic aspect of the signifier in the symbolic is later elaborated by Lacan in his account of "signifierness" in *Seminar XX: Encore* (1972–1973). See more on this subject in Chap. 3.

every time he successfully accomplishes a kill in one of his "adventures." The example of the "primitive hunter" is repeated in the different sessions of *Seminar IX* as well as in later seminars such as *Seminar XI* and is worth being quoted at length:

> I am a hunter ... I kill one of them, it is an adventure, I kill another of them, it is a second adventure which I can distinguish by certain traits from the first, but which resembles it essentially by being marked with the same general line. At the fourth, there may be some confusion: what distinguishes it from the second, for example. At the twentieth, how will I know where I am, or will I even know that I have had twenty of them? (SIX, 6.12.61)

The example of the "primitive hunter" sheds light on the exact *form* of the unary trait. Firstly, the marking of the unary trait on the bone is designated by Lacan as a "general line," a stroke that marks—in the most elementary way—an event that has happened. This stroke precedes the level of the signifier in language as well as that of the ideogram and the image (6.12.61).[6] Accordingly, it bears no distinct meaning associated with its imaginary character in shape or pattern. Its sole property is "unicity," that is, the fact that it is devoid of all "variations" and is thus essentially a mark completely arbitrary in form (22.11.61).[7]

Moreover, the example of the "primitive hunter" demonstrates the exact *symbolic function* ascribed to the unary trait. Lacan argues that the function of the hunter's strokes on the bone is to mark the circumstances of his "adventures."[8] Nevertheless, he emphasizes that, by doing so, they do not provide the hunter with symbolic *content* that conveys the meaning of these adventures but offer a more primitive form of symbolic affirmation preceding the level of the signifier (28.2.62). Accordingly, in its primitive form, the unary trait strips the hunter's adventures of their

---

[6] Lacan explicitly argues that the unary trait is not comparable to an image (a head of a lion for instance).

[7] This complies with Freud's account of the *einziger Zug*, in which Dora chooses to identify with her Father's cough arbitrarily. Dora could have chosen any other feature of his character in order to accomplish this form of identification.

[8] These adventures are related by Lacan to a hypothesized pre-symbolic, real encounter.

immediate phenomenological or sensual content—the type of animal killed, for example. Not only is the content of the hunter's adventures not represented by the markings on the bone, Lacan insists that their *quantitative* dimension is also unavailable to the hunter. One might imagine that the numeration of the repetitive markings on the bone might still hold a certain symbolic value associated with the quantification of the hunter's "adventures" ("third time's a charm"). Conversely, Lacan emphasizes that the primitive hunter does not know how to count (14.3.62), and therefore that the repetitive marking of the unary trait should not be confused with the addition of accumulating numbers (7.3.62).[9] Thus, we see that both the dimension of content and quantification, attributed by Lacan to the level of the signifier, are not part and parcel of the primitive symbolic function of the unary trait.

Nevertheless, Lacan insists that in the repetitive marking of the unary trait in the example of the "primitive hunter" { | + | + | + ... } a unique and "radical subsistence" of difference is engendered, namely that of pure difference (7.3.62). This unique subsistence of difference is not based on the unary trait's *form, content,* or *quantification* but is rooted in the particularity of the hunter's "adventures" that it effaces. In other words, even when the hunter disregards their visual *form,* forgets the *content* of the adventures they represent, and is oblivious as to their *quantification* when he reaches the 20th hunt, the markings on the bone still represent difference when they are grasped in their totality (13.12.61). For, each of the markings stands behind an utterly singular adventure, even if they are represented under the unicity of the unary trait. Lacan associates this difference with the most essential structure inherent to the signifier, through which "the signifier as such serves to connote difference in the pure state" (6.12.61), "difference as such" (21.2.62)—a pure difference.

Lacan gives another explanation of this unique symbolic function when he addresses the notion of a simple tautology.[10] He argues that, while on the level of the signifier, the equation "A is A" can be said to represent a simple tautology, on the level of the inscription of the unary

---

[9] Lacan is insinuating that the level of the unary trait precedes the capacity for counting—which depends on the signifier. This is also implied by his association of the primitive hunter with the human infant unable to count beyond three (SIX, 28.2.62).

[10] When a tautology is defined as the repetitive use of phrases or words that have similar meanings.

trait it engenders a pure difference. Lacan bases this argument by comparing the unary trait to the function of the letter as an "idiotic character" that precedes its being phoneticized or named (20.12.61). Accordingly, Lacan argues that "in as much precisely that if I said above that the 'A is A' is a belief ... I am speaking about A, the letter A." Lacan continues in the same session: "If I pose that there is no tautology possible ... it is in the very status of A that *there is inscribed* that A cannot be A" (6.12.61; emphasis added).[11] In this sense, Lacan demonstrates that, in the repetitive inscription of the unary trait, the hunter does not engender a sequence of simple tautologies but rather a difference rooted in the singularity of the instances of the inscription of the letter that are independent of their signifying value, their sound, or name. Taking us back to the metaphor of the hunter's bone, each marking on the bone signifies that something different has happened. But, when considered as a unary trait, preceding the level of the signifier, the markings do so by signifying difference as such, in the pure state and not difference as it is inscribed in the differential relationships between signifiers.

The Unary Trait and the Constitution of the Symbolic Order

Lacan significantly develops Freud's account of the *einziger Zug* when he argues that the unary trait functions as the marker of the most primal form of identification initiating the subject's access to the symbolic order. For example, in *Seminar IX,* Lacan specifically addresses the unary trait as the "guarantor" of the symbolic order, as "what all signifiers have in common" as their support (22.11.61). In his later *Seminar XVII: The Other Side of Psychoanalysis (1969–1970)*, Lacan proceeds to associate the unary trait with the constitution of the signifier, stating that "the function of the unary trait ... is the function of the simplest form of mark, which properly speaking is the origin of the signifier" (SXVII, p. 46).

Based on Lacan's account of the unary trait, Lorenzo Chiesa, in his paper "Count-as-one, Forming-into-one, Unary Trait, S1" (2006),

---

[11] See original French: "c'est dans le statut même de A *qu'il y a inscrit* que A ne peut pas être A."

describes a progression between three levels of signification in the constitution of the symbolic order.[12] As will be shortly disclosed, Chiesa argues
that the first level is that of the unary trait and of pure difference, the
second level is that of the naming of pure difference, and the third level
is that of the chain of signifiers characteristic of the symbolic order itself.
In this sense, Chiesa provides a more detailed account of the crucial role
that the unary trait plays in the constitution of the symbolic order and its
relation to the subject.

First Level: The Unary Trait

According to Chiesa (2006), on the first level of the constitution of the
symbolic order, the unary trait is inscribed as a singular mark devoid of
any content or form (pp. 78–81). As I have already presented, in Lacan's
example of the primitive hunter, the unary trait functions as the most
initial generic designator of a previous "adventure." Chiesa adds that the
unary trait can only designate the primitive hunter's adventures retroactively, after they have been primordially effaced (p. 81). In this sense,
Chiesa describes the unary trait as the first affirmative symbolic unit situated on the backdrop of what is constitutively and primally lacking in the
symbolic. Furthermore, Chiesa argues that the unary trait takes part in
the initial introduction of a dividing line between the symbolic order and
what is primally repressed and expelled from symbolism—the real (p. 80).
Thus, the unary trait can be described as being situated on the threshold
between the symbolic and the real, for it functions as the marker of their
distinction (Borgnis-Desbordes, 2009, p. 103).

   In the previous chapter, I have argued that the first symbolic inscription achieved in primal repression takes place in *Ausstoßung*. I have also
argued that the mechanism of *Ausstoßung* is divided into a negative aspect,
in which an initial sum of jouissance is primordially expelled; and an
affirmative aspect, in which it is symbolically affirmed as lost through the

---

[12] In this paper, Chiesa (2006) chooses to call these "levels"—a term I preserve in this chapter.
Nevertheless, I do not think that Chiesa is offering here a developmental theory of the constitution
of the symbolic. Accordingly, I propose to view these "levels" as "moments" in a dialectical process
rather than stages of development.

symbol of negation. Correspondingly, Chiesa (2006) explicitly associates the first affirmative designation of the object primordially expelled in primal repression with the initial inscription of the unary trait (pp. 80, 87). In line with Chiesa's interpretation, *I argue that the unary trait can be designated as the first symbolic affirmation of the object primordially excluded in Ausstoßung.* In this sense, the unary trait is designated as the affirmative symbolic product of *Ausstoßung* delivered on the background of the absence of the lost object. Therefore, I argue that the unary trait can be regarded as a concrete manifestation of Hyppolite's "symbol of negation," as a symbolic presence that rises against a "background of absence" in primal repression (É, p. 327).

Second Level: The Name-of-the-Father

As soon as the unary trait is inscribed more than once, it enters "repetition" (SIX, 7.3.62), and the second level of the constitution of the symbolic order comes into play.[13] As was elaborated earlier, the repetition of the unary trait engenders pure difference in the moment the series of marks on the hunter's bone is grasped in its totality (6.12.61; 21.2.62). According to Chiesa (2006), at the moment this series is grasped in its totality, pure difference is designated in the symbolic under a "name" (p. 80). Chiesa addresses the designation of pure difference under a name as a "redoubling" of the operation of the repetition of the unary trait. It provides pure difference with a further ("double") level of symbolic consistency as it is *named as such* (p. 80). In this sense, Chiesa argues that, if the unary trait is that which retroactively signifies the loss of the primordial object, the name is that which allows the subject's further identification with this loss. Chiesa associates the naming of pure difference with Lacan's account of the function of the signifier of the Name-of-the-Father (pp. 89–90). Namely, he argues that the naming of pure difference, engendered in the repetition of the unary trait, transforms the initiatory *particular* dimension of the unary trait to the *universal* authoritative

---

[13] By "repetition," I refer to the consecutive marking of the unary trait on the bone.

dimension of the signifier of the Name-of-the-Father (p. 90).[14] In other words, while the unary trait affirms the dimension of pure difference in a particular signifying element, the signifier of the Name-of-the-Father is the marker of the function of difference in the symbolic order as a whole. It is true then that both the signifier of the Name-of-the-father and the unary trait function as "guarantors" of signification in the symbolic order (SIX, 22.11.61; SIII, pp. 267–268). However, the signifier of the Name-of-the-Father is a *generic* signifier necessarily adopted from the locus of the Other and associated with the whole chain of signifiers in the symbolic order. In contrast, the unary trait is a *particular* mark, singularly adopted by the subject from an arbitrary object, that instates the function of pure difference in the structure of each and every signifier as a distinct signifying unit.

Third Level: The Chain of Signifiers

Chiesa (2006) argues that on the third level of the constitution of the symbolic order, the chain of signifiers is established, and meaning is engendered in the symbolic order through the differential relationships between signifiers (p. 90). These are signifiers that inherently affirm the function of pure difference through their generic relationship to the law of signification instated by the signifier of the Name-of-the-Father.

It is important to note that each of the levels described by Chiesa retroactively affirms the mode of signification achieved on its preceding level. Accordingly, the primordial expulsion of the object of jouissance is only signified in opposition to the unary trait, which only gains its universal value through the inscription of the signifier of the Name-of-the-Father. The signifier of the Name-of-the-Father is, in turn, further affirmed in the relationships between signifiers in the chain of signifiers in the symbolic order, as they originate in its inscription in the unconscious. In other words, pure difference, which is engendered in the

---

[14] "Particular" and "universal" should be taken here according to their terminological function in logic. Accordingly, while the unary trait would affirm that pure difference is embodied in *a* signifier, the signifier of the Name-of-the-Father would affirm that all signifiers in the symbolic order engender meaning through their differential relationships. See more on the universal dimension of the signifier of the Name-of-the-Father in Chap. 3.

repetition of the unary trait, is only truly accessible to a subject that had gone through an alienation in the signifier. On the same note, each of these levels also entails a proactive relationship of dependence: the unary trait is dependent on the initial expulsion of a sum of jouissance in *Ausstoßung*; the signifier of the Name-of-the-Father is dependent on the repetition of the unary trait engendering pure difference; and the chain of signifiers owes its consistency to the law of signification authorized by the signifier of the Name-of-the-Father.

Let us attempt to integrate the conclusions reached so far in this section into the model of primal repression. Elaborating the functioning of primal repression in these terms designates the unary trait as the affirmative symbolic product of *Ausstoßung*, entailing its repetition that engenders pure difference and is then affirmed by the signifier of the Name-of-the-Father in *Bejahung*.[15] These conclusions are summarized in Fig. 6.1:

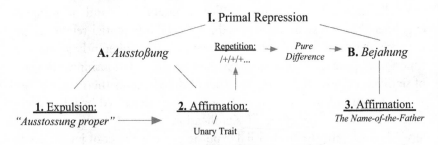

Fig. 6.1 Primal repression, including the repetition of the unary trait and the signification of pure difference

---

[15] It is interesting to think again of the Freudian notion of the judgments of attribution in this context. In Chap. 3, I have presented these judgments as repetitive operations that take part in the constitution of the symbolic. Accordingly, the fact that Freud relates to them in the plural was disregarded. The idea that the unary trait can only engender pure difference in its repetition corresponds to Freud's account of the judgments of attribution in the plural. Accordingly, it provides further prospects for the development of this concept.

The Foreclosure of the Unary Trait

According to Emmanuelle Borgnis-Desbordes, in her paper "Autisme, Transfert et Inventions Subjectives: Deux Cas" (2009), "The [unary] trait has a function on the threshold of the symbolic: it is a *mark* for the subject that conditions its anchoring in the field of the Other and thus conditions its being a speaking subject" (p. 103; brackets added). Borgnis-Desbordes goes on to argue that, in autism we see "a failure … at the threshold of symbolization" (p. 102). This failure causes the subject to lose access to the symbolic order and hinders its functionality. Borgnis-Desbordes explicitly adds: "This failure is situated at the level of what Lacan calls the unary trait—the first symbolic mark for a subject … this unary trait, the autistic subject rejects it" (p. 102). In this sense, Borgnis-Desbordes implies that, without the unary trait, the relationship between the autistic subject and the Other is critically severed, "allowing us to suggest that … [for the autistic] *all of the symbolic is real*" (p. 102; brackets added). Correspondingly, Borgnis-Desbordes adds that with the failure on the level of the unary trait, the autistic subject also loses the capacity to symbolically mediate jouissance and thus encounters the drive object as a menacing presence in the real (p. 106).

The idea that autism involves a failure on the level of the unary trait is generally accepted in the Lacanian field (Borgnis-Desbordes, 2009; Lefort & Lefort, 2003, pp. 28, 56, 59, 126, 154, 169; Maleval, 2009, pp. 81–83, 92, 120, 124, 201, 215). Nevertheless, it is the attribution of this failure to the level of *Ausstoßung* in the course of primal repression—as well as the strong association between the function of the unary trait and Hyppolite's account of the symbol of negation and Laplanche and Leclaire's definition of pure difference—*that brings me to contend that the unary trait can be designated as the object of autistic foreclosure.* The designation of the unary trait as the object of autistic foreclosure has not been proposed so far. Nevertheless, when taken into consideration, one can imagine why the foreclosure of the unary trait interrupts its repetition and therefore hinders pure difference from being engendered in the symbolic order. Without pure difference, the signifier of the Name-of-the-Father is not instated, and the relationship between the subject and the

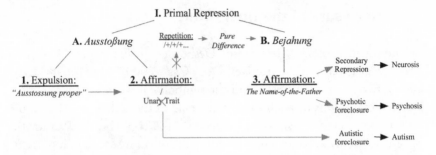

Fig. 6.2 Primal repression, including the foreclosure of the unary trait and the structuration of neurosis, psychosis, and autism

symbolic order is severely impaired. This will also explain why autistic foreclosure necessarily entails in its scope the structuring effect of the foreclosure of the Name-of-the-Father but should not be considered as taking the latter as a direct object of exclusion. Taking into account all of the aforementioned conclusions, we can summarize them in Fig. 6.2.

The Unary Trait in the Clinic of Autism

The goal of this chapter is to present a conceptual analysis of the mechanism of autistic foreclosure and thus not to digress into the study of autistic symptomatology and phenomenology. Nevertheless, the conceptual work provided in this chapter also aims to contribute to the work done with autistic subjects in the clinic. Accordingly, in the end of each of the sections in this chapter, I will briefly present several clinical cases that correspond with the structural hypotheses provided in this chapter. The following section will present clinical cases that give further support for the hypothesis that the unary trait can be designated as the object of autistic foreclosure.

Kanner's "Sameness"

One of the most significant characteristics defining autistic behavior according to Leo Kanner (1943) is "an *anxiously obsessive desire for the maintenance of sameness*" (p. 245). Sameness is designated by Kanner as the tendency of autistic subjects to choose to live in a static world in which change is not tolerated. In his paper "The Conception of Wholes and Parts in Early Infantile Autism" (1951), Kanner provides the following description of this tendency:

> The totality of an experience that comes to the child from the outside must be reiterated, often with all its constituent details, in complete photographic and phonographic identity. No one part of this totality may be altered in terms of shape, sequence, or space. The slightest change of arrangement, sometimes so minute that it is hardly perceived by others, may evoke a violent outburst of rage. (p. 106)

Based on the conclusions presented in this section, the autistic maintenance of "sameness" can also be described as an attempt to keep reality in compliance with the rule of simple tautology.[16] Lacan associates a world composed of simple tautologies with subjects who are not fully alienated in the signifier; more specifically, he associates it with subjects who ignore the manifestation of pure difference in the repetition of the unary trait: "there are beings who are alive and tolerate very well completely ignoring this sort of difference ... this sort of distinction which is particularly manifest in the unary trait" (SIX, 6.12.61). Accordingly, I argue that the autistic compliance with the rule of simple tautology could also be described as an avoidance of the signifying function of pure difference engendered on the basis of the unary trait. Why then would autistic subjects attempt to avoid any the function of pure difference at all costs? Defining the unary trait as the object of autistic foreclosure can answer this question.

According to Lacan, whatever has been foreclosed from the symbolic reappears in the real (SIII, p. 13). Therefore, by hypothesizing that the

---

[16] Yet again, that is, when a tautology is defined as the repetitive use of phrases or words that have similar meanings.

unary trait is the object of autistic foreclosure, we are also inclined to assume that something of its function, which is foreclosed from the symbolic, reappears as a terrifying presence in the real. As a consequence, any repetition engendering anything more than simple tautology can be said to cause the autistic subject to encounter the terrifying presence of pure difference in the real and experience a surge of unbearable anxiety. That would explain why autistic subjects avoid any encounter risking a rupture in the very well-kept sequence of simple tautologies and obsessively maintain—what Kanner described as—sameness.

The Wolf-Child

According to Borgnis-Desbordes (2009), in the clinic of autism, the psychoanalyst aims to slowly introduce the autistic subject to the dimension of pure difference through a supplementary reference to a unary trait (p. 102). This reference is adopted by the subject from the psychoanalyst—situated in the place of the Other—eventually leading to a supplementary form of alienation in language: "We think that the autistic subject, who has rejected the unary trait, can be introduced to the symbolic by being represented by the extrication of a mark, a trace, a trait on the Other" (p. 107). According to the Leforts (1994), the unary trait is usually represented for the autistic subject with the help of actual objects (p. 329).[17] These objects are not akin to signifiers that are elected from the symbolic Other, but are objects that are situated at the threshold of the symbolic and the real:

> A possible treatment of autism must … take as a point of support this *missing* [unary] *trait* … which makes it possible to ensure that the *real is captured in the symbolic* … The work must be situated between the real and the symbolic and aim for a piece of the real to appear in the symbolic. (pp. 102–103; brackets added)

The case of Robert, the Wolf-Child, described by Rosine Lefort in one of the sessions of Lacan's *Seminar I: Freud's Papers on Technique*

---

[17] In the case of Marie François, deliberated in the book *The Birth of the Other* (1994), it was Rosine Lefort's pair of glasses.

(1953–1954), presents such a course of treatment. This case study gains its name due to the child's unique form of identification with the word "Wolf!" at a crucial point of his analysis. During the initial phase of his analysis, Robert exhibits completely disarrayed and scattered behavior. He continuously runs in the counseling room, screaming, opening and closing doors, switching lights on and off, throwing objects, or piling them on Lefort. The turning point in Robert's analysis follows his attempt to cut off his penis with a pair of plastic scissors while standing on his bed in front of other terrified children. During the following sessions, Robert starts to deliberately play with the opening and closing of doors, immediately accompanied by his uttering of the word "Wolf!" In this phase, Lefort describes a progression in which different aspects of Robert's conduct are compiled into a montage of objects and rituals marked by the word "Wolf!" Thus, the word "Wolf!" becomes a major aspect of his conduct, alleviating his aggression and enabling him to regulate his relationship with his surroundings through the use of language (SI, pp. 91–101).

Lacan argues that the assumption of the word "Wolf!" by Robert is a defining factor enabling his transition from being completely immersed in the real to gaining access to some form of symbolic mediation of reality (p. 103). Correspondingly, in his paper "La Matrice du Traitement de l'Enfant au Loup" (2007), Jacques-Alain Miller adds that Robert's use of the word "Wolf!" is accompanied by his attempt to inscribe "a loss, a cut, an annulment, a negation," in the real through the repetitive manipulation of the spatial qualities of objects (inside and outside) (pp. 148–149). He emphasizes that it is the affiliation of this loss with a singular linguistic mark—the word "Wolf!"—that structurally maintains it and progresses Robert in his analysis (p. 147).

When addressing the exact symbolic nature of the word "Wolf!" Lacan argues that it is reducible neither to the signifier nor to a "name" nor to an imaginary manifestation (i.e., the ideal ego or ego-ideal) but rather regarded as a word "reduced down to its core" (SI, p. 104). At this point in his teaching (1953–1954), Lacan had not yet developed his conception of the unary trait. Nevertheless, his account of the word "Wolf!" can be described as an autistic supplement to the unary trait. This would be later corroborated by the Leforts (1988) that view the word "Wolf!" as an initial marker, petrified, lacking a relation to the signifying chain in the

Other, that is adopted by the child as a supplement to the unary trait due to a failure in all forms of identification (p. 616).[18] Accordingly, the case of the Wolf-Child provides further support of the hypothesis that the unary trait can be designated as the object of autistic foreclosure. It demonstrates that the assumption of a supplementary unary trait—engendered with the help of the relationships between objects—can confer on the subject a certain mode of linguistic functionality that enables some mediation of jouissance.

Little Dick

Another example of the role of the unary trait in the clinic of autism can be found in a different part of Lacan's *Seminar I*, devoted to the case of Little Dick that originates from Melanie Klein's paper "The Importance of Symbol-Formation in the Development of the Ego" (1930). While the case of Dick is presented in this seminar as a case of early childhood psychosis, Lacan's assessment of this case is considered to foreshadow the Lacanian approach to autism and will be further developed by his followers in later years (Laurent, 2012a; Maleval, 2003, 2009; Tendlarz, 2003).

In the course of Dick's analysis with Klein, she stages a game with toy trains. In this game she designates one of the trains as "father train" and the other as "Dick train." Dick picks up the "Dick train" and rolls it up to the window, saying, "station." Klein then replies with another opposition: "*The station is mummy*. Dick is going into mummy." These interpretations convey some progress in Dick's analysis. Here is the exact excerpt from Klein's (1930) paper:

> I then took a big train and placed it next to a smaller one and called them "Daddy train" and "Dick train." Thereupon, he picked up the train that I called Dick, and made it roll towards the window, and said "station." I explained, "The station is mummy; Dick is going into mummy." He left the train and ran to the space formed by the inner and outer doors of the

---

[18] The word "Wolf!" in its rendition as a supplementary unary trait reduced to its core can also be associated with what several psychoanalysts refer to as a "holophrase" (Laurent, 2012a, pp. 90–96; Lefort & Lefort, 2003, p. 24; Maleval, 2009, p. 234; Tendlarz, 2003, pp. 60–64).

room, and shut himself in, saying, "dark" and then ran out again directly. He went through this performance several times. I explained: "It is dark inside mummy; Dick is inside dark mummy." Meanwhile he picked up the train again but soon ran back to the space between the doors. While I was saying that he was going into dark mummy, he had said twice in a questioning way, "nanny?" I answered him, "Nanny is coming soon," this he repeated. (p. 242)

Lacan's evaluation of Klein's interpretation is very skeptical as to its symbolic value in terms of the Oedipal myth: "So what did Melanie Klein actually do?—nothing other than to bring in verbalization. She symbolized an effective relationship, that of one named being with another. She plastered on the symbolization of the Oedipal myth, to give it its real name" (SI, p. 85). Therefore, what is at stake in this case study, according to Lacan, is not Klein's crude imposition of Oedipal terms on the child's play but the introduction of the possibility to symbolically designate an opposition between actual objects. This does not open up a metaphorical relationship between Dick, his mother, or his father, but introduces him to the capacity of language to establish meaningful relationships between objects in his world. According to Lacan, "The child symbolizes the reality around him starting from this nucleus, this little palpitating cell of symbolism which Melanie Klein gave him" (p. 85). This cell of symbolism provides "an initial position from which the subject can introduce an interplay between the imaginary and the real and master his development" (p. 86). In the following sessions, based on this initial subjective position, Dick goes from a series of equivalences to a series of equations. He moves to more and more complex objects and later gets to a stage in which he is able to manipulate richer content and use it in order to interact with others.

Similarly to the case of the Wolf-Child, it seems that Lacan attributes the progress in Dick's analysis to the association of a supplementary symbolic marker—the word "station"—with an initial opposition between objects in space. According to Lacan, this association initiates Dick's relationship with language; a relationship that is the defining factor in his capacity to enter into an exchange with Klein. Therefore, we see that Dick's case provides further support for the hypothesis that the unary trait can be designated as the object of autistic foreclosure. For, like in the case of the Wolf-Child, the progress in Dick's analysis entails the supplementary extraction of such a marker through the manipulation of objects.

The Hole as the Object of Autistic Foreclosure

Jacques-Alain Miller invites us to think of it as a certain lack of the hole. I will propose to speak of the foreclosure of the hole, if we agree to extend foreclosure up to this point. (Laurent, 2012a, p. 67)

[Autistic subjects] have access to this terrible dimension where nothing is lacking because nothing can lack. There is no hole, and nothing can be detached to be put in this hole—this hole doesn't exist. (Miller as quoted in Laurent, 2012a, p. 67; brackets added)

A hole in the symbolic Other has a rim, which is not the case with a hole in the real. The autistic version of the hole implies a real absence of a rim ... The hole without rim. (Laurent, 2012a, p. 84)

The notion of the "hole" takes on many roles in Lacan's teaching. Being related to the psychoanalytic notion of lack, it is associated by Lacan with the sexual drives, with desire and more. Lacan's distinction between the notion of the hole and lack can already be found in *Seminar III*. In this seminar, the hole in the symbolic order is identified as a structural outcome of the foreclosure of the signifier of the Name-of-the-Father and a defining feature of psychosis.[19] It is in *Seminar IX* that Lacan provides his first comprehensive distinction of the notion of the hole in terms borrowed from the mathematical study of the properties of space—topology.[20] Briefly introducing this distinction in spatial terms, Miller (2001) argues that when Lacan conceives of lack, space remains. In other words, lack is defined as an absence that is inscribed in a space and obeys the order of spaces. This is why other terms can be inscribed on the backdrop of lack according to Lacan. Miller adds that the hole, as

---

[19] See Chap. 4.

[20] An introduction to the field of topology and its implementation in the distinction of the notion of the hole will be shortly presented in this section.

opposed to lack, implies the disappearance of the order of spaces. It entails the disappearance of space itself as well as its combinatorial rules. In this sense, it implies the foreclosure of the symbolic and represents an effect of the real (pp. 16–17).

Such renditions and, in particular, the explication of the notion of the hole in topological terms, enable Laurent (2012a) to develop one of the most explicit accounts of the object of autistic foreclosure in contemporary Lacanian literature, associating the mechanism of foreclosure at the origin of autism with the radical exclusion of the hole. Laurent's notion of the "foreclosure of the hole" is based both on Lacan's topological account of the hole and on Miller's (2007) account of the autistic inaccessibility to the symbolic dimension of lack. In the fourth chapter of his book *La Bataille De L'Autisme* (2012a), Laurent devotes several pages for the conceptual elaboration of the foreclosure of the hole (pp. 66–69). Nevertheless, while being pioneering, dense, and precise, this account does not exhaustively elucidate the Lacanian roots on which it is based and is mainly initiatory in its structural and formalistic scrutiny. Accordingly, this section will provide a further analysis of Laurent's account of the foreclosure of the hole. It will begin by presenting Lacan's early elaboration of the function of the hole in his account of psychotic foreclosure in *Seminar III*. Next, based on Lacan's dialectics of *need, demand,* and *desire* in *Seminar IX*, it will explicate the crucial role the hole has in the constitution of the symbolic order and its relation to the subject. These dialectics will be elaborated in the scope of Lacan's manipulation of the hole on the topological figure of the torus. By elaborating on the function of the hole on these two levels, this section will support Laurent's association of the object of autistic foreclosure with the figure of the hole and, more specifically, with the symbolic figure of the rim of the hole. Finally, this section will present several case studies from the clinic of autism that support this hypothesis.

The Hole in Primal Repression

Before Lacan began to involve topology in his teaching, the notion of the hole is utilized in *Seminar III* in the elaboration of the mechanism of foreclosure. In this seminar, Lacan implements the notion of the hole in his distinction between the different forms of lack symbolically inscribed in primal repression in neurosis and psychosis.

In Chap. 4, I have explained that the onset of psychosis is dependent on two causal factors that must intersect: a *structural causality* and a *contingent causality* (Recalcati, 2005). In *Seminar III*, Lacan characterizes these two causal factors in psychosis in relation to the notion of the hole. Firstly, regarding the *structural causality* of psychosis, Lacan argues that the foreclosure of the signifier of the Name-of-the-Father produces "a hole in the symbolic" (SIII, p. 156). That is to say that, in neurosis, *Bejahung* warrants the inscription of the signifier of the Name-of-the-father, but, in psychosis, the foreclosure of this signifier produces "a hole, a rupture, a rent, a gap" in place of it (p. 45). In this sense, psychosis is said to be *structurally* prompted by the hole in the symbolic that is thus specified as a defining feature of psychosis. Secondly, regarding the *contingent causality* of psychosis, Lacan argues that when the subject, at a certain point in life, is confronted with the hole in the symbolic, it is at risk of suffering from the onset of psychotic symptoms. This is why Lacan describes the confrontation with the hole in the symbolic as an inherent experiential quality of psychosis: "the feeling that the subject has come to the edge of a hole" (p. 202).

In his paper "La Matrice du Traitement de l'Enfant au Loup" (2007), Miller develops Lacan's notion of the hole in the scope of his understanding of autism. Miller argues that, in autism, similarly to psychosis, the signifier of the Name-of-the-Father is foreclosed. Nevertheless, he emphasizes that in contrast to psychosis, where the foreclosure of the signifier of the Name-of-the-Father creates a hole in the symbolic, in autism, the hole has no symbolic designation at all (p. 148). In this sense, Miller argues that "autistic children … have access to this terrible dimension where nothing is lacking because nothing can lack. There is no hole, and nothing can be detached to be put in this hole—this hole doesn't exist" (Miller as quoted in Laurent, 2012a, p. 67). While Miller characterizes the lack of the symbolic designation of the hole as a major characteristic of the autistic structure, it is Laurent who suggests to associate it with the mechanism of autistic foreclosure: "Miller invites us to think of it as a certain lack of the hole. I will propose to speak of the foreclosure of the hole, if we agree to extend foreclosure up to this point" (p. 67). Accordingly, psychotic and autistic foreclosure are differentiated by Laurent on the basis of their association with the hole. Psychotic foreclosure radically excludes the signifier of the Name-of-the-Father and, in its place, engenders the hole in the symbolic. Autistic foreclosure is considered to radically exclude the hole itself and, thus, grants the subject no access to any form of signification of lack, leaving it to be completely "immersed in the real" where nothing is lacking (p. 67).

In his early account of psychosis in *Seminar III*, Lacan had not yet fully developed the distinction between the notion of lack and the hole. This distinction would be later developed through his recourse to the field of topology which will be elaborated in the next section. When disregarding this development and solely relying on the aforementioned conclusions, one might think that autistic foreclosure follows the functioning of psychotic foreclosure. Namely, one might speculate that, first, psychotic foreclosure engenders the hole in the symbolic, and second, autistic foreclosure radically excludes this hole. Nevertheless, based on the conclusions reached in the previous chapter, a certain progression between the levels of signification associated with the notion of the hole and the signifier of lack can be attested for, thus refuting this assumption.

Lack is engendered in the model of repression in several modalities. Firstly, lack is designated in the negative aspect of *Ausstoßung*, in which an initial sum of jouissance is expelled. In terms of more fitting to our discussion of the hole, this expulsion can be regarded as a primordial "puncturing" on the level of the drive that precedes any form of symbolic designation. Secondly, lack is designated in the affirmative aspect of *Ausstoßung*, in which this initial "puncturing" is symbolically affirmed as the symbol of negation, marking a dividing line between the symbolic and the real (as exterior to symbolization). Lastly, lack is designated in *Bejahung*, where it gains its "minimal" symbolic affirmation as the signifier of the Name-of-the-Father. In this sense, we can draw a line of progression beginning with the real lack, engendered in the negative aspect of *Ausstoßung*, continuing to the symbol of negation, engendered in the affirmative aspect of *Ausstoßung* and ending with the signifier of the Name-of-the-Father, engendered in *Bejahung*. This progression can explain why autistic foreclosure precedes the functioning of psychotic foreclosure in the model of

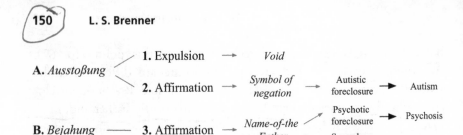

Fig. 6.3 Modalities of lack as signified in *Ausstoßung* and *Bejahung* and their structuring effects

repression and cannot be considered to follow it. Accordingly, I argue that psychotic foreclosure radically excludes the signifier of the Name-of-the-Father and thus regressively assigns the subject with access to the dimension of lack mediated by the symbol of negation; a symbolic unit that, in this section, will be associated with the hole. In contrast, autistic foreclosure radically excludes the symbol of negation itself, engendered prior to *Bejahung*, and thus grants the subject no access to the symbolic designation of the hole but only to its designation as real lack; this real lack will be associated in this section with the figure of the "void." These conclusions are summarized in Fig. 6.3.

The Hole as a Topological Figure

Lacan's interest in topology can be traced back to as early as the 1950s. Since then, his focus on the development of psychoanalysis through the use of topological terms has been a major aspect of his work. Topology can be described as a modern version of geometry, in the sense that it is a study of different forms of space. What distinguishes topology from different types of geometry is the extent to which a figure in space can be manipulated until it loses its essential properties. For instance, in ordinary Euclidean geometry, a circle will retain its identity ("congruence") if it is moved around in space or even flipped but not if it is stretched or bent out of shape. On the other hand, in topology, a circle can be distorted, bent, and transformed, while still retaining its identity. Topology enables us to do so by abstracting certain geometric dimensions from our common understanding of space and representing these dimensions in terms of points, neighborhoods of points, or sets.[21] Based on these terms, a circle can be equated to a triangle or a square simply by pulling and rearranging its circumferences—in the same way one could manipulate a string. What makes topology such a valuable tool in the eyes of Lacan is the fact that it offers a way to conceptualize the internal structure and functioning of almost any form of space. For instance, not only geometric space but also "signifying space," "relational space," and "mental space" can be rendered in topological terms of points, neighborhoods, and sets. Accordingly, Lacan finds topology to be an excellent tool for the depiction of complex psychic phenomena, for example, using a Möbius strip as a way to illustrate the unique relationship between consciousness and the unconscious (SXXIV, 14.12.76). In this sense, topology provides Lacan with an alternative approach to the same Freudian notions that he tackled in the very first years of his career (Ragland, 2004, p. xx).

In *Seminar IX*, Lacan analyzes the topological manipulation of the hole on the surface of the torus in order to provide an intuitive illustration of the structuration of the subject: "the structure of the subject in so far as he speaks … is the one for which I am fomenting for you this topology of the torus that I believe to be very fundamental" (SIX, 21.3.62). On the basis of this topological analysis, Lacan provides a more elaborate account of the relationship between *need, demand,* and *desire* in the structuration of the subject in neurosis, perversion, and psychosis:

> I am bringing all of this to you only as a sort of proposal for exercises, for mental exercises, exercises with which you have familiarized yourself, if you subsequently want to be able to find in the torus the metaphorical value that I shall give it when I shall in every case, whether it is a matter of the obsessional, of the hysteric, of the pervert, even of the schizophrenic, have to articulate the relationship between desire and demand. (11.4.62)

It is my contention that Lacan's analysis of the topological manipulation of the hole on the surface of the torus is the bedrock of Laurent's association of the mechanism of autistic foreclosure with the hole. Therefore, let us begin this section by presenting Lacan's account of the relationship between *need, demand,* and *desire* as it is presented in his

---

[21] These terms are borrowed from set-theory.

paper "The Signification of the Phallus" printed in *Écrits* (2006). This will be followed by Lacan's topological illustration of this relationship in terms of the manipulation of the hole on the surface of the torus as it is presented in *Seminar IX*. This will lead to a final section that will present and develop Laurent's account of the foreclosure of the hole using these terms.

The Dialectics of Need, Demand, and Desire

Lacan's account of the relationship between *need, demand,* and *desire,* described in his paper "The Signification of the Phallus," is an original adaptation of the constitution of the subject in relation to language. It originates in the infant's aim of satisfying its most basic instinctual *needs* and culminates in its realization as a desiring subject.

According to Lacan, infants are born into the world with biologically determined *needs* related to their instincts of survival.[22] Nevertheless, infants are unable to fulfill their *needs* by themselves and are dependent on the efforts of their caretakers in order to survive. Therefore, after birth, when a *need* arises, infants must be quite resourceful in transmitting its urgency to their caretakers in order for it to be fulfilled. In order to do so, infants are required to take on themselves a new relationship with their caretakers by enunciating a *demand*. It is by assuming this early relationship with language that the organic body, composed of the infant's primal instinctual *needs,* is re-appropriated by the signifier and utilized in the enunciation of *demands*.

Lacan's account of the enunciated *demand* is not to be confused with the articulation of *desire* "in socially understandable, if not acceptable, terms," for, at this early stage, the enunciations produced by the infant are quite inarticulable and are mostly fashioned as cries (Fink, 1997, p. 6). Accordingly, the infant's enunciated *demands* cannot be fully associated with a proper meaning (e.g., "I am hungry") but can only be interpreted

---

[22] For example, the need for nourishment, the need to excrete waste, the need for affection, or any other need of which its deprivation may cause the infant's death.

by the caretaker as endowed with meanings that are presented on the backdrop of a real physiological lack (something is lacking and is thus *needed*).

Lacan explicitly associates the initial subordination of the instinctual *needs* to the enunciation of *demands,* with the initial expulsion achieved in primal repression: "What is thus alienated in needs constitutes an *Urverdrängung* [primal repression]" (É, p. 579). Briefly put, according to Lacan, when instinctual *needs* are mediated by language and take the form of *demands,* they undergo a certain alienation by being weaved into the Other of language. Lacan associates this primordial alienation with Freud's (1915b) account of the primal repression of the representatives of the drive (SE XIV, p. 148). In this case, however, it is the infant's instinctual *needs* that are primally excluded (alienated) and affirmed as excluded in the enunciated *demand* (Muller & Richardson, 1985, p. 336). As I have elaborated in the previous chapters, this primordial exclusion is achieved in *Ausstoßung,* functioning on the level of the drive.[23]

One of the defining qualities of the relationship between *need* and *demand* is the fact that it always entails an unbridgeable gap between the two. That is because, according to Lacan, "Demand in itself bears on something other than the satisfactions [of the need] it calls for" (É, p. 579; brackets added). A *demand,* says Lacan, other than being a demand for the satisfaction of a *need,* is also a *demand* for the presence or absence of the caretaker—the "demand for love" (p. 580). In other words, when infants cry out to their caretakers, they could be *demanding* both the satisfaction of their *needs* and the presence and love of their caretakers. In contrast to the *demand* for the satisfaction of a *need,* which is particular and conditional, the *demand for love* is absolute and unconditional and thus can never be satisfied. This insatiable character of the *demand for love* materializes in language in its repetitive enunciation—a questioning directed to the caretaker[24] through which the gap between

---

[23] This form of primordial alienation in language will be thoroughly elaborated in Lacan's later account of alienation and separation in *Seminar XI.*

[24] In Lacan's account of alienation and separation in *Seminar XI,* this is associated with the child's repeated "whys?" These, according to Lacan, do not aim to reveal the reason of things but have to do with questioning the Other's motives and desires (p. 214).

need and *demand* also continuously reappears.[25] Lacan argues that, at a certain point in the repetition of this gap, *desire* is produced as a surplus to both *need* and *demand*: "desire is neither the appetite for satisfaction nor the demand for love, but the difference that results from the subtraction of the first from the second" (p. 580). In other words, *desire* is produced in the place where the enunciated *demand* goes beyond the fulfillment of the original *need* or, put another way, through a signification that surpasses the level of the absence it protests.

Accordingly, we can see the way Lacan describes the relationship between *need*, *demand*, and *desire* as dialectic. On the one hand, *desire* is born out of a contradiction between a *demand* and the *need* it aims to satisfy. It is only through the gap that separates the two that the *object of desire* can find a place to be inscribed in the symbolic (p. 580). On the other hand, *desire* surpasses the level of the enunciated *demand* as it entails different structuring effects that open the subject to different levels of symbolic mediation: "Although it always shows through in demand, as we see here, desire is nevertheless beyond demand" (p. 530). In this sense, *desire* is described as the synthesis that comes in place of the contradiction between *need* and *demand*.

Interestingly enough, in "The Signification of the Phallus," Lacan explicitly claims that, in the relationship between *need*, *demand*, and *desire*, "a topology, in the mathematical sense of the term, appears" (p. 578). And indeed, three years later in *Seminar IX*, Lacan develops this topology, based on the manipulation of the hole on the surface of the torus.

The Hole and the Torus

Lacan introduced the figure of the torus into his discourse on psychoanalysis in a paper delivered at the Institute of Psychology at the University of Rome in the year 1953 (É, p. 264). After its initial presentation, Lacan

---

[25] In, *Seminar IX*, Lacan explicitly terms the repeated enunciation of the *demand for love*: "the repetition of demand" (9.5.62). It is interesting to note that the homology between the repetition of the unary trait, which engenders pure difference, and the repetition of *demand*, which engenders *desire*, is explicitly accounted for by Lacan in this seminar as well (7.3.62).

would go on to employ the unique topological properties of the torus in many instances, developing notions such as *extimacy* (SXXIV, 14.12.76); mental structures such as neurosis (Lacan, 1973, p. 461) and hysteria (SXXIV, 14.12.76); as well as the structure of psychic reality (SIX, 21.3.62). In *Seminar IX*, Lacan specifically focuses on the topological manipulation of the hole on the surface of the torus in order to conceptually develop the relationship between *need, demand,* and *desire* presented in "The Signification of the Phallus." Let us first introduce the different figures taking part in the construction of the torus and then proceed to Lacan's use of these figures in his development of this relationship.

The Topology of the Torus

According to Lacan, "a torus is quite simple: a ring" (SIX, 14.1.62). In simple topological terms, the "ring torus" is defined as a surface having "genus one," that is, possessing one single hole. The single-holed ring torus can be constructed from a flat rectangle by gluing both pairs of opposite edges together. The ring torus is usually rendered in three-dimensional space and is shaped like a donut (Weisstein, 2013). See Fig. 6.4.

In the center of the donut torus we find a hole. A hole is defined as a topological structure that prevents a surface from being continuously shrunk to a point. Accordingly, a hole is also called a "disconnectivity in space," because it infuses a topological space with a measure of separation (Weisstein, 2013). In order to intuitively understand what this means, let

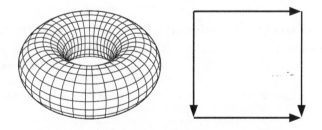

Fig. 6.4 The ring torus and its construction from a flat rectangle

us take for an example a structure without holes, such as a sphere. Any circle we could draw on the surface of the sphere is shrinkable to a point—nothing stops it from shrinking ad infinitum. In contrast, on the surface of the torus, there are some circles that cannot be reduced to a point; for example, the circle surrounding its central hole. The hole in the center of the torus functions as a topological "peg" stopping the circle that revolves around it from shrinking into a point. In other words, the central hole of the torus will always engender a space that is interior to the confines of this circle.

A hole is determined by the space that is included in its circumference. When addressing the circumference of the hole, Laurent (2012a) refers to it as the "rim" of the hole.[26] A rim, according to Laurent, is described as a circumference designating a hole in space or, in other words, a line demarcating the disconnectivity engendered by a hole in space. Digressing from exact topological terminology, one could imagine that, in the case of the "donut" torus, the body of the torus functions as the rim of its central hole.

Lacan argues that one can identify two holes in the topological figure of the "donut" torus. In accordance with the definition of a hole, each of these is necessarily enclosed by at least one circle (rim) that is not shrinkable to a point. Lacan claims that in the case of the *circle enclosing the thickness of the torus*:

> This circle is not reducible, which means that if you suppose it to be realized by a string still passing through this little arch which would allow us to tighten it we cannot reduce it to something like a point; whatever its circumference may be, there will always remain at the center, the circumference of what one could call here the thickness of the torus. (SIX, 11.4.62)

The circle enclosing the thickness of the torus can be designated by drawing a line that goes through the central hole of the torus, passes to

---

[26] The topological notion of a "rim" is not identical to the one Laurent proposes in his book *La Bataille De L'Autisme* (2012a). The closest topological figure that can be associated with Laurent's account of the rim is the "closed disc," defined as follows: "a disc is the region in a plane bounded by a circle. A disk is said to be closed if it contains the circle that constitutes its boundary and open if it does not" (Arnold, 2011, p. 58).

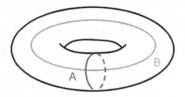

Fig. 6.5 The "empty" (B) and "full" (A) circles on the ring torus

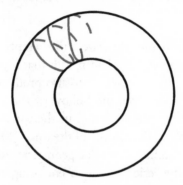

Fig. 6.6 Spring-like trajectory of the "full" circle on the torus

the other side of the central hole, and comes back around. Lacan names this circle the "full circle" of the torus (7.3.62)—see circle A in Fig. 6.5.

Lacan adds that the thickness of the torus is composed of a series of similar circles enclosing it in the form of a spring (30.5.62)—see Fig. 6.6.

He argues that their spring-like trajectory can be geometrically represented on a square by making a cut on the circumference of the thickness of the torus, allowing the alteration of the torus into the shape of a pipe or a sleeve (see sleeve in Fig. 6.7). The hollow of this sleeve designates the first modality of the hole presented in the topological model of the torus—the hole of the thickness of the torus. This sleeve can then be cut in the middle (along line B in Fig. 6.7) so as to produce a geometric square demonstrating the "movement" of this series on the surface of the torus (see arrows on square in Fig. 6.7).

Lacan remarks that in the figure of the torus we identify another disconnectivity attributed to the central hole of the torus. It can be designated by drawing a circle that does not pass through the central hole but

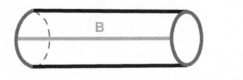

Fig. 6.7 The hollow sleeve designating the hole of the thickness of the torus and its geometric representation

goes around it. Lacan names this circle the "empty circle" of the torus (7.3.62) (see circle B in Fig. 6.5). Lacan adds that if you make a cut along the circumference of this circle, you will also produce a sleeve but a very short and wide one. This time, the hollow of the sleeve designates the second modality of the hole presented in the topological model of the torus—the central hole in the middle of the torus (11.4.62). Cutting this sleeve vertically will produce a similar geometric square demonstrating the "movement" of the series of circles enclosing the thickness of the torus (see Fig. 6.7).

Need, Demand, and Desire in the Torus

In *Seminar IX*, Lacan implements the topological manipulation of the hole on the surface of the torus for the conceptual development of his account of the dialectics of *need*, *demand*, and *desire*. I doing so, Lacan associates the "full circle" of the torus (the spring-like circuit demarcating the thickness of the torus) with the level of the drive and, more specifi- cally, with the enunciation of the infant's *demand*: "the circles encompass- ing the thickness of the torus as such could very intelligibly serve to represent this dimension of demand" (11.4.62). Lacan associates the spring-like circular movement of this circuit with the repetitive enuncia- tion of the insatiable *demand for love* (see Fig. 6.8). Accordingly, Lacan claims that we can quickly see "how easily the demand in its repetition, its identity and its necessary distinction, its unfolding and its return onto itself, is something which easily finds something to support it in the structure of the torus" (11.4.62).

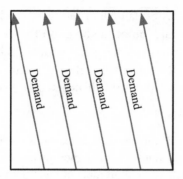

Fig. 6.8   Geometric representation of the repetitive enunciation of the *demand for love*

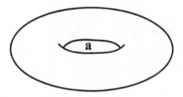

Fig. 6.9   The central hole of the torus designating the contours of the object of desire

Correspondingly, Lacan associates the "empty circle" (see circle B in Fig. 6.5) with the dimension of *desire* and argues that its circumference, marking the central hole of the torus, designates the contours of the object of desire (11.4.62)—see Fig. 6.9.

Lacan argues that the most compelling aspect of the topological depiction of the dialectics of *need, demand,* and *desire* is manifest in the reciprocal relationship between the full and the empty circles on the surface of the torus (11.4.62). As will shortly be presented, it enables Lacan to provide a more accurate illustration of the dialectic relationship between *need, demand,* and *desire* than is presented in "The Signification of the Phallus."

As has been presented in the previous section, according to Lacan, *desire* is necessarily engendered in the repetition of the enunciated *demand.* However, while in "The Signification of the Phallus" this necessity is not explicitly explained, in *Seminar IX*, it is illustrated through the topological manipulation of the holes on the surface of the torus. In a passage worth being quoted at length, Lacan basically claims that, in the topological model of the torus, when the full circuit of *demand* closes on itself after at least two repetitions, it necessarily gives rise to the empty circle of *desire*:

> In this movement, this dimension appears to us through which desire is what supports the no doubt circular movement of the always repeated demand, but of which a certain number of repetitions can be conceived—this is the use of the topology of the torus—as achieving something. The bobbining movement of the repetition of demand closes somewhere even virtually, defining another loop which is completed by this very repetition and which sketches out what? The object of desire … this object does not remain an object of need; it is from the fact of being caught up in the repetitive movement of demand, in the automatism of repetition, that it becomes the object of desire. (SIX, 9.5.62)

The fact that the repeating circuit of *demand* gives rise to the circle of *desire* is rendered explicit when attributed to the topological figure of the torus. It is enough to imagine the circuit of *demand* as the rim of the circle of *desire* in order to grasp their interrelation.[27] According to Lacan, by doing so, it better portrays the constitutive relationship between *demand* and *desire* as well as the distinction between the object of *need* and the object of *desire*. In his paper "Torus and Identification" (2016), Michael Friedman provides an intuitive example demonstrating this relationship in geometric terms. Friedman argues that the geometric square produced by the two cuts on the surface of the torus (see Fig. 6.7) already, in fact, illustrates that the trajectory of the circuit of *demand* necessarily sketches out the circle of *desire*. He claims that on this square, the vertical vectors represent the trajectory of the circuit of *demand* (D), while the horizontal axis represents the circle of *desire* (d)—see Fig. 6.10:

---

[27] One might imagine this circuit of *demand* as a long circular string composed of many twists—a spring. Pulling the string reveals a larger circle representing the circle of *desire* included in the circuit of the spring.

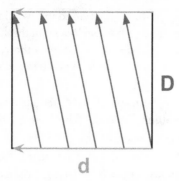

Fig. 6.10 Geometrical representation of the circuit of *demand* (D) and the circle of *desire* (d)

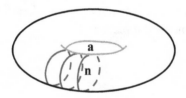

Fig. 6.11 The movement of the circuit of demand circumvents both the place of the object of desire (*a*) in the central hole of the torus and the object of need (*n*) in the hole of the thickness of the torus

Friedman adds that the "full circle," viewed in this illustration as the sum of repetitions of *demand* around the central hole of the torus—D+D+D+…+D—implicitly but necessarily includes the circumference of the circle of *desire*—D+D+D+…+D+d. Accordingly, Friedman claims that "the summand *d*, the desire, is being revealed a posteriori through the demands. It is a missed loop, which has no place between the different demands but has to appear through them" (p. 170).

Therefore, we see that, with the figure of the torus, Lacan is able to portray the unique way in which *desire* springs up from the repetition of the enunciated *demand*. It is through the movement of the circuit of *demand* that the place of the object of *desire* is circumvented in the central hole of the torus, as a place exterior to the hole of *demand* that marks the place of the object of *need* (see *n* and *a* in Fig. 6.11, correspondingly):

> The object of desire can in no way be evoked in this void ringed here by the loop (*boucle*) of the demand. It is to be situated in this hole that we will call the fundamental nothing to distinguish it from the void of demand, the nothing from which the object of desire is called to become. (SIX, 30.5.62)

In other words, Lacan associates the circular circuit of *demand* with the rim demarcating the object of need (the hole of the thickness of the torus), and the circle composed of the thickness of the torus itself with the rim demarcating the object of *desire*. Lacan adds that there is a certain "succession of these circles" (11.4.62). That is because the central hole of the torus gains its topological designation only after the hole of the thickness of the torus is demarcated by the repetition of the circuit of *demand*. This succession is akin to the one between the object of *desire* and the repetition of the enunciated *demand* presented earlier but now is better illustrated in its topological representation.

The Inverted Eight

A further development of Lacan's topological illustration of the relationship between *need, demand,* and *desire* can be found in his analysis of the "inverted eight" (11.4.62). The inverted eight is a topological figure that can be put together by taking a loop, twisting it in the middle to the shape of an eight, and inverting one of the two loops of the eight so that it becomes internal to the other—see Fig. 6.12:

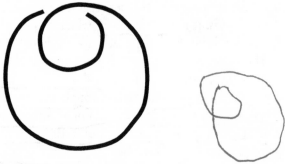

Fig. 6.12 The inverted eight

On first glance, the inverted eight seems to represent two concentric circles; the inside circle touches on the limit of the outside one. Nevertheless, Lacan emphasizes that "the line here of the outside circle continues into the line of the inside circle" (11.4.62). In other words, Lacan argues that the small circle is a continuation of the circumference of the larger circle, and accordingly, the inverted eight represents one circle and not two. As a result, Lacan claims that the relationship between these two presumed circles can be considered to represent the difference between the same circle and itself:

> What does this inverted eight, this circle which continues itself inside itself, what is it, if not a circle which at the limit redoubles itself and takes itself again, which allows there to be symbolized … in so far as it takes itself up again, as it identifies itself to itself. Reduce more and more the distance which separates the first loop, let us say, from the second and you have the circle in so far as it takes itself. (11.4.62)

Lacan argues that the unique self-referential quality of the inverted eight is useful for the further illustration of the relationship between the circuit of *demand* and the circle of *desire* on the surface of the torus: "This sort of loop has an altogether privileged interest for us; because it is what is going to allow us to support, to depict, the relationships of demand and desire as structural" (11.4.62). Lacan does so by associating the smaller loop in the figure of the inverted eight with the trajectory of the circuit of *demand* and the larger loop with the circle of *desire*. He argues that every circle formed in the spring-like trajectory of the circuit of *demand* can also manifest in a second circle revolving the central hole and thus tracing the circle of *desire*. By doing so, it can be considered to depict both the demarcation of the contours of the torus and the contour of the object of *desire*—see Fig. 6.13.

The figure of the inverted eight is sketched out on one topological dimension (on one surface using a single line) but also demarcates two dimensions of lack that are independent and designated by two distinct holes. In other words, it portrays the *extimate* relationship between

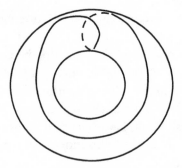

Fig. 6.13 Internal to the figure of the inverted eight, the circuit of *demand* manifests in a second circle revolving the central hole of the torus and tracing the circle of *desire*

demand and *desire*, in which they take on themselves strictly distinct roles in the constitution of psychic reality but are nevertheless composed of the same symbolic chain.[28] Moreover, the unique character of the inverted eight illustrates the way in which the "redoubling" of the smaller loop of the torus can be said to necessarily engender the bigger loop in its own repetition, thus engendering difference in relation to itself: "Here the two loops [of the inverted eight] represent the reiteration, the reduplication of demand and so involve this field of difference to itself, of self-difference" (11.4.62; brackets added). In other words, it emphasizes that the repetition of the circuit of *demand* engenders the circle of *desire* on the basis of "self-difference"—or pure difference, as it has been presented so far in the previous section—going as far as defining the inverted eight "the symbol of self-difference" (11.4.62).[29] In this sense, it is the figure of the inverted eight that illustrates the way pure difference is engendered in the repetition of the circuit of *demand*, bringing about the demarcation of the contours of the object of *desire*.

---

[28] See *extimacy* in Chap. 3.

[29] Interestingly enough, this is homologous to the case of the unary trait, presented in the previous section of this chapter, in which pure difference is engendered in the repetition of the unary trait.

The Foreclosure of the Hole of Demand

After inquiring into the two modalities of the hole in the topological elaboration of the torus, we can now further explicate Laurent's (2012a) account of the foreclosure of the hole in autism. As was just elaborated in the previous section, in *Seminar IX*, Lacan designates two modalities of the hole on the surface of the torus. The first, demarcating the thickness of the torus, is associated with the circuit of *demand*, and the second, at the center of the torus, is associated with the contours of the object of *desire*. Lacan explicitly argues that there is a succession in the constitution of the circuit of *demand* and the circle of *desire* on the torus, and thus, the hole of *demand* precedes and conditions the formation of the hole of *desire*. This relationship of dependence implies that, in case the hole of *demand* is nullified, this will prevent the hole of *desire* from being formed. Accordingly, it is my hypothesis that Miller's (2007) contention that autistic subjects have no access to the symbolic dimension of lack can be associated with the nullification of these two holes in Lacan's topological account of the torus. Moreover, *I argue that Laurent's account of the foreclosure of the hole can be considered to entail the nullification of the hole of demand that prevents the formation of the hole of desire.* Without access to the dimension of the enunciated *demand*, the subject's relationship to the symbolic order is severed in its inception. As a result, the subject cannot gain access to the dimension of *desire* in its mediated symbolic form.

This hypothesis complies with the model of primal repression presented in the previous chapter. As was stated earlier, in the course *Ausstoßung*, a sum of jouissance is first expelled and then affirmed as lost in the symbolic order. In the terms of the dialectics of *need, demand,* and *desire*, something at the level of the infant's instinctual *needs* is excluded and signified as lost in the enunciation of a *demand* (É, p. 579). In the terms of the topological model of the torus, the circuit of *demand* marks out the hole of the thickness of the torus—this hole being the topological analogy of the exclusion on the level of *need*. The foreclosure of the affirmative symbolic product of *Ausstoßung* would thus be associated with the foreclosure of the circuit of *demand*, leaving the subject without access to the hole demarcating the contours of the object of *desire*. Moreover, also supporting this hypothesis is Lacan's association of the concept of pure difference with the figure of the inverted eight. As was previously elaborated, in the figure of the inverted eight, pure difference is engendered on the basis of the repetition of the enunciated *demand*. Therefore, similarly to the case of the unary trait, the foreclosure of the circuit of *demand* prevents its repetition from engendering pure difference, thus hindering the further inscription of the contours of the object of *desire*. Its compliance with these two models strengthens the hypothesis that in autism we are dealing with a structural foreclosure on the level of the hole of *demand*.

The Foreclosure of the Rim

In, *La Bataille De L'Autisme* (2012a), Laurent offers a distinction between the notion of the hole in its symbolic and real designations—naming them "hole" and "void" respectively (p. 84). Laurent argues that while this distinction might seem to be paradoxical, it is resolved when we "topologically distinguish the hole and the void according to the presence or absence of a rim." He adds that "A hole in the symbolic Other has a rim, which is not the case with a hole in the real … [The latter] implies a real absence of a rim … The hole without rim" (pp. 83–84; brackets added). Accordingly, Laurent associates the topological figure of the "void" with the conception of the "hole in the real" that is then classified as a "hole without rim." On the other hand, Laurent associates the topological figure of the "hole" with the conception of the "hole in the symbolic" that is classified as a hole *with* a rim (see Fig. 6.14). In other words,

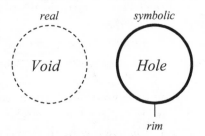

Fig. 6.14 The "void" as the hole in the *real* without a rim and the "hole" as the hole in the *symbolic* with a rim

Laurent implies that a hole gains its designation in topological space only when it is demarcated by a rim, in the same way that a lack gains its designation in the symbolic only when it is represented by a signifier.

Laurent's distinction between the "void" and the "hole" complies with a distinction Slavoj Žižek (2012) introduces between a "pre-symbolic emptiness" and "emptiness marked as such within the symbolic space" (p. 602). The first is akin to an empty space lacking all elements that can fill it and the second to an empty space whose emptiness is its content—absence is itself demarcated in it.

Laurent (2012a) argues that while in autism we see a foreclosure of the symbolic figure of the "hole," the subject still has access to its real designation as a "void" (pp. 83–86). Accordingly, *we see that Laurent's account of autistic foreclosure does not entail the radical exclusion of the hole in all of its manifestations but only the radical exclusion of its symbolic designation.*

As has been elaborated earlier, in the Lacanian framework, only signifying units can be objects of foreclosure and not actual psychic faculties or domains. According to Lacan, this is true for any psychic mechanism of *constitutive exclusion* because they are all pre-determined by an object that conditions their operation. Basing myself on Laurent's (2012a) elaboration of the function of the rim, *I argue that Laurent's account of autistic foreclosure cannot be directly described as the "foreclosure of the hole" but should be classified as the foreclosure of its designator in the symbolic: the rim.* And indeed, Laurent explicitly claims that: "To say that there is no hole is also to say that there is no rim limiting this hole" (p. 69). Therefore, even in Laurent, we see that the foreclosure of the rim necessarily entails the nullification of the hole.

In *Seminar IX*, Lacan accounts for two rims demarcating two holes in the figure of the torus. First, he identifies the rim of the hole of *demand* with the smaller loop of the inverted eight that passes through the central hole of the torus. Second, he identifies the rim of the hole of *desire* with the larger loop of the inverted eight that revolves around the central hole of the torus. Taking into consideration that the repetition of *demand* is a pre-condition for the formation of the object of *desire*; and, in topological terms, the rim of the hole of *demand* conditions the rim of the hole of *desire; I argue that, in this topological depiction, the rim of the hole of demand can be designated as the object of autistic foreclosure.* This would also imply that the foreclosure of the rim in autism is, in fact, the foreclosure of any symbolic demarcation designating the totality of the series of enunciated *demands.* Without the rim of *demand,* the thickness of the torus cannot be designated in space and therefore cannot function as the rim of the hole of *desire,* thus collapsing the structure of the torus as a whole and—in more psychoanalytic terms—radically hindering the formation of any symbolic signification of lack in psychic reality.

The aforementioned hypothesis also complies with the model of primal repression presented in the previous chapter. Accordingly, the affirmative aspect of *Ausstoßung* is associated with the inscription of the symbolic figure of the rim—a figure that transforms the real lack of the object (the void) into a hole that materializes as a lack in the symbolic. This affirmation is followed by *Bejahung,* in which the signifier of the Name-of-the-Father further signifies this hole, anchoring the subject to the symbolic. In autistic foreclosure, the symbolic figure of the rim is radically excluded before the signifier of the Name-of-the-Father is instated in the place of the hole. Its radical exclusion leaves the subject with sole access to the dimension of the "hole in the real"—the hole with no rim—the void. These conclusions are summarized in Fig. 6.15:

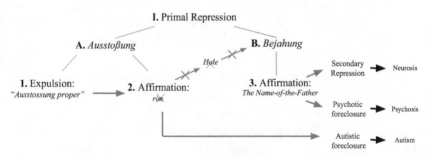

Fig. 6.15 Primal repression, including the foreclosure of the rim of the hole and the structuration of neurosis, psychosis, and autism

The Hole and the Rim in the Clinic of Autism

The following section will present clinical evidence attesting to the unique autistic relationship with the void in the real. It will present Laurent's account of the consequence of the foreclosure of the hole for the autistic conception of space as well as account for the autistic recourse to a "castration in the real." These will provide further support for the hypothesis that the rim of the hole of *demand* can be designated as the object of autistic foreclosure.

Identification with the Void

Both of Lacan's linguistic and topological accounts of the structuration of the subject presume that the dimension of lack is imperative to the formation of any subjective structure. Therefore, if we assume that autistic foreclosure radically excludes the dimension of lack in its entirety from psychic reality, this would imply that, in autism, there is no subject. One of the basic axioms of the Lacanian understanding of autism is that autistic individuals are in fact subjects. Accordingly, we must assume that the foreclosure of the rim in autism does not utterly eradicate the dimension of lack from psychic reality. I have previously argued that while autistic foreclosure radically excludes the symbolic designation of the hole, it still remains a pivotal aspect in autistic subjective reality through its manifestation in the real. This hypothesis complies both with Miller's (2007) contention that autistic subjects have no *symbolic* access to the dimension of lack and with the re-adaptation of Laurent's (2012a) account of the foreclosure of the hole as the foreclosure of the rim.

As was presented in the previous section, in *Seminar IX*, Lacan designates two modalities of lack in his account of the topological figure of the torus—the thickness of the torus and the central hole of the torus. Accordingly, I have argued that, due to the foreclosure of the rim of the circuit of *demand*, autistic foreclosure brings about the nullification of both of these modalities of lack from psychic reality. But, if these two modalities of lack are foreclosed in autism, in what way does lack manifest in autistic psychic reality? We can provide an intriguing answer to this question by using the three figures Laurent (2012a) associates with the manipulation of the hole on the torus:

1. The void—a non-demarcated void.
2. The rim—demarcating a void.
3. The hole—a demarcated void (by a rim).

These three figures enable us to differentiate between three distinct modalities of lack that take part in autistic foreclosure:

1. The hole of the thickness of the torus (symbolic): the hole of the circuit of *demand*. This hole is demarcated by a rim signifying the repetition of enunciated *demands*. I have suggested that the rim of this hole is the object of autistic foreclosure.
2. The hole in the center of the torus (symbolic): the hole of the object of *desire*. This hole is demarcated by a rim composed of the circuit of *demand*. I have suggested that autistic foreclosure prevents its affirmation due to the foreclosure of the rim of the hole of the circuit of *demand*.
3. The void in the center of the torus (real): the void that is engendered after the functioning of autistic foreclosure. This void stands in the place where the foreclosed circuit of *demand* designated a hole prior to autistic foreclosure. In this sense, it only is retroactively situated in the space demarcated by the circuit of *demand* before it was foreclosed (the hole of the center of the torus). Nevertheless, it has no rim and, therefore, has neither a limit nor a proper designation in space—see Fig. 6.16:

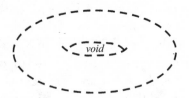

Fig. 6.16 The void with no rim

The notion of a void that is situated in the place where a hole was marked by a rim is accounted for by Lacan in *Seminar VII: The Ethics of Psychoanalysis (1959–1960)*.

> Now if you consider the vase from the point of view I first proposed, as an object made to represent the existence of the emptiness at the center of the real that is called the Thing, this emptiness as represented in the representation presents itself as a *nihil*, as nothing. And that is why the potter, just like you to whom I am speaking, creates the vase with his hand around this emptiness, creates it, just like the mythical creator, *ex nihilo*, starting with a hole … the fashioning of the signifier and the introduction of a gap or a hole in the real is identical. (p. 121)

In this passage, Lacan directs our attention to the fact that while we conventionally think of a vase as a vessel that contains an internal hole, it is in fact the void that initially enables the potter to mold the surrounding vase. In other words, Lacan argues that the emptiness or nothingness—preceding the construction of the vase—exceeds it in its scope. Correspondingly, I argue that one can account for the presence of the void in the real without its symbolic designation by a rim, following autistic foreclosure.

Laurent's (2012a) account of the void in the real with no rim complies with Lacan's argument presented in the above passage. It is a void defined as a nothingness that lacks its symbolic designation by a rim (the vase). Nevertheless, it is important to note that the void in the real does not actually precede the formation of the rim. In direct reference to Martin Heidegger, Lacan argues that the void—when it is addressed on the level of the real—gains a distinct designation only after the potter molds the vase. In this sense, the void embodies the "thingness" of the vase, only retroactively, after the potter molds the vase that demarcates it (Heidegger, 1971, p. 167). Therefore, in the same way that the symbol of negation retroactively gains its symbolic designation through the inscription of the signifier of the Name-of-the-Father, the void in the real retroactively gains its designation only after it has been demarcated by a rim. Thus, *I argue that the void in the real is a figure that can only be engendered retroactively in autism, sequentially following both (1) its initial demarcation by a rim and (2) autistic foreclosure that radically excludes the rim demarcating it.* This point is important to stress yet again. In other words, I argue that the void in the real must be first "eclipsed" by the signifier in order to appear as a hole in the symbolic (É, p. 691). Only after the hole is symbolically designated by the rim, and following the foreclosure of this rim, can the void in the real be considered to embody an actual presence in subjective reality.

In *La Bataille De L'Autisme* (2012a), Laurent associates his notion of the void in the real with the Kleinian conception of the autistic experience of the "black hole," originally associated with Frances Tustin's (1986) work on autism. As will be immediately presented, this "black hole" or "great black nothingness" (Rey-Flaud, 2010)—the outcome of autistic foreclosure—can be associated with Lacan's account of the autistic mode of identification presented in his analysis of the case of Little Dick in *Seminar I.*

The Leforts, Maleval, and Laurent all agree that in autism there is a radical failure in the subject's capacity for identification (Laurent, 2012a, p. 39; Lefort & Lefort, 2003, pp. 102, 169; Maleval, 2009, pp. 81–83, 215). And indeed, when addressing the case of Little Dick, Lacan argues that he does not have access to the most primordial forms of identification: "Dick cannot even engage in the first sort of identification, which would already be an essay in symbolism. He is, paradoxical as it may seem to say it, eyeball to eyeball with reality, he lives in reality" (SI, p. 69). However, Lacan adds that one mode of identification is left open for Dick: "a single and unique primary identification, with the following names—the void, the dark" (p. 69). Lacan argues that this primordial identification with the void precedes "the so-called genital phase, in which reality is then fixed" (p. 69)—referring to secondary repression and the working of the reality principle. Accordingly, he argues that Dick achieves neither secondary nor primal repression; he resides in a reality constructed not on a "humanized" symbolic level but rather on a "dehumanized" form of "fixed symbolization" (p. 69). According to Lacan, the fixed figure of the void is the only human aspect of Dick's reality and is the only place where his objects can take form in a quasi-symbolic way: "In this gap, he can count only a very limited number of objects, which he cannot even name" (p. 70). It is on the basis of the identification with this void that Dick is able to gain some access to language, based on the distinction between objects manipulated in this space (pp. 86–87).[30]

Accordingly, we see that Lacan's account of the identification with the void in the case of Little Dick exemplifies the importance of the void in the real in autistic psychic reality. According to Laurent, the void is the sole manifestation of lack in the structuration of autistic reality following autistic foreclosure. In the case of Dick we see that it functions as the supplementary locus for the dynamics of autistic subjectivity. Instead of achieving an identification on the imaginary or symbolic level, Dick identifies with the void in the real—the product of autistic foreclosure—thus bringing about the structuration of autistic psychic reality as a space where a limited number of objects can be addressed and manipulated.[31]

Autistic Space

Already in his paper on the mirror stage printed in *Écrits* (2006), Lacan argued that the subject's primordial identification dictates its apprehension and positioning in space (É, pp. 77–78). Correspondingly, in his paper "Autism and Psychosis: Further Dialogue with Robert and Rosine Lefort" (2012b), Laurent suggests that the identification with the void in the real manifests in a unique topology defining the autistic construction of space and relationship with objects in space. In this unique construction, the foreclosure of the rim reveals a topology that excludes the limitation and distinction between objects as well as between the subject's body and exterior objects:

> We are led to suppose a space that is not constructed with an inside and an outside ... but a space that is structured like a torus, where from the point of view of its surface, the interior and the exterior of the torus circle are

---

[30] See account of this progression in the case of Dick in the previous section on the unary trait in this chapter.

[31] See further account of the autistic object in Chap. 7.

always exterior. Looking towards the interior, one is always looking at infinity. (p. 18)

This time, Laurent uses the figure of the torus in order to exemplify the continuity that characterizes autistic space. He argues that, in the topology of autistic space, there is no rim that provides the distinction between the inside and the outside (of the body, for instance). Without such a distinction, space is materialized when both the interior and exterior are continuous. Laurent associates this topology with the surface of the torus and argues that if the subject would be situated on such a surface, then looking into the hole of the torus would entail looking outside of it, while looping on the inside, ad infinitum. This exemplifies a space "in which infinity and proximity are the same" (p. 18).

In his paper "Autism and Topology" (2000), Bernard Burgoyne attributes the topological characteristics of autistic space to an arrest in the development of symbolic means of spatial separation. Burgoyne provides a compelling mathematical illustration of such a setback in the constitution of the symbolic order rooted in set-theory. He argues that in the structuration of the symbolic, the subject commonly obtains four different symbolic measures of separation, whereas in autism the subject is only disposed to the first one. Burgoyne is, in fact, proposing that the symbolic function of the rim materializes in the progression between several levels of spatial separation; this progression culminates in what Laurent calls "metric space," characteristic of the world inhabited by the neurotic subject. The foreclosure of the rim in autism thus explains why autistic subjects have no access to these symbolic means of separation. Instead, autistic subjects are situated in a space endowed with an infinite sense of continuity, in which "the Other is always able to invade the subject's body with a terrible *jouissance*, in catastrophic ways, without rims which could mark a regulated pulsation [of the drive]" (Laurent, 2012b, p. 18; brackets added). This explanatory framework, based on the function of the rim in the construction of space, explains a variety of corporeal symptoms apparent in autism (Leekam, Nieto, Libby, Wing, & Gould, 2007). One example is the propensity for "aloneness"—described by Kanner (1943)—that can be explained as an attempt at preserving a state of radical separation from the outside world.

Castration in the Real

Losing all access to the symbolic mediation of lack also entails losing all access to castration. Accordingly, in his paper "Extension du Spectre de l'Autisme" (2015), Maleval goes as far as arguing that in autism there is a "foreclosure of castration" (p. 779). However, in another text, Maleval (2009) insists that "Autistic subjects are affected by the negativity of language" (p. 102). In the case of the foreclosure of the rim, this negativity would entail the presence of the void in the real. Facing this dimension of lack brings autistic subjects to experience unbearable anxiety that they associate with a "pure presence of death" (Laurent, 2012a, pp. 67–69, 84). Laurent adds that the void in the real materializes for autistic subjects in their encounters with objects conceived as holes, such as doors, toilets, windows, and in the separation of feces from the body. Laurent terms the autistic aversion to these holes as the "intolerance of the hole" (p. 68) and associates it with Lacan's neologism *troumatisme* (hole-trauma) (SXXI, 12.2.74).

In order to surmount this terrible anxiety or *troumatisme*, while having no access to symbolic castration, the autistic subject is disposed to achieve a "castration in the real" (Laurent, 2012a, p. 67). The case of the Wolf-Child, presented in Lacan's *Seminar I* by Rosine Lefort, exemplifies such an attempt. Attempting to master the void in the real, which he encountered in the course of his analysis, Robert opposes it by trying to cut off his penis using a pair of plastic scissors. In terms borrowed from the account of the foreclosure of the rim, Robert attempts to demarcate the rim of the void in the real by making a rim on his body—with a cut. In his paper "Avoir un Corps" (1992), Antonio Quinet argues that by doing so, Robert attempts to introduce his body to the dimension of castration; he attempts to signify the unbearable real lack of the phallus by opposing it with the real cutting of the penis. Through the introduction of this opposition in the real, he attempts to inscribe something of the real lack in his body in order to gain access to the phallic signifier. Miller (1988) names this attempt a "*real*ization of the symbolic" (*réelisation*), containing the word "real," which refers to the register of the real. Accordingly, I argue that Robert's attempted *real*ization of the rim in the real of his body is a clear attempt to supplement for its radical exclusion from the symbolic in autistic foreclosure. As will be presented in the following chapter, in the Lacanian clinic of autism, subjects are encouraged to achieve such supplementary inscriptions but not at the cost of the integrity of their bodies, rather in ways that rely on their unique mode of access to language.

The Voice as the Object of Autistic Foreclosure

What binds me to the Other is the voice in the field of the Other. (Miller, 1989, p. 184)

The position of the autistic subject therefore seems to be characterized by not wanting to yield invocatory jouissance. As a result, the incorporation of the Other of language does not take place. The autistic does not place his voice in the void of the Other, which would allow him to inscribe himself under the unary signifier of primordial identification. (Maleval, 2009, p. 81)

At all levels of the development of autism, the same problem persists to varying degrees: the extreme difficulty, not in acquiring language but in assuming a position of enunciation … The dissociation between voice and language is at the heart of the matter in autism. (Maleval, 2009, pp. 87–88)

In his book *L'Autiste et sa Voix* (2009), Jean-Claude Maleval associates the origin of autism with the "retention" of the object of the invocatory drive—the voice object. In doing so, Maleval ventures beyond the structural theory of autistic foreclosure and goes on to investigate this unique gesture on the level of the drive, thus explaining the origin of autism in more dynamic terms. According to Maleval, autistic subjects retain invocatory jouissance in an attempt to avoid the traumatic separation from the voice object when it is constitutively invested in the Other. Moreover, he argues that its retention manifests in the subject's refusal to assume any form of enunciative role, sometimes resulting—in the most severe cases—in a state of autistic mutism.

This section will elaborate the role that the voice object plays in the constitution of the autistic subjective structure. In it, Maleval's dynamic interpretation will be reformulated in more structural terms that will be in line with the discussion of autistic foreclosure presented so far. This

section will demonstrate that the *rim,* in its manifestation in the invocatory drive circuit, can be designated as the object of autistic foreclosure.
Moreover, it will propose that the foreclosure of the rim is achieved following the third stage of the circuit of the invocatory drive, thus hindering the materialization of the voice object and, as a result, severing the
relationship between the subject and the Other.

This section will begin by introducing Lacan's interpretation of the
Freudian conception of the drive (*Trieb*). Firstly, it will introduce the
distinction between drive and instinct, followed by a presentation of
Lacan's description of the drive object as it is accounted for in *Seminar
X.* This section will then proceed to depict Lacan's adaptation of the
Freudian model of the stages of the drive in the schema of the drive circuit as it is presented in Lacan's *Seminar XI.* This discussion will be followed by a thorough elaboration of the singular function of the voice
object in this model and especially in the constitution of the relationship
between the subject and language. Following this elaboration, this section will address the function of the voice object in autism. It will firstly
present Maleval's account of the retention of the voice in dynamic terms.
It will then go on to reformulate this account in structural terms borrowed from the discussion on the foreclosure of the rim presented so far.
This section will conclude by presenting a further analysis of Maleval's
account of the retention of the voice based on other psychoanalytic perspectives and provide several points of critique.

Drive and Instinct

One of the major misunderstanding of the Freudian conception of the
drive (*Trieb*) is rooted in a translation error in *The Standard Edition of the
Complete Psychological Works of Sigmund Freud.* In this canonic corpus,
editor James Strachey inaccurately uses only one word—"instinct"—
when he translates two distinct terms used by Freud to denote: the
instinct (*Instinkt*) and the drive (*Trieb*). Protesting this reductionist translation, in *Seminar XI*, Lacan explicitly argues: "*Trieb* and *instinct* have
nothing in common" (SXI, p. 49). This contention is not only based on
Lacan's interpretation of Freud but is actually included in Freud's original

writings in German, in which he meticulously differentiates between the conception of the *Trieb* and the *Instinkt*—drive and instinct, respectively.

According to Miller and Laurent (1998), the Freudian conception of the instinct (*Instinkt*) is akin to a hardwired biological program that compels the organism to ensure its survival. It forces the organism to act with the aim of fulfilling its instinctual needs (such as hunger and thirst) by raising tension levels when they arise and providing satisfaction that appeases these tensions when these needs are fulfilled. Thus, the instincts are said to function on the basis of the natural rhythms of the body, in a pattern that can be associated with a sinus wave (pp. 15–35).

The drive (*Trieb*), on the other hand, cannot be reduced to the level of the instinctual need. The drive is a product of the encounter between the biological organism and language. It is composed of both of these dimensions as it incorporates the mutual effects language and the body have on each other. Accordingly, Lacan argues that the drive originates from a rupture in the instinctual organization of the natural world of the organism. It thrusts the organism from the real into the domain of symbolic reality, initially introducing the order of the signifier (SXI, p. 162).

One can say that the drive emerges as an excess produced by "the cut that the signifier introduces into the real" (Dravers, 2011, p. 7). This cut is closely linked to the operation of *Ausstoßung*, in which the primal object is expelled and then affirmed as lost. Accordingly, we see that the drive emerges on the level of primal repression—in the symbolic affirmation of an expulsion of an initial sum of jouissance. This expulsion initiates the dynamic of the drive circuit in its constant movement revolving around an object corresponding to the different orifices of the body. Freud identifies two such orifices in the body and, accordingly, two initiatory drives—the oral and the anal.[32] Lacan adds to this list the scopic and the invocatory drives.[33] The subject's body is initially reduced to these four fundamental erogenous zones, through which four corresponding drive objects are engendered in the psyche. Freud establishes a list of these lost objects, each corresponding to one of the aforementioned drives: the

---

[32] Freud also adds the phallic drive as well as the genital drive which unifies the functioning of the other drives at the end of the subject's course of libidinal development.

[33] Lacan also takes off the list the phallic and genital drives, as he insists that all drives are partial; therefore, there cannot be a drive object holistically unifying the others (SXI, p. 177).

breast (oral drive) and the excrement (anal drive). Lacan adopts this list and adds two more objects to it that correspond to his two additional drives: the gaze (scopic drive) and the voice (invocatory drive).

The Drive Object

Ever since Freud's conception of the drive, the term "object" is used to describe not only external objects in space but also the dimension of the drive object. In order to accentuate their particularity, in *Seminar X*, Lacan provides an explicit account of the distinction between the psychoanalytic notion of "objectality" (related to the drive object) and the general notion of "objectivity." Lacan explicates this distinction on the basis of two major characteristics of the drive object—the *constitutive cut* and the *cause* of desire:

> Our vocabulary has endorsed for this object the term *objectality*, in so far as it stands in contrast to the term *objectivity*. To encapsulate this contrast in some brief formulas, we shall say that objectivity is the ultimate term in Western scientific thought, the correlate to a pure reason which, at the end of the day, is translated into—is summed up by, is spelt out in—a logical formalism. If you've been following my teaching over the last five or six years, you know that objectality is something else. To bring it out in its vital point and forge a formula that balances up with the previous one, I will say that objectality is the correlate to a pathos of the cut … As a lost object, at the different levels of the bodily experience where its cut occurs, it is the underpinning, the authentic substrate, of any function of cause. (SX, pp. 214–215)

In this excerpt Lacan argues that while the level of objectivity denotes external objects in space, on the level of objectality we distinguish objects in relation to *constitutive cuts* applied on the body, corresponding to the four erogenous zones. These cuts involve the submission of a "pound of flesh" (p. 124) that "falls away" from the body and is inserted into the signifying dialectics (p. 167).[34] In other words, they are a result of a symbolic operation in which the body of the subject is cut and then invested with a fragmented form of jouissance corresponding to the four erogenous drive orifices (Dravers, 2011, p. 10).[35] These cuts are applied on both the subject's body and the Other who provides their symbolic support.[36]

The fact that these constitutive cuts are applied on both the body and the Other dictates that the drive object belongs neither solely to the body nor to the Other but is, in fact, a remainder that is equally subtracted from both of them (Harari, 2013, p. 179; SX, p. 220). This intermediary surplus dimension is illustrated in Freud's account of the relationship between the infant and the mother's breast. According to Freud (1924), infants initially consider the mother's breast as part of themselves as well as part of the mother and, thus, experience its distancing as a gap between the mother and their own being (SE XIX, p. 175). Lacan provides another compelling example, demonstrating the structural nature of such an object, in his account of the placenta. The placenta is not strictly considered to be a part of the mother or the infant; rather, it occupies an intermediary space between the two in the form of a detached remainder. This remainder embodies a strange form of excess, belonging to both the infant and the mother but, at the same time, not solely belonging to either of them (SX, pp. 166–167).

Being situated "in between" the body and the Other, the drive object plays a crucial role in the mediation of the subject's relationship with the Other. It does so by establishing itself within the field of demand, where the subject's instinctual needs are initially determined by signifiers that attach them to the field of the Other (Dravers, 2011, p. 8; É, p. 579). As

---

[34] As will be presented in the following chapter, Maleval (2009) describes this operation as a "yielding" (*cédant*) of jouissance to the Other (p. 99).

[35] Lacan is quite explicit in his objection to the post-Freudian idea of the stages of drive maturation eventually replacing polymorphous perversity with genital normality. For Lacan the drives are always partial, that is, fragmented, and are never unified. Accordingly, for Lacan, the fragmentation of jouissance is the "normal" disposition of the subject in psychoanalysis.

[36] It is interesting to think of the cut in the body and the Other through the scope of the operation of *Ausstoßung*. The initial cut on the body would be associated with the expulsion of a sum of jouissance, while the cut in the Other will be associated with the signification of lack through the symbol of negation.

noted in the previous section, the subtraction of the instinctual need from the enunciated demand aiming to fulfill it always has a remainder—the precursor of the subject's desire.

This brings us to another crucial aspect of the drive object presented by Lacan in the aforementioned excerpt: its affiliation with the function of the *cause* of desire (SX, pp. 214–215). According to Marie-Hélène Brousse (2007), the notion of the "cause" can also be elaborated on the basis of Lacan's distinction between objectivity and objectality. In the domain of objectivity, the function of the cause is linked to significant connections, relationships, laws, and equations. In the domain of objectality, which is to say, the domain of the drive, "the cause is what takes the place of the hole, of the considerable gap or absence that is the characteristic of desire" (p. 8). In other words, Brousse argues that the drive object, marking the initial cut in the Other, is a necessary condition and cause for the structuration of the subject as desiring.

The function of the drive object as the cause of desire calls for a further distinction between the "objectal cause" in its manifestation as the *object of the drive* and its embodiment as the *object of desire*. In his paper "Object *a* in Social Links" (2006), Žižek provides an interesting account of such a distinction:

> In the case of *objet a* as the object cause of *desire*, we have an object which is originally lost, which coincides with its own loss, which emerges as lost, while, in the case of *objet a* as the object of the drive, the "object" *is directly the loss itself*. In the shift from desire to drive, we pass from the *lost object to loss itself as an object*. That is to say, the weird movement called "drive" is not driven by the "impossible" quest for the lost object, but by a push to directly enact the "loss"—the gap, cut, distance—itself. (p. 117)

In this excerpt, Žižek associates two distinct symbolic designations of lack with the object of the drive and the object of desire. The object of desire is engendered as lost in the Other; it is a symbolic designation of the lost object. On the other hand, the object of the drive signifies in the Other the primordial loss itself. Thus, the object of the drive mediates between the real of the body and the symbolic order. It does so by engendering a remainder in the symbolic that marks the place of a loss outside of symbolization. This remainder in the symbolic is the place where the object of desire can be symbolically designated. That is why it is its *cause*.

While Lacan describes four distinct drive objects, they are all considered to take part in the (1) *constitutive cut* that initiates the (2) *cause* characteristic of desire. This shared functional capacity is associated by Lacan with the "object cause of desire" (SX, p. 189) which is also called *objet petit a* (SXI, p. 17). Lacan uses the algebraic letter *a* to try and strip the particular meanings attributed to the actual body organs associated with the drive objects. For example, attributing the object of the oral drive to the breast carries with it several additional meanings, such as being a mammary gland, of feeding, warmth, and motherhood. According to Lacan, "The algebraic notation has precisely the purpose of giving us a pure identity marker, we having stated already that marking something out with a word is only ever metaphorical" (SX, p. 86). Therefore, the *a* stands for both the function of the *cut* and the function of the *cause* associated with the drive object. We will return to the elaboration of the function of *objet petit a* in the following discussion of the voice object but, right now, we will turn to the role of the drive object in the circuit of the drive.

The Partial Drive and Its Circuit

The Four Components of the Drive

In *Seminar XI*, Lacan presents a "deconstruction of the drive" using the four Freudian components of the drive—*Drang* (thrust), *Quelle* (source), *Objekt* (object), and *Ziel* (aim) (pp. 161–173). Let us characterize and then integrate these components into Lacan's account of the drive circuit.

Lacan describes the *thrust* of the drive as a constant tendency to discharge that is produced by an internal stimulus. This tendency differentiates the drive from the instinct on two levels. Firstly, Lacan argues that the stimulus that initiates the *thrust* of the drive cannot be equated to the excitation marking an instinctual need, for example, hunger or thirst. This is because instinctual excitation engages the "organism as a whole" (p. 164), whereas drive-stimulus is always partial and divided into the erogenous zones of the body. Secondly, Lacan emphasizes that "the characteristic of the drive is to be a *konstante Kraft*, a constant force" (p. 164). Therefore, contrary to the "instinctual thrust" that functions according to a biological rhythm, the *thrust* of the drive is incessant: "it has no day or night, no spring or autumn, no rise and fall. It is a constant force" (p. 165). Thus, contrary to a sinus wave that exemplifies the instinctual rhythm, the drive perpetually moves in a straight line.[37]

Lacan associates the *aim* of the drive with the course or trajectory that provides the drive with its satisfaction. Nevertheless, Lacan insists that, in the satisfaction of the drive, there is a dissociation between the drive's *aim* and its *object*, as the drive *aims* for a satisfaction that is totally indifferent to the identity of its object (p. 168). On the level of the instinct, a specific object always corresponds to the "aim" of a need. For example, the baby's hunger is "aimed" at the consumption of food. Nevertheless, on the level of the drive, there is no distinct natural *object* designated as its *aim*—any *object* can be adopted as a drive *object*. For example, in the domain of the oral drive, it is not the stuffing of the mouth with food that necessarily provides drive satisfaction but it could be the mouth ordering from the menu. Lacan calls this type of satisfaction "impossible" and "paradoxical" (pp. 166–167). As will be explained shortly, in the drive circuit, the drive *aims* around the *object*, gaining satisfaction in the demarcation of its contours, thus reaching its *goal* without attaining its *object*.

Lacan associates the *source* of the drive with the "rim-like structure" of the erogenous zones of the body (p. 169). These are not strictly associated by Lacan with their biological function but rather with their role in the mediation of the subject's relation to the Other.

These four elements combine together into a series of imaginary and symbolic constructs, binding the instinctual biological aspect of sexuality to the logic of the unconscious unraveled in the Other, thus correlating two completely heterogenous aspects: the subject's sexuated being and language (Brousse, 1995, p. 112). Lacan describes these drive constructs as "montages"—open to an infinite amount of internal

---

[37] As will soon be demonstrated, this movement is described as a circular circuit by Lacan.

transformations—calling them the "surrealist collage" of human sexuality (SXI, pp. 169, 176).

The Drive Circuit

In the 14th chapter of *Seminar XI*, "The Partial Drive and Its Circuit," Lacan presents a schema that adds another explanatory layer to his original interpretation of the inter-relations between the four components of the drive. This would come to be known as Lacan's schema of the drive circuit—see Fig. 6.17.

In the center of the schema we can identify the drive *object* (*a*). On the right, the *source* of the drive is replaced by the figure of the *rim*. The *thrust* of the drive is represented by the arrow, moving in a circular trajectory. It originates from within the *rim*, *aims* its trajectory around the *object*, finally returning to its *source*—represented in the schema by the *goal*.[38] The schema thus accentuates the dissociation between the drive's *aim* and its *object*, this time demonstrating that the drive's *goal* is not the attainment of the *object* but the return to the *source* (pp. 161–170).

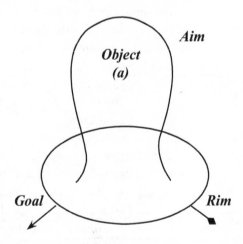

Fig. 6.17   Lacan's schema of the drive circuit. (Based on Lacan 2001, p. 178)

---

[38] Lacan specifically uses the English word "Goal" to play on its double meaning: as an aim or objective or the rim of a goal as in the game of soccer.

The circuit of the drive presented in this schema is described by Lacan as being circular and thus continuous. It originates from the erogenous zone and continues to circumvent the *object* of the drive by returning to the erogenous zone, from where it sets out on its path yet again. Thus, according to Lacan, with the drive, we are dealing with "something that emerges from a rim, which redoubles its enclosed structure, following a course that returns, and of which nothing else ensures the consistency except the object, as something that must be circumvented" (p. 181). Lacan emphasizes that the continuous circular movement of the circuit of the drive hinges on the unattainability of the drive object: "The *objet petit a* … is introduced from the fact that no food will ever satisfy the oral drive, except by circumventing the eternally lacking object" (p. 180). The fact that the *object* is not attainable means that drive satisfaction is always partial and makes the *thrust* revolve around the *object* indefinitely as a constant force. Accordingly, not only can we characterize the satisfaction of the drive as never reaching its *object*, we can also say that drive satisfaction is directly derived from the failure to reach it (Dravers, 2011, p. 18).

Lacan adds that the drive *object* has a crucial role in ensuring the consistency of the functioning of the drive circuit: "nothing else ensures the consistency [of the drive circuit] except the object, as something that must be circumvented" (SXI, p. 181; brackets added). The drive *object* does so by functioning as the hinge that conditions the relationship between the *rim* in its manifestation as *source* and *goal*. In the schema, the circular movement of the *thrust* originates in the *rim* (as *source*) and also returns to it (as *goal*); thus, the *rim* is rendered as both the *source* and the *goal* of the drive, which are tied together by the *thrust* revolving around the *object*. The *rim* has been a major focus in the previous section of this chapter and will also take center stage in this section. The *rim* as *source* and *goal* represents the erogenous zones on the body and the Other respectively. It marks a cut on both the surface of the body and the Other, while not exhaustively belonging to any of them. The *object*, situated in the schema right between these two surfaces, holds them together. Like a rock tucked under two sheets around which a rope is tied, it ensures the two remain linked.

In his paper "Instincts and Their Vicissitudes" (1915a), Freud uses the example of sadism and masochism in order to differentiate between three different stages in the development of drive functioning—*active, reflexive,* and *passive.* In the first stage, the force of the drive is *actively* aimed outward toward an extraneous object ("to see"). In sadism, this would manifest in the exercise of power over another person as an object. The second stage entails the reversal of the drive's aim from an *active* to a *reflexive* aim, thus aiming it to the subject's own body ("to see oneself"). In masochism, this would include giving up the exterior object and replacing it with the subject's own body as object. In the final stage, another subject is sought after that can take over the role of the subject in the first stage ("to be seen" or "to make oneself be seen"). This is the *passive* stage, where Freud insists there is an "introduction of a new subject" into the equation that actively takes the original subject as its object: "to whom one displays oneself in order to be looked at by him" (SE XIV, p. 129).

In his account of the circuit of the drive, Lacan emphasizes that the three stages Freud presents in his paper are signified by the fundamental movements that are presented in his schema (SXI, pp. 177–179). The outward trajectory of the drive, emerging from the *rim* in the general direction of the object, represents the first *active* stage. The second *reflexive* stage, the reversal, is represented by the 180 degrees turn of the drive's trajectory—changing its outward course to an inward one, thus marking the contours of the *object.* The third and final *passive* stage is represented by the return of the drive circuit to its *source.* Lacan explicitly remarks that it is the third stage that is crucial for the constitution of the subject in relation to the Other: "it is in this way that the subject attains what is, strictly speaking, the dimension of the capital Other" (p. 194). That is because, in Lacan's interpretation of the stages of drive functioning, the "new subject" introduced in the third stage is the Other. The relationship between the subject and the Other is established through their mutual association with the drive *object.* Accordingly, on the third stage of the drive circuit, the subject situates itself in the place of the *object,* by making itself be seen, heard, excreted, or devoured by the Other (p. 195; Dravers, 2011, p. 20).[39] A good example is the well-known image of a child gaining satisfaction when his foot is being nibbled by his mother. This image represents the third stage of the circuit of the oral drive, in

---

[39] In relation to the scopic, invocatory, anal, and oral drives respectively.

which the subject gains satisfaction by making itself be "eaten" by the Other (Laznik, 2009, pp. 50–51). Lacan finally adds that it is only on the third stage that the drive *object* is fully inscribed in the field of the Other and ensures the consistency of the drive circuit as a whole: "It is only with its appearance at the level of the other that what there is of the function of the drive may be realized" (SXI, pp. 178–179).

Finally, Lacan's interpretation of the three stages of the drive circuit also sheds light on the way in which the drive *object* is involved in the initiation of the relationship between the registers of the symbolic and the real. The involvement of the drive object in the initiation of this relationship is captured in Lacan's contention that in the circuit of the drive—"*la pulsion en fait le tour*" (p. 168).[40] Playing on the double meaning of the word *tour*, in French, Lacan is implying that the drive "revolves around something" but also plays a "trick" on something. This would be the drive *object*, around which the circuit of the drive "revolves" and on which the "trick" of the drive works. In her paper "The Drive (II)" (1995), Brousse argues that, in the drive circuit, "the drive tricks the real because, as you revolve around the object, you make it your prisoner, that is, you bring a little bit of it inside the symbolic structure" (p. 113). Accordingly, we see that the drive *object* functions as a type of facilitator between the symbolic and the real registers. It enables the initial incorporation of jouissance in the signified body of the subject and, thus, the further symbolic mediation of this jouissance:

> The drive is thus, as Lacan says, an apparatus by which to bring some sexuality as real into the field of the imaginary and the symbolic … That's what the drive is made for, and this is the kind of link it makes with sexuality as defined in terms of the real. (p. 113)

The Voice Object

In his account of autistic subjectivity, Maleval (2009) mainly focuses on the initiatory relationship between the subject and the drive object. Focusing on the level of the invocatory drive, Maleval claims that it is a

---

[40] This basically untranslatable phrase is presented in the original French in the English translation of *Seminar XI*.

refusal on the level of this drive that is situated at the origin of autism (pp. 77–85). In order to understand this claim, we must first characterize the object of the invocatory drive—the voice object.

All drive objects embody the constitutive function of the *objet petit a*. That is the constitutive *cut* that warrants the relationship between the subject and the Other and provides the *cause* of subjective dynamism. Nevertheless, Lacan argues that each of the drive objects constitutes a particular aspect in this relationship—being situated in a different way between the subject and the Other (SX, p. 291). In Roberto Harari's (2013) words: "one object *a* is not the same as another, since, as we shall see, each one relates the subject (S) differentially with the Other (A), as a remainder of the latter due to the constitution of the former" (p. 210). Going back to Lacan's "*fait le tour*," we can say that the drive "revolves around" or "tricks" the object in a different way, bringing something else of the real into the field of the imaginary and the symbolic (Brousse, 1995, p. 113). The particular relationship each drive object initiates between the subject and the Other is accounted for by Lacan in *Seminar X*. Nevertheless, because the discussion in this section focuses on the constitutive cut created by the voice object, only the nature of this drive object will be elaborated.[41]

The Nature of the Voice Object

It is quite hard to designate the exact nature of the voice as a drive object. That is because it is very much distinct from the conventional notions we have of the voice. Let us initially say that, first of all, the voice as a drive object cannot be fully identified with the voice we hear when one speaks. It is reducible neither to the intonation of speech nor to its vocality nor to the register of sound (Maleval, 2009, p. 78). Secondly, the voice as drive object does not fully coincide with the meaning conveyed in speech; namely, it cannot be reduced to the chain of signifiers. Finally, the voice as drive object is also not reducible to the materiality of a speaking body, to the movements of the mouth, or to vibrations of sound created by the

---

[41] A thorough account of the nature of the other three drive objects can be found in *Seminar X*, pp. 189, 291–292, 315, 328.

mouth cavity (Dolar, 1996, p. 10; 2006, p. 73). Therefore, at the outset of its explication, one can argue that the voice, as drive object, is precisely what is subtracted from the subject's speech in all of these dimensions together (Harari, 2013, p. 205).

In order to explicate the exact nature of the voice object in *Seminar X*, Lacan refers to the "Shofar"—an ancient musical instrument, typically made of a lamb's horn, that is used in the Jewish religious rituals of the New Year and day of atonement (SX, pp. 243–255). The Shofar is blown several times at each of the above-mentioned rituals. It produces a continuous tone that is abruptly cut several times, lacks melody, and resembles an animal's cry. Lacan takes inspiration in Theodor Reik's analysis of the role of the Shofar in the Freudian myth presented in *Totem and Taboo* (1913). According to Reik (1946), the Shofar is used to voice the cry of the dying primal Father to the unconscious psychic life of the listener, as well as its presence as the totemic God with whom the listener identifies. Through the voice of the Shofar the community of listeners comes to yield itself to this God and its Law. Conversely, according to Lacan's account of the Shofar, the voice of the Shofar does not belong to the primal Father himself but is a remainder of his authority, left over after his murder. It is presented as the pure authority of his Law, devoid of its content (SX, p. 250). To this Mladen Dolar (1996) add that the voice of the Shofar is akin to "that part of him which is not quite dead, what remained after his death and testifies to his presence—his voice—but also to his absence, a *stand-in for an impossible presence*, enveloping a central void" (p. 26).

The initial introduction of the authority of the Law through the voice of the Shofar is associated by Lacan with the constitution of the symbolic order and, more specifically, with "the subject's relation to the signifier in what might be called … a first assimilation" (SX, p. 249). Lacan relates this "first assimilation" to the instatement of the "primordial signifier," not only as it is affirmed in the symbolic but also as it is endowed with jouissance and voiced by the subject.[42] According to Lacan, when such a

---

[42] This is where the voice object exceeds the account of the primordial signifier of the Name-of-the-Father: as it further elaborates of the function of jouissance in the instatement of the initial relationship between the subject and the Other.

signifier "passes into an utterance, a new dimension is involved, an isolated dimension, a dimension unto itself, the specifically vocal dimension" (p. 249). Just like the voice of the Shofar embodies the remainder of the assimilation of the primal Father's unbridled jouissance by the symbolic Law (the killing of the primal father); the voice as drive object is a remainder of the assimilation of the subject's jouissance in language. It is a manifestation of the impossible intersection between language and jouissance, embodied in the isolated dimension of the drive (Dolar, 1996, p. 27). It produces an effect indicating that something was separated from both of these domains at the moment of speech (Brousse, 2007, p. 12).

In his book *A Voice and Nothing More* (2006), Dolar provides a compelling account of the function of the voice object in the impossible intersection between language and jouissance. Dolar argues that, in every utterance, one can identify the dimension of signification in language as well as the dimension of jouissance that does not follow the signifying logic. Dolar claims that the voice object is situated in the intersection between the part of the jouissance excluded from language and the part of language excluded from jouissance:

> So the voice stands at a paradoxical and ambiguous topological spot, at the intersection of language and the body, but this intersection belongs to neither. What language and the body have in common is the voice, but the voice is part neither of language nor of the body. (p. 73)

Dolar adds that the voice object is what detaches itself from the body when an utterance is made. Thus, on the one hand, while not being of the body, the voice object still remains a corporeal object and, on the other hand, it upholds the subject's relationship with language while not being a signifier. Dolar proposes to imagine an intersection of two circles—the circle of language and the circle of the body—and situates the voice object at the place where the intersection of the two circles is *extimate* to both, that is, eclipsed by both circles but belonging to neither of them—see Fig. 6.18.

According to Maleval (2009), "Compared to the three other drive objects, oral, anal and scopic, the voice has the privilege of commanding

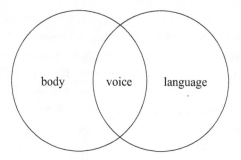

Fig. 6.18 The voice object is situated at the intersection of the two circles but belongs to neither of them

the investment in language." To this, he adds: "The voice as a drive object is … that which carries the subject's presence in its speech" (p. 78). Maleval thus furthers Lacan's account of the constitutive function of the voice as drive object, as he adds that, in this constitution, language is elected to designate the subject's being in speech. Basing himself on Lacan's contention that "A voice … is not assimilated, but incorporated" (SX, p. 277), Maleval claims that the voice "incorporates" the subject's being in the Other. In other words, by yielding the voice object to the Other, the Other is constituted as a place able to receive a signifier that carries the enunciative being of the subject (Maleval, 2009, p. 81). As will be thoroughly elaborated in the following section, this entails the subject yielding a sum of invocatory jouissance and situating it in the Other, thus gaining its designation as a "subject of enunciation."

In the aforementioned account of the voice object, Maleval is relying on Lacan's distinction between the "subject of enunciation" and the "subject of the statement" (pp. 127, 234). This distinction is presented in Lacan's paper "Remarks on Daniel Lagache's Presentation" (É, pp. 543–574). In this account, Lacan differentiates between the subject of the unconscious that speaks through the symptom and the subject around whom speech revolves—the one captured in the content of speech. The latter, also called the "subject of the statement," is equated by Lacan to the way in which a person and the others surrounding him or her consciously perceive him or her. This is the subject that articulates the conscious discourse. In other words, it is "the person who is actually speaking at the moment I say *I*" (Lacan, 2008, p. 36). Lacan associates the subject of the statement with Roman Jakobson's (1971) conception of linguistic "shifters" (p. 132). According to Lacan, the subject of the statement is similar to shifters in language—like "I," "you," "he," "she," and so on—that identify the circumstances of speech (É, p. 556). These linguistic elements cannot be discerned without reference to the message in which they are included. For example, in the sentence, "I am a good boy," the shifter, "I," signifies a subject only in relation to the predicate, "good boy," because, without it, the "I" would signify nothing. Accordingly, Lacan argues that the subject of the statement is the conscious subject in so far as it thinks of itself under predication—as a "good boy" for example. It is associated with the ego and a specific ideal image with which the subject identifies. The "subject of enunciation," on the other hand, is not related to the level of the enunciated statement but, rather, to the act of enunciation itself. It is not captured by a statement that includes predicates that are related to a shifter—for Lacan insists that not all statements include shifters. Accordingly, the subject of enunciation appears through language, even in cases where the subject of the statement is not singled out in speech. It is the subject insofar as it is a by-product of speech: "the subject not insofar as it produces discourse but insofar as it is produced, cornered even, by discourse" (Lacan, 2008, p. 36). According to Lacan, it manifests in the symptom, appearing as a force that disrupts the subject's conscious discourse. Thus, it embodies the aspect of the subject that is rooted in the unconscious, for, according to Lacan, "the presence of the unconscious, being situated in the locus of the Other, can be found in every discourse, in its enunciation" (É, p. 707).

Maleval's (2012) contribution to Lacan's distinction between these two subjective agencies lies in his contention that the subject of enunciation materializes in discourse when the voice object is incorporated in the Other (p. 38). It materializes in speech whenever a sum of invocatory jouissance is yielded to the Other and situated in discourse. Miller (1989) supports this contention when he argues that "The voice is that part of the signifying chain that is not assumable by the subject as '*I*' and subjectively assigned to the Other" (p. 183). Therefore, at this point, we consider the voice object as: what carries the presence of the subject of enunciation as not-*I* in speech; what subjectifies the symbolic order; and what renders it as a place for the subject's being beyond the conscious discourse of the ego.

The Voice Object in the Constitution of the Symbolic Order

In *Seminar X*, Lacan attempts to clarify the way in which the constitution of the subject's relationship with language relies on the functioning of the circuit of the invocatory drive. By metaphorically alluding to the acoustic void characteristic of the physiology of the ear, Lacan describes the constitutive function of the third stage of the circuit of the invocatory drive (SX, p. 275). Lacan explains that when the voice reaches the ear cavity, it resonates and, by doing so, marks out the contours of its internal void— the place from where it returns to the subject as being heard. In the invocatory domain of the drive, following the *active* and *reflexive* stages (*speaking* and *hearing oneself speak*, respectively), the drive circuit reaches the third stage in which the subject *passively makes himself be heard*. In this stage, the subject still uses its own voice but introduces the Other into the equation. Namely, introducing the Other as the place in which the voice resonates and, by doing so, constituting the Other as the locus from which the subject's voice is heard (SXI, p. 195).

But Lacan takes the metaphor of the ear cavity one step further when he claims that this void should not be strictly addressed in its spatial form:

> If the voice in the sense we understand it [as a drive object] holds some importance, it's not on account of resonating in any spatial void. The simplest intrusion of the voice in what in linguistic terms is called its phatic function ... resonates in a void that is the void of the Other as such, properly speaking *ex-nihilo* ... It is proper to the structure of the Other to constitute a certain void ... the voice resonates in this void as a voice that is distinct from sonorities. It is not a modulated voice, but an articulated one. (SX, pp. 275–276; brackets added)[43]

---

[43] The following discussion concerning the constitutive relationship between the void and the voice object can also be associated with the constitutive function of the void in Lacan's account of the vase presented in the previous section of this chapter on the foreclosure of the hole.

In this excerpt, Lacan emphasizes that the function of the void—in the third stage of the invocatory drive circuit—should not be strictly equated with the return of an echo from any spatial void. In the case of the spatial void, the voice is duplicated as an echo. In the case of the voice as drive object, its resonance in the void of the Other entails an excess beyond duplication—a creation *ex-nihilo*. Lacan associates this excess with what linguist, Roman Jakobson, terms the "phatic function" of language. According to Jakobson (1960), this function entails the establishment of a line of communication regardless of the content communicated in this line—a function "primarily serving to establish, to prolong, or to discontinue communication" (p. 355). Accordingly, Lacan argues that, when the voice resonates in the void of the Other, it returns to the subject not only in its purely auditory or meaningful function but also in its "phatic function"—the emblem of the constituted relationship with the Other. In other words, it echoes back to the subject from the Other, "incorporating" the latter's alterity in the original speech of the subject (SX, p. 277). By carving out a void in the Other and resonating within this void, the voice is constituted as an excess to the original speech of the subject. As Dolar (2006) puts it, in this constitutive moment, "the non-sonorous resonance endows what is said with alterity" (p. 160). This is why the voice object, in the third stage of the invocatory drive, is considered to initiate the relationship between the subject and language, by introducing the Other as the place from which the subject is to be heard.

The Foreclosure of the Voice Object

The Traumatic Separation from the Voice Object

According to Maleval (2009), "alienation in the Other of language produces a traumatic separation, a yielding of the object of primordial jouissance, allowing for the localization of the latter outside of the body" [*hors-corps*] (p. 90). This process is called by Lacan "symbolic castration" (SX, pp. 275–276). In the domain of the invocatory drive, it involves yielding the object of invocatory jouissance and localizing it in the Other.

Maleval (2009) adds that, by making language the place in which a signifier can carry the subject's enunciative being, "Symbolic castration erases the presence of the voice in the real" (p. 82). The erasure of the presence of the voice in the real is experienced by autistic subjects as extremely distressing—as "a mutilation or even as a cataclysm" (p. 85). Accordingly, autistic subjects adopt two defensive strategies in order to protect themselves from this terrible anxiety. The first is adopted on a more fundamental structural level and involves the retention of the voice object from the field of the Other. The second is a lateral tactical approach that entails avoiding any encounter with the signification of invocatory jouissance manifest in enunciative presence.

The Retention of the Voice Object

In his book *L'Autiste et sa Voix* (2009), Maleval claims that autism originates in a deficiency on the level of the invocatory drive (p. 99). Maleval associates this deficiency with the subject's refusal to inscribe invocatory jouissance in the Other: "The voice is a drive object that has the specificity of controlling primordial identification, so that the refusal to yield invocatory jouissance undermines the subject's inscription in the field of the Other" (pp. 82–83). Maleval articulates this refusal in terms of the subject's "retention of the voice" (Maleval, 2012, pp. 37–38). In this sense, he associates it with an active refusal to constitute the Other—the symbolic order as the locus of signifiers—as a place in which the voice object is to be inscribed.

The retention of the voice hinders the imperative function of the voice object in the constitution of the relationship between the subject and language. Therefore, Maleval (2009) argues that due to its fundamental role in the knotting of the subject and the Other, the retention of the voice object causes a radical break from the field of the Other. It prevents the autistic subject from having any access to phallic signification and leaves it with no access to the symbolic Other. Thus, Maleval states that the autistic subject "rejects any dependence on the Other ... so as to radically resists the alienation of its being in language" (p. 81). Resisting the alienation in language is one of the fundamental structural attributes characterizing autistic subjectivity. As will be elaborated in the next chapter, it takes form in a unique mode of access to language that fore-closes the dimension of the signifier.

Avoidance of Enunciative Presence

Other than the refusal to yield the object of invocatory jouissance to the Other, autistic individuals do everything in their capacity to avoid an encounter with the enunciative presence of the voice—which is to say, any encounter with the signification of invocatory jouissance which car-ries the alterity of the subject's enunciation. In the previous section I have associated the enunciative presence of the subject in speech with Jakobson's (1960) notion of the "phatic function." Namely, the purely inter-subjective dimension in speech, independent from the meaningful content communicated between subjects. In the clinic of autism, we encounter a variety of tactics that are employed in an attempt to speak without actively engaging in the phatic function. Some autistic individu-als use a very monotonic voice, devoid of affect; some use a very high-pitched voice; some use dolls, portraying them as the actual enunciator when they speak through them "in-proxy"; and some repeat sentences and words in the exact intonation and order in which they first heard them. All of these are implemented in an attempt to engage the voice in a unique form of speech that solely conveys information and is utterly devoid of the enunciative presence of the subject in speech (Grandin, 2006). In more severe cases of autism, we see subjects who distance them-selves from the enunciative presence in speech to such a degree that can manifest in a state of complete solitude: "Solitude is a clear indication of a refusal to appeal to the Other in connection with a fundamental diffi-culty for the autistic to place himself in the position of enunciator" (Maleval, 2009, p. 96). The autistic state of solitude is also utilized as a defense from the intrusive and horrifying enunciative presence of others. In this sense, the autistic subject puts itself under the protection of what Frances Tustin (1992) termed the "autistic shell" (pp. 191–207)—a dynamic shield that also aims to protect the subject from any encounter with the enunciative presence of other subjects.

The Foreclosure of the Rim in the Circuit of the Invocatory Drive

According to Maleval's dynamic interpretation, autism originates in the retention of the voice object from the field of the Other; in other words, in autism we originally find an active refusal to yield invocatory jouissance and inscribe it in the Other. In the following sections, Maleval's dynamic interpretation will be translated into more structural terms, terms used so far in this book to describe the functioning of autistic foreclosure. Correspondingly, at the very outset of this section, it seems reasonable to assume that—when it is transposed into the framework of autistic foreclosure—the retention of the voice might be said to entail the radical foreclosure of the voice object. However, this assumption does not comply with the Lacanian framework presented so far. As has been stated earlier in this section, the drive object has a unique status in the relationship between the subject and the Other. While knotting the subject's sexuated body and the Other, the drive object cannot be reduced to either the dimension of the body or the signifier. Because foreclosure is a psychic mechanism that radically excludes a signifying unit from the symbolic, the voice object—not being able to be reduced to a symbolic unit—cannot be considered to be the object of autistic foreclosure.

A compelling paragraph written by the Leforts in their book *La Distinction De L'Autisme* (2003) strongly supports this assumption:

> What is lacking, therefore, due to the absence of a return of the circuit, is the source of the drive, the erogenous zone of the mouth and its goal. What remains? Otherwise, only the thrust whose constant force is evident and the object that, far from lacking, appears in the foreground of an intolerable real. (p. 16)

In this excerpt, the Leforts emphasize that it is neither the *object* nor the *thrust* of the circuit of the drive that is lacking in autism. According to the Leforts, it is the *source* and *goal* of the drive—integrated in the figure of the *rim* in the Lacanian schema—that are foreclosed and thus lacking in autism. Without a *rim*, the drive circuit loses its *aim* and is

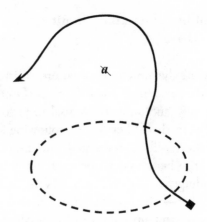

Fig. 6.19 The drive circuit *thrust* into an *aimless* movement, unable to inscribe the drive *object* in the symbolic without the *rim*

thus *thrust* into an "aimless" movement—unable to inscribe the dimension of the drive object in the symbolic—see Fig. 6.19.

I have already argued that the *rim* represents the *source* and *goal* of the drive circuit in their symbolic manifestation in the erogenous zones on the subject's body as well as in the Other. Accordingly, when the Leforts claim that in autism the *source* and *goal* of the drive circuit are lacking, this could be understood as the foreclosure of their symbolic designation—the foreclosure of the *rim* of the drive circuit.

The aforementioned hypothesis might seem markedly parallel to the previously proposed interpretation of Laurent's account of the foreclosure of the rim of the hole. However, while Laurent addresses the figure of the rim in its topological and structural function, the Leforts approach it through its role in the dynamics of the drive circuit—an approach that corresponds to Maleval's account of the retention of the voice object. Accordingly, *I argue that the symbolic inscription of the rim in the circuit of the invocatory drive can be designated as the object of autistic foreclosure.* Without the *rim*, the drive circuit is "short-circuited"—lacking a *source* and unable to return to its *goal*, thus hindering the inscription of the voice object in the Other. Without the voice object inscribing a void in the Other, the dimension of lack cannot be instated in the Other, as well as on the subject's body. On the side of the Other, this manifests in what Maleval (2012) calls a "real Other, without the hole"—an Other utterly divorced from the domain of the symbolic (p. 65). On the side of the subject's body, it is what Laurent (2012a) calls a body "without holes" or a "body without organs," in the sense that all the organs of exchange are utterly "plugged"—that is, they lack a hole (pp. 13, 42).[44]

The foreclosure of the *rim* in the invocatory drive circuit does not truly absolve the autistic subject from dealing with the unbearable anxiety the voice object provokes. On the contrary, according to the Leforts (2003), this foreclosure causes the voice object to be permanently experienced as an intolerable intrusion in the real (p. 16). The Leforts base themselves on Lacan's contention that "whatever is refused in the symbolic order, in the sense of *Verwerfung*, reappears in the real" (SIII, p. 13). According to this formula, the foreclosure of the *rim* in the drive circuit hinders the symbolic inscription of the void in the Other, causing it to reappear in the real and give rise to an unbearable anxiety that is experienced by the subject as mutilation.[45]

Further Developments in the Understanding of the Function of the Invocatory Drive in Autism

In the next chapter, a variety of clinical cases attesting to the retention of the voice in autism will be thoroughly presented. Therefore, at the conclusion of this section, instead of presenting clinical evidence that supports this model, several contemporary developments of the Lacanian understanding of the function of the invocatory drive in autism will be presented. These would be based on interdisciplinary studies conducted by Lacanian psychoanalysts that also take part in evidence-based research investigating the underlying cause of autism.

---

[44] It is interesting to note, on a clinical level, that, among autistic children, the erogenous zones seem to lack a rim-like structure. Other than the unbearable anxiety revolving the movement of jouissance through them, autistic children can be seen to dribble saliva and suffer from uncontrollable sphincters (Laznik, 2009). More on the autistic body as the body without organs in Brenner (2021).

[45] See account of *troumatisme* (hole-trauma) and the "black hole" in a previous section of this chapter on the foreclosure of the hole.

Foreclosure of the Rim in the Third Stage of the Invocatory Drive Circuit

In her paper "The Lacanian Theory of the Drive: An Examination of Possible Gains for Research on Autism" (2009), Marie Christine Laznik claims that the onset of autism can be traced back to failure on the third stage of the drive circuit (p. 43). In order to base this claim, Laznik goes on to briefly explain the role of the three stages of the drive according to Freud:

> Of these three stages, the first, for Freud, is active. The infant ... goes towards an external object, the breast or the bottle. The second stage is reflexive when the infant takes as an object a part of his own body, for example the finger, or the pacifier. In the third stage, which Freud describes as passive, the infant makes of himself the object of an other, this famous new subject, for example, the mother. (p. 49)

According to Laznik, autistic children frantically avoid situations in which they let themselves be the object of the Other—let themselves be eaten, looked at, or heard: "The future autistic child will not know this third stage of the circuit of the drive, that moment when he will make himself the object of a new subject ... the circuit of the drive does not close" (pp. 50–51).

In order to further address the failure in the third stage of the drive circuit in autism, Laznik proposes to integrate the model presented by Freud in "Instincts and Their Vicissitudes" (1915a) and in *Project for Scientific Psychology* (1950). She believes that, by bringing these two texts together, "we have constructed for ourselves a valuable tool which allows us to understand the initial putting into place of the psychic apparatus and the failings inherent in autism" (Laznik, 2009, p. 53). On the basis of these two texts, Laznik notes that in the third stage of the drive circuit "something of the representation of the drive (*Wunschvorstellung*) will inscribe itself in the hallucinatory pole of primary satisfaction" (p. 53). Laznik refers to an inscription that instantiates something of the desire of the Other—what is later in her paper explicitly associated with the lack in the Other (p. 57). Laznik gives an example from the domain of the oral drive in which the hallucinatory experience of the infant's satisfaction also includes the mother's laughter signifying her pleasure. In other words, in the third stage of the drive circuit the drive object is inscribed in the Other and kicks off the subject's relation to the desire of the Other. Laznik bestows on this stage a "humanizing role," as it retroactively establishes the place of the subject as a desiring subject in the first and second stages of the drive circuit as well (p. 54).[46]

According to Laznik, autistic subjects do not have access to the third stage of the drive circuit. This means that autistic subjects cannot make themselves the object of the Other. Without the third stage, the drive circuit remains "open" and the drive object "unsignified." As has already been elaborated, this hinders the subject's relationship with the symbolic order, leaving the jouissance of the drive in an unmediated state. This is turn affects the structure of the unconscious and the whole system of representations as well as the world of perception in its "humanized" organization. Laznik adds: "If this third stage is not reached … then nothing can guarantee that auto-erotism will not be devoid of the mark of the link to the other, which is eros. Now, if we remove eros, auto-eroticism is to be interpreted as autism" (p. 54).[47]

In Lacan's schema of the drive circuit, the *rim* embodies both the function of the *source* and the *goal* of the drive. By adhering to Laznik, we can now argue that in the first stage of the drive circuit the *rim* is established as *source*, whereas in the third stage of the drive circuit it also manifests as *goal*. In this sense, the *source* of the drive is associated with the orifices of the body in their manifestation as *biological sources of excitation* prior to their symbolic mediation. In contrast, the *goal* of the drive is associated with the orifices of the body in their manifestation as the *erogenous zones* following their symbolic mediation. Accordingly, by arguing that, in autism, the third stage of the drive circuit is not reached, we conclude

---

[46] Laznik argues that "as soon as one has passed through the third stage, there is *eros* in the second." In this sense, she implies that the closing of the circuit of the drive initiates the domain of desire in psychic reality—*eros*. She adds that, previous to the third stage of the drive, there is only the dimension of the drive object—of the death drive, *Tantalus* (Laznik, 2009, p. 54).

[47] Laznik is playing here on the similarity of the word "eros" and the "erotism" in "auto-erotism." Accordingly, "auto-erotism" without "eros"—namely, without the "erotism"—remains "autism."

that, in autism, the *rim* is lacking in its symbolic designation as *goal* but *not* as *source*. This would explain why autistic subjects are still disposed to unbearable intrusions of jouissance but have no capacity to mediate it using symbolic means. If we abide by this assumption, the previous hypothesis concerning autistic foreclosure can be slightly revised accordingly. It is *not* that autistic foreclosure radically excludes the *rim* of the drive circuit as a whole. Instead, *autistic foreclosure radically excludes the rim solely in its symbolic manifestation as goal and not as source*. Or, stated otherwise, *autistic foreclosure radically excludes the rim in its manifestation in the third stage of the invocatory drive circuit, hindering the inscription of the voice object in the Other.*

The Primacy of the Voice Object

In the aforementioned paper, Laznik (2009) delivers another hypothesis that is explicitly developed in her previous paper, *"La Voix Comme Premier Objet de la Pulsion Orale"* (2000). According to this hypothesis, the voice as a drive object has an identificatory role that is prior to that of the oral, anal, and scopic drives. According to Laznik:

> [The mirror] stage only comes about if there has previously been an experience of prosody in the mother's voice, or in the voice of some significant other. This experience will have allowed the infant to note his own presence as being the object cause of desire of this barred Other (that is to say, an Other marked by a lack). (Laznik, 2009, pp. 57–58; brackets added)

Going against several of Lacan's specifications in his conceptualization of the drive object presented in *Seminar X*, in this excerpt, Laznik claims that the closing of the circuit of the invocatory drive is a mandatory condition for the identification with the object of the mother's gaze in the mirror stage. In other words, Laznik argues that the inscription of invocatory jouissance in the third stage of the drive circuit is imperative for the establishment of the scopic drive circuit that plays a central role in the identification achieved in the mirror stage. This point is further substantiated in Laznik's earlier paper (2000) in which she promotes the idea that the most initial inscription of the subject in relation to the Other is achieved in the domain of the invocatory drive. She seems to adopt a developmental approach to the functioning of the drives—emphasizing the primary role of the oral drive in this progression—and suggests situating the voice object as the "primary object of the oral drive" (p. 1). Laznik bases herself on several studies that investigate early stages of linguistic acquisition among autistic infants (Cassel et al., 2013; Fernald & Simon, 1984; Mahdhaoui et al., 2009, 2011; Saint-Georges et al., 2013). In these studies, the researchers discover that infants demonstrate higher levels of oral activity when exposed to a specific form of motherly talk that they name *motherease.* They note that even when a newborn infant, who has not yet started breastfeeding (i.e., not yet learned the experience of oral satisfaction), hears the unique vocalization of *motherease*, it becomes more attentive and demonstrates suckling movements with its lips. Laznik claims that this demonstrates that the infant has a "hunger" for the mother's voice, even before the oral drive circuit has been established. Accordingly, she goes on to claim that it is the establishment of the circuit of the invocatory drive that enables the child to develop his oral tendencies (as well as anal and specular).[48]

Critique of Laznik's Dynamic Interpretation

Laznik provides an explanatory framework that accounts for the pervasiveness of autism at a very early age.[49] Nevertheless, several points of critique should be taken into account and incorporated into this framework. Firstly, as has been elaborated in Chap. 4, it is my contention that psychic mechanisms of *constitutive exclusion* are "reactive" and function "after the fact," meaning they take as their object of exclusion a signifying unit previously affirmed in the psyche. The symbolic affirmation of the

---

[48] Laznik (2000) also refers to the case of Marianne, a child that was born unable to devour food orally, but yet demonstrates the completion of the third stage of the invocatory drive circuit manifest in her linguistic functionality (pp. 5–7).

[49] The infant's lack of appeal to the caretaker, even in cases of hunger; the lack of crying; and an avoidance of eye contact from a very early age are all accounted for by several of the psychoanalysts mentioned in this book (Benoist, 2011; Laurent, 2012a, p. 91; Maleval, 2009, pp. 88, 96; Miller, 2010, p. 135).

rim of the drive is accomplished only retroactively after the third stage of the drive circuit. Accordingly, in opposition to Laznik, who claims that in autism the third stage of the drive circuit "is not reached" (Laznik, 2009, p. 54), it is my contention that the drive circuit must first reach its third stage in order for autistic foreclosure to operate. It is only after the initial instatement of the third stage of the drive circuit that autistic foreclosure can take the *rim* as its object and radically exclude its symbolic designation. Therefore, *I argue that the symbolic manifestation of the rim, as the product of the third stage of the invocatory drive circuit, can be designated as the object of autistic foreclosure only after the initial closing of this circuit.* After its initial inscription in the Other, this *rim* is foreclosed from the symbolic order as part of the subject's attempt to defend itself against the traumatic separation from the voice object.

Secondly, and very importantly, in her attribution of an initiatory function to the invocatory drive in the further instatement of the other drive circuits, it seems that Laznik adheres to a theory of the progressive maturation of the drives. Contrasting Laznik, it is important to note that Lacan opposes post-Freudian theories of sequential maturation of the drive.[50] Lacan explicitly argues that: "There is no relation of production between one of the partial drives and the next … [nor] the slightest relation of deduction or genesis. There is no natural metamorphosis of the oral drive into the anal drive" (SXI, p. 180; brackets added). Therefore, I argue that each of the domains of the drive entails a singular relation to jouissance and the Other. Furthermore, I contend that the partial drives materialize in each subject on the basis of its particular history and the unique ways in which it is inscribed in the Other as a sexuated being. Consequently, in contrast to Laznik, I maintain that we cannot assume that the "voice object is the primary object of the oral drive" (Laznik, 2000), let alone assume that it is situated earlier in a hypothesized sequence of the psychosexual development of the drives. On the other hand, we can assume that the circuit of the invocatory drive instates the function of *objet petit a* in relation to the Other in a singular way. It does so on the basis of the particularity of each subject's history that dictates

---

[50] As suggested by Karl Abraham (1925), who developed it into a corresponding theory of the development of the drive from the stage of polymorphous perversity to genital normality.

the way jouissance is inscribed in the body (Dravers, 2011, p. 10). This inscription is crucial for the establishment of the relationship between the subject and language and, due to its unique function, might have an effect on the functioning of other drive circuits.

Works Cited

Abraham, K. (1925). The Influence of Oral Erotism on Character-Formation. *International Journal of Psycho-Analysis, 6*, 247–258.

Aristotle. (1995). In J. Barnes (Ed.), *Organon, Complete Works of Aristotle.* Princeton, NJ: Princeton University Press.

Arnold, B. H. (2011). *Intuitive Concepts in Elementary Topology.* Mineola, NY: Dover Publications.

Benoist, V. (2011). L'Autre dans L'Autisme. *International Psychology, Practice and Research*, (2), 1–13.

Borgnis-Desbordes, E. (2009). Autisme, Transfert et Inventions Subjectives: Deux Cas. In J.-C. Maleval (Ed.), *L'autist, son double et ses objets* (pp. 101–114). Rennes, France: Presses Universitaires de Rennes.

Brenner, L. S. (2021). Is the Autistic Body a Body without Organs? In E. Daffron & B. Mclaughlin (Eds.), *The Body in Theory: Essays with Lacan and Foucault.* Chapel Hill, NC: McFarland Press & Company.

Brousse, M.-H. (1995). The Drive (II). In H. Sussman (Ed.), *Reading Seminar XI: Lacan's Four Fundamental Concepts of Psychoanalysis* (pp. 99–108). New York: SUNY Press.

Brousse, M.-H. (2007). Strange Objects, Immaterial Objects: Why Does Lacan Include the Voice and the Gaze in the Series of Freudian Objects. *International Lacanian Review*, 1–16.

Burgoyne, B. (2000). Autism and Topology. *Drawing the Soul: Schemas and Models in Psychoanalysis, 1*, 190–217.

Cassel, R. S., Saint-Georges, C., Mahdhaoui, A., Chetouani, M., Laznik, M. C., Muratori, F., et al. (2013). Course of Maternal Prosodic Incitation (Motherese) During Early Development in Autism: An Exploratory Home Movie Study. *Interaction Studies, 14*(3), 480–496.

Chiesa, L. (2006). Count-as-one, Forming-into-one, Unary Trait, S1. *Cosmos and History: The Journal of Natural and Social Philosophy, 2*(1–2), 68–93.

De Saussure, F. (1959). *Course in General Linguistics.* New York: Philosophical Library.

Deleuze, G. (1994). *Difference and Repetition*. New York: Columbia University Press.

Dolar, M. (1996). The Object Voice. In R. Salecl & S. Žižek (Eds.), *Gaze and Voice as Love Objects* (pp. 7–31). London: Duke University Press.

Dolar, M. (2006). *A Voice and Nothing More*. Cambridge, MA: MIT Press.

Dravers, P. (2011). The Drive as a Fundamental Concept of Psychoanalysis. *Psychoanalytical Notebooks*, (23), 117–149.

Fernald, A., & Simon, T. (1984). Expanded Intonation Contours in Mothers' Speech to Newborns. *Developmental Psychology*, *20*(1), 104–113.

Fink, B. (1997). *The Lacanian Subject: Between Language and Jouissance*. Princeton, NJ: Princeton University Press.

Freud, S. (1913). Totem and Taboo. In *The Standard Edition of the Complete Psychological Works of Sigmund Freud, Volume XIII (1913–1914): Totem and Taboo and Other Works* (pp. 7–162).

Freud, S. (1915a). Instincts and Their Vicissitudes. In *The Standard Edition of the Complete Psychological Works of Sigmund Freud, Volume XIV (1914–1916): On the History of the Psycho-Analytic Movement, Papers on Metapsychology and Other Works* (pp. 109–140).

Freud, S. (1915b). Repression. In *The Standard Edition of the Complete Psychological Works of Sigmund Freud, Volume XIV (1914–1916): On the History of the Psycho-Analytic Movement, Papers on Metapsychology and Other Works* (pp. 141–158).

Freud, S. (1921). Group Psychology and the Analysis of the Ego. In *The Standard Edition of the Complete Psychological Works of Sigmund Freud, Volume XVIII (1920–1922): Beyond the Pleasure Principle, Group Psychology and Other Works* (pp. 65–144).

Freud, S. (1924). The Dissolution of the Oedipus Complex. In *The Standard Edition of the Complete Psychological Works of Sigmund Freud, Volume XIX (1923–1925): The Ego and the Id and Other Works* (pp. 171–180).

Freud, S. (1950). Project for a Scientific Psychology (1950 [1895]). In *The Standard Edition of the Complete Psychological Works of Sigmund Freud, Volume I (1886–1899): Pre-Psycho-Analytic Publications and Unpublished Drafts* (pp. 281–391).

Friedman, M. (2016). Torus and Identification. In *Psychoanalysis: Topological Perspectives: New Conceptions of Geometry and Space in Freud and Lacan* (p. 153). Bielefeld, Germany: Transcript-Verlag.

Grandin, T. (2006). *Thinking in Pictures, Expanded Edition: My Life with Autism*. New York: Vintage.

Harari, R. (2013). *Lacan's Seminar on Anxiety: An Introduction.* New York: Other Press.

Heidegger, M. (1971). *Poetry, Language, Thought.* New York: HarperCollins.

Jakobson, R. (1960). Closing Statement: Linguistics and Poetics. In T. A. Seboeok (Ed.), *Style in Language.* Cambridge, MA: MIT Press.

Jakobson, R. (1971). Shifters, Verbal Categories, and the Russian Verb. In *Selected Writings, vol. II, Word and Language.* The Hague, Netherlands: Mouton.

Kanner, L. (1943). Autistic Disturbances of Affective Contact. *Nervous Child, 2*(3), 217–250.

Kanner, L. (1951). The Conception of Wholes and Parts in Early Infantile Autism. *American Journal of Psychiatry, 108*(1), 23–26.

Klein, M. (1930). The Importance of Symbol-Formation in the Development of the Ego. *The International Journal of Psycho-Analysis, 11*, 24–39.

Lacan, J. (1973). L'Étourdit. In *Autres Écrits* (pp. 449–496). Paris: Seuil.

Lacan, J. (1988). In J.-A. Miller (Ed.), *The Seminar of Jacques Lacan, Book I, Freud's Papers on Technique (1953–1954).* New York: Norton & Company.

Lacan, J. (1992). In J.-A. Miller (Ed.), *The Seminar, Book VII, The Ethics of Psychoanalysis (1959–1960).* New York: Norton & Company.

Lacan, J. (2001). In J.-A. Miller (Ed.), *The Seminar, Book XI, The Four Fundamental Concepts of Psychoanalysis (1964).* New York: Norton & Company.

Lacan, J. (2006). In B. Fink (Ed.), *Écrits.* New York: Norton & Company.

Lacan, J. (2007). In J.-A. Miller (Ed.), *The Seminar of Jacques Lacan, Book XVII, The Other Side of Psychoanalysis (1969–1970).* New York: Norton & Company. https://doi.org/10.2307/1347895

Lacan, J. (2008). *My Teaching.* London: Verso.

Lacan, J. (2014). In J. Miller (Ed.), *The Seminar of Jacques Lacan, Book X, Anxiety (1962–1963).* Cambridge, UK: Polity.

Lacan, J. (n.d.-a). *The Seminar of Jacques Lacan, Book IX, Identification (1961–1962).* Trans. Gallagher, C. Unpublished.

Lacan, J. (n.d.-b). *The Seminar, Book XII, Crucial Problems for Psychoanalysis (1964–1965).* Trans. Gallagher, C. Unpublished.

Lacan, J. (n.d.-c). *The Seminar, Book XXI, The Names-of-the-Father (1973–1974).* Trans. Gallagher, C. Unpublished.

Lacan, J. (n.d.-d). *The Seminar, Book XXIV, Final Sessions (1976–1977).* Trans. Gallagher, C. Unpublished.

Laplanche, J., & Leclaire, S. (1972). The Unconscious: A Psychoanalytic Study. *Yale French Studies,* (48), 118–175.

Laurent, É. (2012a). *La Bataille de l'Autisme*. Paris: Navarin.

Laurent, É. (2012b). Autism and Psychosis: Further Dialogue with Robert and Rosine Lefort Psychoanalytical Notebooks, (25), 11–26.

Laznik, M. C. (2000). La Voix Comme Premier Objet de la Pulsion Orale. Psychanalyse et Enfance Du Centre Alfred-Binet. *Paris*, 1–18.

Laznik, M. C. (2009). The Lacanian Theory of the Drive: An Examination of Possible Gains for Research in Autism. *Journal of the Centre for Freudian Analysis and Research, 19*, 79–91.

Leekam, S. R., Nieto, C., Libby, S. J., Wing, L., & Gould, J. (2007). Describing the Sensory Abnormalities of Children and Adults with Autism. *Journal of Autism and Developmental Disorders, 37*(5), 894–910.

Lefort, R., & Lefort, R. (1994). *Birth of the Other*. Oxford, UK: University of Illinois Press.

Lefort, R., & Lefort, R. (2003). *La Distinction de L'Autisme*. Paris: Seuil.

Mahdhaoui, A., Chetouani, M., Cassel, R. S., Saint-Georges, C., Parlato, E., Laznik, M. C., et al. (2011). Computerized Home Video Detection for Motherese May Help to Study Impaired Interaction Between Infants Who Become Autistic and Their Parents. *International Journal of Methods in Psychiatric Research, 20*(1), e6–e18.

Mahdhaoui, A., Chetouani, M., Zong, C., Cassel, R. S., Saint-Georges, C., Laznik, M.-C., et al. (2009). Automatic Motherese Detection for Face-To-Face Interaction Analysis. In *Multimodal Signals: Cognitive and Algorithmic Issues* (pp. 248–255). Springer.

Maleval, J.-C. (2003). L'Objet Autistique à la Machine: Les Suppléances du Signe. *Fabienne Hulak, Pensée Psychotique et Création de Systèmes, ERES « Hors Collection »*, 197–217.

Maleval, J.-C. (2009). *L'Autiste et sa Voix*. Paris: Seuil.

Maleval, J.-C. (2012). Why the Hypothesis of an Autistic Structure? *Psychoanalytical Notebooks, 25*, 27–49.

Maleval, J.-C. (2015). Extension du Spectre de l'Autisme. *L'évolution Psychiatrique, 90*, 764–781.

May, T. (1997). *Reconsidering Difference: Nancy, Derrida, Levinas, and Deleuze*. University Park, PA: Penn State Press.

Miller, J. (2010). *L'Avenir de L'Autisme*. Paris: Navarin.

Miller, J.-A. (1988). A Propos des Structures de la Psychose. In R. Lefort & R. Lefort (Eds.), *Les Structures de la psychose: L'enfant au loup et le Président*. Paris: Seuil.

Miller, J.-A. (1989). Jacques Lacan et la Voix. *La Voix*, 179–180.

Miller, J.-A. (2001). Lacan's Later Teaching. *Lacanian Ink, 20*, 4–41.

Miller, J.-A. (2007). La Matrice du Traitement de l'Enfant au Loup. *La Cause Freudienne, 2*(66), 141–151.

Miller, J.-A., & Laurent, É. (1998). The Other Which Does not Exist and Its Ethical Committees. *Almanac of Psychoanalysis*, (1), 15–35.

Muller, J. P., & Richardson, W. J. (1985). *Lacan and Language: A Reader's Guide to the Écrits*. New York: International Universities Press.

Quinet, A. (1992). Avoir un Corps. In *L'Enfnat et la Psychanalyse*. Paris: Eolia.

Ragland, E. (2004). *Logic of Sexuation, The: From Aristotle to Lacan*. New York: SUNY Press.

Recalcati, M. (2005). The Empty Subject: Un-Triggered Psychoses in the New Forms of the Symptom. *Lacanian Ink, 26*.

Reik, T. (1946). *Ritual: Psycho-Analytic Studies*. Oxford, UK: Farrar, Straus and Giroux.

Rey-Flaud, H. (2010). *Les Enfants de l'Indicible Peur: Nouveau Regard sur l'Autisme*. Paris: Flammarion/Aubier.

Saint-Georges, C., Chetouani, M., Cassel, R., Apicella, F., Mahdhaoui, A., Muratori, F., et al. (2013). Motherese in Interaction: At the Cross-Road of Emotion and Cognition? (A Systematic Review). *PloS One, 8*(10), e78103.

Sturrock, J. (1979). *Structuralism and Since: From Lévi-Strauss to Derrida*. Oxford, UK: Oxford University Press.

Tendlarz, S. E. (2003). *Childhood Psychosis: A Lacanian Perspective*. London: Karnac Books.

Tustin, F. (1986). *Autistic Barriers in Neurotic Patients*. London: Karnac Books.

Tustin, F. (1992). *The Protective Shell in Children and Adults*. London: Karnac Books.

Weisstein, E. W. (2013). "Ring Torus" & "Hole."

Žižek, S. (2006). Object a in Social Links. In J. Clemens & R. Grigg (Eds.), *Jacques Lacan and the Other Side of Psychoanalysis* (pp. 107–128). London: Duke University Press.

Žižek, S. (2012). *Less than Nothing: Hegel and the Shadow of Dialectical Materialism*. New York: Verso Books.

7

The Autistic Linguistic Spectrum

In the previous chapter, autistic foreclosure was explicated using the coordinates of Freud's model of repression as well as provided with several interpretations as to the nature of the object it radically excludes. This chapter will provide an account of the consequences of the functioning of autistic foreclosure on the structuration of the symbolic order and its relationship with the subject. As will be shortly presented, it will provide an account of the varying degrees of the unique autistic mode of access to language that is rooted in a fundamental refusal of the domain of signifiers. The first section of this chapter will provide an account of the autistic lack of access to the locus of the Other that is commonly associated with the psychoanalytic notion that in autism "there is no Other." The second section will unravel a comprehensive account of the notion of the "sign" in Lacan's teaching and its distinction from the "signifier." On the basis of this distinction, the unique autistic mode of access to language will be associated with the subjective recourse to the sign. The final section will provide an integrative model through which the varying degrees of autistic linguistic functionality can be understood. This section will provide an alternative framework for the understanding of the varying degrees of symptomatic severity confronted in the clinic of

© The Author(s) 2020
L. S. Brenner, *The Autistic Subject*, The Palgrave Lacan Series,
https://doi.org/10.1007/978-3-030-50715-2_7

autism—commonly designated today, in the psychiatric domain, on the "autism spectrum" (APA, 2013). The conclusions reached in this chapter, alongside those reached in the previous chapters, will provide compelling evidence for the designation of autism as a singular subjective structure in the final chapter of this book.

There Is No Other in Autism

One of the most well-known Lacanian psychoanalytic observations regarding the autistic subjective structure is the fact that in autism "there is no Other." The number of available accounts of this defining characteristic is vast among Lacan's followers. For instance, in his paper "L'Autre dans L'Autisme" (2011), Benoist explicitly argues that "the assertion that 'there is no Other' defines the structure of autism in general" (p. 5). Laurent, in *La Bataille de l'Autisme* (2012a), proposes that, in autism, "The Other can 'be there' and, at the same time, have no existence for a subject … as 'the Other that does not exist' " (p. 29). The Leforts, who are considered to be the ones to have inaugurated the formula presented above, provide in *La Distinction de la Autisme* (2003) several formulations for this psychoanalytic notion. One of the most poignant formulations is worth quoting at length:

> The fundamental etiological point of this structure is that there is no Other for it. In the transference, I am there and I do not exist as the Other, whether it is the Other of the image, the Other of the signifier, or the Other that is the bearer of the object. (p. 14)

In this compelling excerpt, the Leforts assert that the Other does not exist for the autistic subject in three different modalities. They claim that, in autism, there is no Other of the image—nothing from the Other is reflected in the mirror. They argue that there is no Other of the signifier—the signifier shows no signs of alterity. Finally, they argue that there is no Other in relation to which the drive object can be inscribed. Let us then attempt to understand how the lack of the Other in the three afore-mentioned modalities can be related to the functioning of autistic fore-closure presented in the previous chapter.

No Other of the Image

The Leforts' notion of the "Other of the image" can be associated with the locus in which the subject's specular image is inscribed in the course of its imaginary identification in the mirror stage (É, pp. 75–81).[1] In this sense, the Other of the image would be described as the place from which the (lower-case) other, or the specular image, is reflected—corresponding with the symbolic inscription of the ideal ego and the ego-ideal in Lacan's account of the subject's identification (SI, p. 125).[2] Appropriately, Laurent (2012a) attributes this setback in the subject's identification in the mirror stage to a failure on the level of the imaginary register, arguing that "autistic subjects undermine any imaginary identification" (p. 39). A compelling account of the autistic setback in imaginary identification can be found in Lacan's *Seminar I: Freud's Papers on Technique (1953–1954)*, in a section devoted to the case of "Little Dick," provided by Melanie Klein (1930).[3] In relation to Dick's access to the dimension of identifica-tion, Lacan argues that "Dick cannot even engage in the first sort of identification, which would already be an essay in symbolism. He is, paradoxical as it may seem to say it, eyeball to eyeball with reality, he lives in reality" (SI, p. 69). In this excerpt, Lacan argues that Dick has no access to the most initial form of identification and thus loses all access to the symbolic order through which reality is mediated. In the previous chapter, I have argued that instead of achieving an identification on the imaginary or symbolic level, Dick identifies with the void in the real—the product of autistic foreclosure—thus bringing about the structuration of autistic psychic reality. Accordingly, the Leforts'

---

[1] It is important to note that the Leforts use the upper-case Other. Accordingly, I infer that they are not implying that the specular image is directly lacking in autism but the place from which it is inscribed or reflected, that is, the Other as mirror.

[2] Both the ideal ego and ego-ideal are lacking in autism according to the Leforts (2003, pp. 34–35).

[3] See more on the case of Little Dick in Chap. 6.

contention that in autism the Other of the image is lacking can be understood as being rooted in the functioning of autistic foreclosure that gives rise to a crucial setback in the subject's imaginary identification, radically hindering its access to symbolic identification and the function of the symbolic order in the mediation of reality.

No Other as the Bearer of the Object

The Leforts' notion of the "Other that is the bearer of the object" can be associated with the locus in which the drive object is symbolically inscribed. As I have already elaborated in the previous chapter, autistic foreclosure hinders the functioning of the drive circuit by radically excluding the symbolic inscription of the . The foreclosure of the rim originates in the subject's refusal to yield the jouissance of the drive to the Other. By refusing to inscribe the jouissance of the drive in the Other, the subject revokes the function of the Other as the bearer of the drive object. According to Maleval (2009), in autism, the function of the Other is specifically revoked in its role as the bearer of the object of the invocatory drive (pp. 81, 85). Accordingly, the Leforts' contention that in autism the Other that is the bearer of the object is lacking can be understood as being rooted in the functioning of autistic foreclosure that hinders the inscription of the drive object in the Other and, thus, gives rise to a failure in the drive circuit in general and the invocatory drive circuit in particular.

No Other of the Signifier

The Leforts' notion of the "Other of the signifier" can be associated with Lacan's diversified account of the big Other as the locus of language, the intersubjective domain of human culture, and, finally, the Freudian unconscious (Chiesa, 2007, p. 35). Let us address these three modalities of the Other in relation to autistic foreclosure and its effect on their functioning in autism.

No Other as Language

According to Lacan, language precedes the existence of an individual in the sense that it exists before he or she is born and subsists after his or her death. As Fink emphasizes in his book *The Lacanian Subject* (1997), before a child is born, he or she is already endowed with a name as well as assigned with a personality, all of which are imagined by his or her parents through their use of signifiers. These signifiers—used to endow the child with an existence in language—are not uniquely invented by the parents but are acquired from a symbolic order that has been accumulating for centuries preceding his or her conception (p. 5). This system of signifiers is governed by a set of laws and is determined by Lacan as the "Other of language" (SVI, p. 226).[4]

The problems autistic subjects have with the acquisition and management of language are well documented and vastly accounted for. In the Lacanian field, these problems are attributed to the subject's refusal to being alienated in the signifier (Lefort & Lefort, 2003, pp. 27, 52, 56; Maleval, 2009, pp. 81, 88, 90)[5] as well as a failure of the initial form of identification enabling access to the dimension of the signifier (SI, p. 69; Lefort & Lefort, 2003, pp. 66, 102, 169; Maleval, 2009, pp. 81–83, 92, 215; Laurent, 2012a, p. 39). The setback in alienation and identification with the signifier significantly restricts the autistic subject's mode of access to the Other of language and, as a result, interferes with the capacity of the symbolic order to mediate the subject's reality through the use of signifiers. This crucial setback persists from a very early age, manifesting in the poverty of babbling (Maleval, 2018b, pp. 7–9) as well as in the fact that autistic infants make no verbal appeals to their caretakers (crying, for instance) in order to pacify their needs (Maleval, 2009, pp. 97–99; 2015; Miller, 2010, p. 135). In the previous chapters, I have associated the aforementioned with the functioning of autistic foreclosure, a foreclosure

---

[4] In his paper "The Signification of the Phallus," Lacan associates these laws with the metonymic and metaphoric axes that govern the interactions between signifiers (É, p. 578).

[5] This refusal is not to be understood in terms of a casual choice between two options but associated with the voluntary dimension Freud (1894) attributes to repression (SE III, p. 46) or with Lacan's account of the forced choice (SXI, p. 212).

that hinders the subject's recourse to the symbolic order on a level preceding that of the "minimal" signification achieved in *Bejahung*.

No Other as Culture

Another crucial aspect of the "Other of the signifier" is its role in instating the laws that determine what can and cannot be openly articulated in language, in other words, its role in determining which signifiers can be conscious, and which must be repressed (Chiesa, 2007, p. 101). These laws materialize in the cultural norms governing intersubjective reality. The Other thus creates order in the intersubjective domain, enabling the members of a culture to be invested in a shared sense of the coherence of the world. Lacan argues that the symbolic cultural laws cannot be reduced to the linguistic laws governing the interaction between signifiers. He claims that this is most evident in the Oedipus complex where the prohibition of incest instates something in the psyche that is independent of the dimension of the laws of metonymy and metaphor (É, p. 576).

As a result of autistic foreclosure, the autistic subject loses access to the dimension of the cultural norms in the Other. Without access to this dimension, autistic subjects have great difficulty in entering the social bond and commonly find themselves outside the scope of social exchange (Maleval, 2009, pp. 105, 216; 2015, p. 772; Laurent, 2012a, p. 75). In the most severe cases, the autistic detachment from the social bond can manifest in a state of complete solitude starting from a very early age. This state entails a complete disregard of the presence of those surrounding the child, including his or her caretakers. These would be children who do not express interest in being close to or loved by their parents—never meeting the eyes of others, avoiding their gaze at all costs, and never crying in distress (Lefort & Lefort, 2003, pp. 14, 92; Maleval, 2009, pp. 97–99, 107; 2011, p. 79, 81). In some cases, autistic children grow up to be completely engulfed in their own shell, unable to acknowledge the presence of others. Correspondingly, Kanner (1943) notes that for autistic subjects a "profound aloneness dominates all behavior" (p. 247), that is, "an *extreme autistic aloneness* that, whenever possible, disregards, ignores, shuts out anything that comes to the child from the outside" (p. 242).

No Other as the Locus of the Unconscious

Lacan bestows on the signifier a crucial role in the constitution and functioning of the unconscious: "The unconscious is fundamentally structured, woven, chained, meshed, by language. And not only does the signifier play as big a role there as the signified does but it plays the fundamental role" (SIII, p. 119). In his paper "The Signification of the Phallus," Lacan even goes on to claim that the function of the signifier is the only way to truly grasp what Freud has anticipated in his account of the unconscious (É, p. 578). Being composed of signifiers, the unconscious functions according to the linguistic laws that govern their interrelations: "laws that govern this other scene, which Freud … designates as the scene of the unconscious" (p. 578).

Because autistic foreclosure diminishes the subject's access to the dimension of the signifier, it seems to necessitate a critical re-assessment of the general definition of the unconscious when it has to do with autistic subjects. First, because Lacan characterizes the unconscious as fundamentally dependent on the use of signifiers, one might speculate that autistic subjects have no unconscious. Nevertheless, Lacan also describes the unconscious as being "structured like a language" (SXI, p. 20). In this sense, one can speculate that the autistic unconscious is structured like a language that is not composed of signifiers but is composed of other linguistic units. As will be elaborated in the following section, these linguistic units are "signs." In cases where signs are organized into a linguistic network, they construct what later in this chapter will be called the "supplementary" or "synthetic Other." Accordingly, I propose that the synthetic Other—as the locus of the sign—can be considered as the support for a different mode of linguistic functionality that underlies the workings of the autistic unconscious. Second, it is a very basic Freudian (1925) principle that dictates that, in order for there to be an unconscious, there must be repression (SE XIX, p. 236). In the previous chapters, I have argued that the autistic subject is constituted on the basis of a more "radical" form of foreclosure than we see in psychosis. I have demonstrated that this foreclosure hinders the functioning of repression on all of its levels. And indeed, Maleval (2009) agrees that in autism there is a total "absence of repression" (p. 211).[6] With no repression, not even primal repression, the subject is not rendered as split between consciousness and the unconscious. Therefore, if we assume that there is an autistic unconscious, we infer that it is always accessible to consciousness—brought "out into the open" (*à ciel ouvert*) (SIII, p. 59). Correspondingly, in her autobiographical book about autism, Temple Grandin (2006) contends: "Since I think with the subconscious, repression does not occur and denial is impossible. My search engine has access to the entire library of detailed sensory based memories" (p. 219). Grandin's testimony is further corroborated by Lefort and Lefort (2010) who argues that, in autism, "the sexual reality of the unconscious is read as an open book and passes to the front of the stage: the unconscious is there and no longer functions as such" (p. 144).

The autistic unconscious, being structured like a language but not being split from consciousness, can be topologically represented. Commonly, Lacan is considered to associate the Möbius strip with the topological representation of the Freudian unconscious (SXIV, 24.12.76). Alternatively, the autistic unconscious can be topologically represented by the torus. Both of the above-mentioned topological figures are composed of one surface. On the surface of the Möbius strip, every point seems to designate an interior and exterior while actually being composed of only one surface. This represents the "extimate" relationship between consciousness and the unconscious as well as their inherent distinction. In contrast, on the surface of the torus, there is no such distinction between the interior and the exterior. According to Laurent (2012b), from the vantage point of its surface, looking into the hole of the torus entails looking outside of it—looping on the inside, ad infinitum. This fusion between the interior and the exterior on the surface of the torus can be said to provide a more accurate topological representation of the autistic unconscious where "the interior and the exterior of the torus circle are always exterior" (p. 18).

In summary, we see that as a result of autistic foreclosure the subject loses access to the Other in all of its symbolic modalities. Accordingly, in

---

[6] Maleval (2015) also argues that the autistic propensity for memorization attests to this absence (p. 776)

autism we say that there is no Other through whom the image is inscribed; no Other who is the bearer of the drive object and the mediator of jouissance; no Other as language; no symbolic Other giving access to the social bond; and no unconscious composed of signifiers and split from consciousness.

Autistic Sign Language—"Rather Verbose"

Abnormalities in language and speech development are considered to be a defining feature characterizing subjects who are diagnosed today as autistic. Accordingly, a very common misconception about autism states that some autistic subjects never enter language (Maleval, 2009, p. 75; 2011, p. 77). Conversely, in the Lacanian field, even though they are considered to have no access to the domain of signifiers, autistic subjects are not deemed to be "out-of-language" (Maleval, 2009, p. 99), not "exiled from language" (Maleval, 2012, p. 37). Borrowing a term coined by Lacan (1989) in one of his only explicit accounts of autism, autistic subjects are viewed as being "rather verbose" (p. 20).

Lacan's Assertion of Autistic Verbosity

Lacan never addressed the subject of autism explicitly in his seminars or printed papers. Nevertheless, he provided us with two explicit accounts of autism in two different conferences that took place in 1975. In both of these conferences, Lacan's remarks on the subject of autism were brief and conveyed one crucial point: autistic subjects are subjects of language.

In a symposium held in the city of Geneva in 1975, entitled "The Symptom," Lacan explicitly addresses the subject of autism for the first time. In the course of his lecture, Lacan presents his account of the "speaking being" (*parlêtre*) (SXXIII, p. 27). He insists that the essential nature of the subject in psychoanalysis is to be found in its relationship with language—its receptiveness to the field of the Other. Lacan (1989) adds that, while this receptiveness is associated with the mother's voice, it is not restricted to the auditory field and, more than anything, implies a receptiveness to the signifier (p. 19).

In response to this argument, Lacan is questioned by several members of the audience. One question directly addresses the subject of autism, claiming that autistic subjects do not seem to hear anything around them in the sense that they lack a receptiveness to the signifier: "I was thinking of autism, for instance. This would be a case in which the receiver is not in place, and in which hearing doesn't work" (p. 19 [A question posed by a member of the audience]). In response, Lacan gives the following answer:

As the name indicates, autistics hear themselves. They hear lots of things. Normally this even leads to hallucination, and hallucinations have always a more or less vocal character. Not all autistics hear voices, but they articulate lots of things, and what they articulate, it is a matter of discovering where they heard it. (p. 19)

Lacan continues and insists that if it seems that autistic subjects do not hear us, it is only because: "They don't manage to hear what you have to say to them, in so far as you are caring for them ... But, in the end, surely there is something to say to them" (p. 20). Lacan agrees that something is "frozen" in autistic language (same as in the case of psychosis) but that this does not mean that autistic subjects are divorced from language—that they are not speaking beings:

It is a matter of knowing why there is something in the autistic or in the schizophrenic which freezes, if I can put it like that. But you can't say that he doesn't speak. That you have trouble hearing, grasping the point of what they say, doesn't prevent these people from being rather verbose. (p. 20)

With these remarks, Lacan provides the us with an imperative. By claiming that autistic subjects are "rather verbose," Lacan not only determines them as subjects under the mark of the speaking being but also implies that psychoanalysts can ameliorate their suffering in the clinic through the mediation of language but not necessarily through speech.[7]

---

[7] The distinction between language and speech is presented by Lacan in *Seminar I*, in his account of the case of Little Dick. In a passage concerning Dick's linguistic functionality, Lacan argues that

As will be presented in the following sections, the work with autistic subjects in the Lacanian clinic entails an engagement with objects that is
supported by language but does not involve speaking of one's suffering
and receiving interpretations.

The second and last time Lacan explicitly addressed the subject of
autism was in a conference at Columbia University in the year 1975,
titled "Conferences and Conversations at North American Universities."[8]
In this lecture, Lacan (1975) addresses the relationship between the autistic subject and language in the following way:

> There are some for whom saying words is not easy. One calls this autism.
> This is a bit hastily said. It is not necessarily that. They are simply people
> for whom the weight of words is very serious and who are not disposed to
> take their ease with these words. (p. 3)

Here Lacan once again insists that autistic subjects are subjects of language. He argues that they have access to words but have some difficulties
using them. Accordingly, he implies that there is something about their
relationship with language that is difficult for them to handle. By using
the specific term "words," Lacan could be implying that the singular relationship autistic subjects have with language is not dependent on "signifiers" but on other linguistic units which stand in for complete words
(these will be associated with "signs" in the following section).[9]

Clinical Evidence for Autistic Verbosity

Statistically speaking, more than half of the children diagnosed today as
being on the "autism spectrum" present some sort of verbalization at a
young age (Pickett, Pullara, O'grady, & Gordon, 2009). These numbers
were already attested for in Kanner's (1943) and Asperger's (1991)

"Language and speech are not the same thing—this child is, up to a certain point, a master of
language, but he doesn't speak" (p. 84).

[8] This lecture was published in French and translated to English by Jack W. Stone but not published.

[9] Already in his account of the case of the Wolf-Child, Lacan refers to the linguistic units at his
disposal as words that are essentially speech reduced down to its core (SI, p. 104).

inaugural studies, in which the majority of autistic children and adults under their care could use and understand language. From the age of six months, most autistic children display some forms of babbling, but of an atypical nature: they are low in frequency, poorly coordinated with the gaze, less socially oriented, appear monotonous, and lack enthusiasm and intention (Maleval, 2018b, p. 42). After the age of five years, children diagnosed on the lower end of the autism spectrum usually display forms of ritualistic vocalizations, sounds accompanying "stereotypy" (stereotypical behavior),[10] "echolalia,"[11] and other forms of controlled verbalization. These are all verbalizations that are not implemented by autistic children for communication but are aimed solely at achieving a personal and solitary form of vocal satisfaction (Baggs, 2007). In less severe cases, we see autistic individuals who regularly utilize unique forms of speech. These forms of speech are indirect, artificial, non-expressive of affect as well as displaying difficulties with intonation, pitch, speed, fluency, and emphasis on words. In these cases, autistic subjects use language in order to interact with other people as well as to progress in a variety of occupational fields.

But how can a subject utilize language when all access to the Other has been foreclosed? Under these circumstances, how can a child gain access to the dimension of the signifier? In his book *L'Autiste et sa Voix* (2009), Maleval provides a possible answer to these questions: "Not being fully disposed to the signifier, the autistic seems to develop the resources he can draw from the sign" (p. 185).[12] Therefore, Maleval argues that the autistic subject's "entry into language is made by the assimilation of signs" (p. 95)—that autistic language is a "sign language" and not a language composed of signifiers.[13] Before elaborating on the exact effects autistic

---

[10] Repetitive behavior which includes tapping of ears, snapping fingers, and vocalizations.

[11] Senseless repetition of words or syllables.

[12] It is interesting to note that in Lacan's (1989) lecture on the symptom, right after referring to the autistic mode of language, he addresses the "sign language" adopted by deaf and mute individuals (p. 20).

[13] It should be noted that, since the publication of *L'Autiste et sa Voix* in 2009, Maleval had softened his approach regarding the autistic sole recourse to the sign. For instance, in a paper from 2018, Maleval argues that autistic subjects do have a passive and reduced mode of access to the domain of signifiers (Maleval, 2018b, pp. 43–44). However, in this book, I preserve Maleval's initial hypothesis and provide it with further supports.

foreclosure has on autistic linguistic functionality in the next section, let us begin by reviewing the semiotic roots of the conception of the sign and then go on to present Lacan's adaptation of these roots in his renewed distinction between the sign and the signifier. This will lead us to the next section that will present Maleval's further contribution to Lacan's conception of the sign based on his work with autistic subjects.

The Signifier and the Sign

The Semiotic Roots of Lacan's Conception of the Sign

Charles Sanders Peirce's "Sign Theory" or "Semiotics" comes to account for the signification, representation, reference, and meaning established through the use of signs in language (Atkin, 2013). Peirce defines the most basic structure of the sign in the following way: "I define a sign as anything which is so determined by something else, called its object, and so determines an effect upon a person, which effect I call its interpretant, that the latter is thereby mediately determined by the former" (Peirce, 1977, p. 80). In this excerpt, Peirce argues that the signification inherent to the functioning of the sign structurally entails three distinct elements. The first element is a sign in its sensory form (*representamen*).[14] The representamen could be a written word, an image, or even the sight or smell of smoke (signaling a fire). The second element is the *object*, which is whatever the representamen refers to. Peirce emphasizes that the object is not identical to a "real" object in the world but is based on approximate knowledge of an object and is thus called a "semiotic object." A semiotic object could be the concept to which a written word refers, or, yet again, the notion of fire evoked by the sight or smell of smoke. The third element is the *interpretant*. According to Peirce, the interpretant is the agent mediating between the representamen and the object. It is only through its interpretation that signification can be achieved in the structure of the sign. According to Peirce, the interrelation between these three elements

---

[14] It should be noted that Peirce provides several other terms in order to differentiate the sign as a signifying element from the sign as a structure entailing a multiplicity of elements. These are "representamen," "representation," and "ground."

is the bedrock of the capacity of language to signify meaning. As I will shortly demonstrate, it is captured by Lacan's famous aphorism in which he classifies a sign as that which "represents something for someone" (SXI, p. 207).

Peirce (1982) classifies three distinct types of signs—the icon, the index, and the symbol. The icon is a sign that refers to a semiotic object by virtue of its resemblance or similarity to one of its visual qualities (color, tone, brightness, etc.). This could be the way a portrait is associated with the person it depicts, or the way the figure on a sign on the door of a restroom resembles the male/female form.[15] The index is a sign that refers to a semiotic object through a necessary causal relationship or physical connection. That could be the way a weathercock is associated with the direction of the wind or the way smoke is associated with fire. The symbol is a sign that refers to a semiotic object by virtue of some observed or general social convention. This means that a symbol does not entail any necessary resemblance or natural link with its semiotic object and, thus, necessitates the appropriation of the intersubjective cultural context that grounds their relationship (pp. 53–56). Symbols would be words such as *homme* and "man" associated with the same semiotic object as well as the name "google" signifying the global corporation as well as the act of searching for information on the internet.

In his account of the sign, Lacan appropriates the framework provided by Peirce and augments it with his understanding of Ferdinand de Saussure's account of the signifier. According to de Saussure (1959), the "sign" is the most basic unit in language and is composed of two elements—a conceptual element (concept) designated as the "signified" and a phonological element (sound-image) designated as the "signifier." De Saussure illustrates the relationship between these two elements in a diagram representing their structural unity—see Fig. 7.1.

According to de Saussure, there is no natural connection between a signifier and a signified. For instance, the word "cat" does not have any immediate relationship to anything "cat-like" in the world or to the concept "cat." Thus, while the bond between a signifier and a signified might

---

[15] This resemblance is debatable, as Lacan suggests in "The Instance of the Letter in the Unconscious" (É, pp. 416–418).

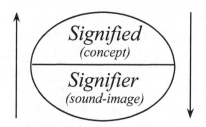

Fig. 7.1   De Saussure's illustration of the relationship between the signifier and the signified. (Based on De Saussure 1959, p. 66)

seem unbreakable after it has been established in a specific language, it is—in its essence—utterly arbitrary and changes with time.[16]

Peirce and de Saussure are considered to be the founding fathers of the field of semiotics. Nevertheless, while similarities can be drawn between the frameworks they present, they are definitely not identical. On the one hand, both thinkers designate the sign as the most basic unit in language as well as identify two corresponding aspects inherent to it—a representamen or a signifier; and a semiotic-object or a signified. Moreover, both thinkers attest to the strict psychological dimension characterizing these two elements and do not confuse the semiotic-object or signified with actual objects in the world. On the other hand, Peirce identifies the additional dimension of the interpretant inherent to the structure of the sign. This dimension provides three different classifications of the interpretive procedure that dictate a different relationship between the representamen and the semiotic-object—the icon, the index, and the symbol. In contrast, de Saussure describes the relationship between the signifier and the signified as being strictly rooted in the natural course of development of a language along its history.

Lacan's Adaptation of Semiotics

Lacan bases his account of the signifier and the sign on the framework provided by Peirce and de Saussure while generously augmenting selected parts in both. One of Lacan's first major augmentations of Peirce and de

---

[16] This is marked in Fig. 7.1 by the horizontal line splitting the signifier from the signified.

Saussure's semiotics is drawing a clear distinction between the signifier and the sign. More specifically, while for de Saussure the signifier is considered to be a component of the sign, for Lacan, the signifier and the sign are designated as two distinct linguistic units with different characteristics. Diverting his focus to the functioning of the signifier in the production of the signified, Lacan classifies it as the most fundamental signifying unit in a natural language instead of the sign (SIII, pp. 119–120). He relegates the figure of the sign to the rank of a signifying unit that embodies the direct biunivocal relationship between an index and a referent, a unit more akin to Peirce's understanding of the sign. As a result, Lacan argues that—unlike the signifier—the sign does not characterize the way in which a natural language functions (p. 167) but is habitually used in more instinctive forms of communication—for instance, the way a certain color can automatically trigger a certain sexual response among animals (É, p. 77).

Robinson Crusoe

Lacan's most comprehensive account of the distinction between the signifier and the sign can be found in *Seminar III: The Psychoses (1955–1956)*. In a compelling session of the seminar, in which Lacan depicts a scene from Daniel Defoe's *Robinson Crusoe* (1719), he elaborates on his assertion that "the signifier has its own coherence and nature which distinguish it from every other species of sign" (p. 167). Several passages from this session are worth quoting at length and will be explored in the following section:

> Let's begin with the biological sign. In the very structure, in the morphology, of animals there is something that has this captivating value due to which its receiver, who sees the red of the robin redbreast for instance, and who is made for receiving it, undertakes a series of actions or henceforth unitary behavior that links the bearer of this sign to its perceiver. Here you have what gives us a precise idea of what may be called natural meaning. Without otherwise seeking how this might take place in man, it is clear that by means of a series of transitions we can manage to purify, neutralize, the natural sign. (p. 167)

In this introductory passage, Lacan argues that, contrary to the signi-fier, the "biological sign" refers to its (semiotic) object through a "natural" relationship. Lacan associates this "natural sign" with an instinctual code language used in the interaction between animals and their environment. He provides an example in which the relationship between a sign (the red breast of the robin) and the appropriate reaction (mating behavior) is hardwired into the robin's biology. He argues that, in this domain, mean-ing has no ambiguity—a natural sign demonstrates there is a direct equivalency between the sign and its referent.[17] Lacan continues:

> Then there is the trace, the footprint in the sand, the sign about which Robinson Crusoe makes no mistake. Here sign and object separate. The trace, in its negative aspect, draws the natural sign to a limit at which it becomes evanescent. The distinction between sign and object is quite clear here, since the trace is precisely what the object leaves behind once it has gone off somewhere else. Objectively there is no need for any subject to recognize a sign for it to be there—a trace exists even if there is nobody to look at it. (p. 167)

Lacan continues by addressing a "transitive" relationship between a sign and its referent. In comparison to the direct relationship between the sign and the object in the example of the "natural sign," the *trace sign*—described in this passage—entails a transitive relationship between a sign (A), functioning as a trace (B) of an effaced object (C). In other words, Lacan argues that in the domain of the trace sign, an object is not directly indicated by the sign but is mediated by a trace entailing a necessary rela-tionship with an effaced object. Lacan provides the example of the foot-print on the sand, which is a sign that there is another man somewhere on Robinson Crusoe's island (Friday). Lacan emphasizes that with the trace sign we are still not in the domain of the signifier and insists that it does not necessarily indicate the presence of any subject. Finally, Lacan concludes:

---

[17] The automatic reaction of animals to visual cues is mentioned by Lacan as early as in his paper on the mirror stage printed in *Écrits* (2006, pp. 75–81).

When have we passed over into the order of the signifier? The signifier may extend over many of the elements within the domain of the sign. But the signifier is a sign that doesn't refer to any object, not even to one in the form of a trace, even though the trace nevertheless heralds the signifier's essential feature. It, too, is the sign of an absence. But insofar as it forms part of language, the signifier is a sign which refers to another sign, which is as such structured to signify the absence of another sign, in other words, to be opposed to it in a couple. (p. 167)

In this final passage, Lacan provides one of his most explicit distinctions between the signifier and the sign. He argues that although the signifier shares with the trace sign the absence of the object as one of its fundamental features, it is qualitatively distinct. That is to say that the trace sign conveys meaning on the basis of the absence of an actual referent—a foot of a man, Friday—while the signifier does not require a semiotic object as its absent referent in order to convey meaning. That is because, according to de Saussure, in the process of signification, a signifier engenders meaning strictly through its differential relationships with other signifiers; all of which, when standing by themselves, are absent of meaning (pp. 32, 54, 119, 167).[18]

In this sense, Lacan (1977) argues that the signifier always entails "the murder of the thing" (p. 104); for, the signifier is radically independent of the function of the referent in its capacity for signification. In contrast to this, Maleval (2012) adds: "A major characteristic of such signs is that they do not totally efface the thing designated, since they remain in a relation of similarity or contiguity with them. The referent of signs can be found in the world of things" (p. 41). In this sense, we see that, in opposition to the signifier, the sign is a linguistic unit that does not allow the murder of the thing (Maleval, 2009, p. 218).

Going back to Peirce's distinction between the icon, index, and symbol, Maleval adds that Peirce's account of the icon and the index can be associated with the newly contrived definition of the Lacanian "natural sign" and trace sign, respectively. The direct connection between the "natural sign" and its object is akin to Peirce's account of the iconic sign, in

---

[18] See more on Lacan's account of the function of differential relationships between signifiers in the process of signification in Chap. 6.

which a painting functions as a sign for the painted character. Correspondingly, the indirect, but necessary, relationship between the trace sign and its effaced object is akin to Peirce's account of the indexical sign, in which smoke functions as a sign for fire in its absence. Finally, it is Peirce's account of the symbol, in its capacity for abstraction as well as its arbitrary and changing character, that can be partially associated with Lacan's interpretation of the signifier (p. 184).

The arbitrary character of the symbol in its re-adaptation in the relationship between the signifier and the signified is further developed by Lacan in *Seminar VI: Desire and Its Interpretation (1958–1959)*. In this seminar, Lacan returns to his depiction of the scene from the book *Robinson Crusoe*:

> I spoke to you about Robinson Crusoe and the trace of Friday's footstep. Is that trace already a signifier? I told you that the signifier begins not with a trace, but with the fact that one effaces the trace. Nevertheless, an effaced trace does not constitute a signifier. What inaugurates the signifier is the fact that it is posited as capable of being effaced. Stated otherwise, Robinson Crusoe effaces the trace of Friday's footstep, but what does he put in its place? If he wishes to remember where Friday's foot was, at the very least he makes a cross at that spot—in other words, a bar [or: line, *barre*] and another bar on top of that one. This is what specifies the signifier. The signifier presents itself both as being able to be effaced and as being able, in the very operation of effacement, to subsist as such. (SVI, p. 80; brackets added)

In this excerpt, Lacan adds another layer to his distinction between the signifier and the sign. According to Lacan, in a case in which Robinson Crusoe encounters the trace sign in the form of the footprint and then proceeds to erase this sign and inscribe in its place an arbitrary marker (a cross), this would entail an entry into the domain of the signifier.[19] Lacan implies that what makes the cross a signifier rather than a sign is the fact that its relation to the signified is completely arbitrary. The signifier does not need to look like a foot or have any necessary relation to the presence

---

[19] Lacan provides a further account of Crusoe's effacing of the footprint and marking of the cross in its place in *Seminar V: The Formations of the Unconscious (1957–1958)*, p. 322.

of a man on the island in order to signify something. In order to do so it only necessitates a relationship to another signifier. This is, emphasized yet again, due to the fact that signifiers engender meaning strictly through their differential relationships with other signifiers. The sign, on the other hand, entails a permanent and necessary relationship between the representamen and the semiotic-object in order to convey meaning for the interpretant.

The Subject and Someone

Another crucial aspect in Lacan's distinction between the signifier and the sign is their different relationship with the subject. Two of Lacan's formulations provide its exact designation: "the signifier is not the sign … The signifier, as I told you, is, contrary to the sign which represents something for someone, what represents the subject for another signifier" (SIX, 27.2.67). The definition of the sign as that which "represents something for someone" and the definition of the signifier as that which "represents the subject for another signifier" are canonical in Lacan's corpus and reappear extensively in his seminars and printed papers. As will be immediately demonstrated, the difference in phrasing is key to the understanding of their distinction.

Let us begin with Lacan's definition of the signifier. According to Lacan, the signifier is unique in its capacity to represent a *subject* for another *signifier*. As already presented in the previous chapters, according to Lacan, the subject in psychoanalysis is constituted in the encounter between language and jouissance. It is in this encounter that primal repression takes place and constructs the subject's relation to the symbolic order as well as provides the means for the mediation of jouissance. By doing so, it also introduces the subject as divided between consciousness and the unconscious. In his paper "Position of the Unconscious," printed in *Écrits* (2006), Lacan strictly associates this division with the function of the signifier. Basing himself on Freud, he argues that this division establishes a distinction between the subject as it is presented in conscious discourse and the subject in its manifestation in the structure of all unconscious formations (p. 269). The fact that the signifier introduces this division in the subject implies that it represents a subject for another signifier in two distinct ways. The first is associated with the subject as it is presented in Lacan's account of the "subject of the statement." As I have already argued in the previous chapter, Lacan determines the subject of the statement as the conscious subject in so far as it thinks of itself under predication. It is associated with the ego and a specific ideal image that the subject identifies with. In this sense, Lacan's formulation of the signifier—as that which represents the subject for another signifier—suggests that the election of a master signifier (S1) portraying the self ("good boy" for example) enables the inscription of the subject of the statement in the symbolic only when it establishes a relationship with other signifiers (S2). That is because a signifier can engender meaning only through its differential relationships with other signifiers (Hook & Vanheule, 2016). The second way in which the signifier represents a subject for another signifier is associated with Lacan's account of the "subject of enunciation." As I have already argued in the previous chapters, Lacan describes the subject of enunciation as the product of discourse, as a force contradicting the conscious discourse of the ego and manifesting in symptoms. Lacan's formulation of the signifier designates the subject of enunciation as a fleeting presence encapsulated in the relationship between signifiers. It is between the signifiers in the chain of signification that "it speaks" (*Ca Parle*) (SIII, p. 41). In other words, it is through the mediation of signifiers that the unconscious can manifest itself in consciousness, dreams, slips of the tongue, jokes, and so on. (É, p. 269).

While Lacan's formulation of the signifier assumes a relationship to the subject, his formulation of the sign does not use the term "subject," but, rather, the term "someone" to designate the function of Peirce's interpreter. This is because Lacan explicitly argues that the sign entails a relationship to its object, even in the case of the complete absence of a subject: "Objectively there is no need for any subject to recognize a sign for it to be there—a trace exists even if there is nobody to look at it" (SIII, p. 167). In his paper "Position of the Unconscious," Lacan states this quite explicitly. Firstly, by arguing that "the fact that the signifier reveals to the subject his own division should not make us forget that this division derives from nothing other than that very same play, the play of signifiers—signifiers, not signs" (É, p. 269). He then continues in regard to the sign:

> Signs are polyvalent: they no doubt represent something to someone, but the status of that someone is uncertain … This someone could, by some stretch of the imagination, be the universe, insofar as information, so we are told, circulates therein. Any center in which information is added up [se totalise] can be taken for a someone, but not for a subject. (p. 269)

In this excerpt, Lacan explicitly attests to the "de-subjectification" of the sign. He argues that the "someone" in the formula of the sign is not necessarily a subject but could be any locus in which information is collected. This is why the sign does not entail the incorporation of the subject in language like the signifier does.[20]

In summary, the sign can be said to be distinct from the signifier in three different ways. Firstly, the sign entails a "natural" (natural sign) or "transitive" (trace sign) relationship to its referent (semiotic-object), while the signifier has no referent and engenders meaning through its relationships with other signifiers (it entails the murder of the thing). Secondly, the relationship between the sign and its referent is permanent, while the relationship between the signifier and the signified is fluid and ever changing.[21] Finally, in contrast to the signifier, the sign neither splits the subject nor implies the presence of the subject.

Maleval's Contribution to Lacan's Conception of the Sign

In a variety of papers, ranging from the year 2003 up to this day, Maleval had provided several interpretations that develop Lacan's conception of the sign. Maleval's interpretation of the sign is rooted in his analysis of autistic linguistic functionality that, according to him, is strongly disposed to the use of signs. Abiding with Lacan's clear distinction between the signifier and the sign, Maleval goes to great length to further

---

[20] This argument is supported in a similar manner in *Seminar XI*, p. 207.

[21] Lacan argues that the fluid relationship between the signifier and the signified is characterized by the "incessant sliding of the signified under the signifier" (É, p. 419).

differentiate the sign from any other signifying unit presented in Lacan's teaching as originating in the Other.[22] Coming to the conclusion that the sign is not adopted from the field of the Other, Maleval (2009) argues that its assumption originates in a purely autarchic decision on behalf of the subject (pp. 78, 101–102). In other words, that the coupling between a sign and a referent is not based on a previously contrived convention that is shared by the users of a language but is determined under terms independently assigned by the subject. Accordingly, I argue that Lacan's contention that the sign represents something for some*one*, can also be understood as its propensity to represent something for *one* person alone, and, thus, that any intersubjective agreement about the "meaning" of a sign can be achieved only by recourse to the signifier. That being the case, we infer that a language composed solely of signs would be akin to a private "code language" that is truly accessible only to its fabricator (Maleval, 2009, p. 180; 2011, p. 85).[23]

Moreover, Maleval (2009) agrees with Lacan that the sign does not split the subject. Namely, he argues that, when relying on the sign, "The autistic resists the advent of a subject divided by the signifier" (p. 103). Accordingly, he suggests that the autistic subject does not meet Lacan's strict definition of the subject as represented by one signifier for another. Maleval's exact designation of autistic subjectivity is rooted in one of Lacan's definitions of the subject presented in *Seminar IX: Identification (1961–1962)*: "The first definition that one can give of a someone is: someone who is accessible to a sign. It is the most elementary form, if one can express oneself in that way of subjectivity" (6.12.61). In this sense, Maleval (2009) argues that the autistic subjectivity is the "most

---

[22] Briefly stated, Maleval demonstrates that the sign cannot be confused with Lacan's account of the master signifier (*S1*) as well as with his account of the signifiers composing the signifying chain (*S2*) (Maleval, 2003, p. 209; 2009, p. 218; 2018, p. 62). He also insists that the sign cannot be confused with Lacan's account of the letter—that which constitutes the Freudian unconscious (Maleval, 2003, pp. 214, 216; 2009, p. 214). Finally, he demonstrates that the sign cannot be associated with any form of symbolic inscription of the *objet petit a* (Maleval, 2018a, p. 62).

[23] As I have already mentioned, Maleval softens his approach regarding the autistic sole recourse to the sign in later publications (2018b, pp. 43–44). The fact that autistic code language can also be used for communication with others demonstrates that the sign does function as a supplement for the signifier on some levels and, accordingly, that autistic subjects might not be utterly divorced from some functions warranted by the use of signifiers.

elementary form of subjectivity"; that is, someone who is accessible to a sign but not divided by the signifier (p. 103).

Finally, Maleval adds that the sign is utterly alien to the dimension of symbolic loss (p. 214). This contention can be understood on two levels. The first level is that of signification, in which the signifier initially introduces the dimension of lack by losing all access to any referent outside the domain of signifiers. As I have already argued, according to Lacan, the signifier breaks the link with what it signifies and derives its value only through the difference that it introduces in relation to other signifiers. Conversely, the relationship between the sign and its referent is unavoidable and generally permanent. Maleval (2009) argues that the sign does not in any way lose the link with its object but remains "parasitic" to the referent in the sense that it does not erase the thing represented (p. 188). Accordingly, the sign and the referent are petrified into a "rigid sequence" of memorized equivalences determining the relationship at stake (pp. 191, 207).[24] Not only is the sign petrified to a specific referent, Maleval adds that it also tends to "stick" to the specific context under which it was initially acquired (p. 208). That is why changes in specific circumstances challenge the knowledge established by the sign because the link between a sign and its referent is unlikely to change when the context changes. For example, the sign "cat" might refer to a specific Persian cat encountered on a rainy day, and, thus, the same cat encountered on a sunny day would not be acknowledged by the same sign (Grandin, 2006, p. 12). As will be elaborated in the following section, the rigid relationship between the sign, its referent, and the context under which they were acquired makes it inadequate in its capacity to convey abstractions, ambiguities, and other concepts lacking a distinct referent. Accordingly, a language composed of signs tends to be "precarious," as in comparison to the fluidity and associative flexibility of the signifier, any change in the context of a situation or in the characteristics of a thing conveys a threat to the consistency of the knowledge acquired by signs (Maleval, 2003, p. 214;

---

[24] The equivalence between the sign and its referent is described by Gérard Berquez (1983) in the following way: "The linguistic sign is not distinct from the material referent, the sign and the thing are the same, there is no space between the sign and reality, between the representation and the thing represented, there is for the autistic child total adequacy between the sign and the thing" (p. 123).

2009, pp. 86, 187). Because the sign does not entail the gap between the signifying element and its referent, it does not introduce the subject to the dimension of lack inherently associated with the signifier. That is why Maleval argues that, while the signifier always entails "the murder of the thing," the sign "does not allow the murder of the thing" (p. 218). The second level in which the sign is alien to the dimension of loss is that of jouissance. This is a result of autistic foreclosure, radically excluding the most initial symbolic affirmation of the loss of jouissance taking place in primal repression. As was elaborated in the previous chapters, according to Maleval, autism is characterized by a "refusal to yield invocatory jouissance," a refusal that "undermines the subject's inscription in the field of the Other" (pp. 82–83). With no recourse to the field of the Other, the autistic subject has no access to the signifier as a means to symbolically mediate jouissance and is solely disposed to the sign in this effort. However, according to Maleval, signs do not provide a good means for the symbolic mediation of jouissance. As will be presented in the following section, he argues that due to the fact that signs are limited in their access to the dimension of the drive, they can only enable a supplementary inscription of the initial loss of jouissance necessary for the construction of psychic reality (Maleval, 2011, p. 89).[25] That is why Maleval views the autistic recourse to the sign as entailing a fundamental "failure of the knot between jouissance and language" (Maleval, 2009, p. 216).

After presenting Lacan's account of the sign, as well as Maleval's further contribution to this account, the following section will provide an explication of the exact way in which a "sign language" is adopted by autistic subjects. In this section, several modalities in its construction will be presented, as well as a model for the distinction between the varying degrees of the severity of the symptomatic manifestations of autism, based on the level of linguistic functionality adopted by the subject.

---

[25] In the next section, this supplementary inscription will be defined as the "delimitation" of jouissance, in contrast to the "ciphering" of jouissance achieved through the use of signifiers.

The Development of the Rim and Autistic Linguistic Functionality

In psychoanalysis, a specific symptom is considered to correspond to an underlying subjective structure established by the functioning of a psychic mechanism of *constitutive exclusion*. Contrary to psychiatry, where a diagnosis is usually based on the severity of apparent symptoms, in psychoanalysis, the severity of a symptom does not necessarily dictate the diagnosis of a subjective structure. In this sense, in the psychoanalytic clinic, a subject can be diagnosed as psychotic even without exhibiting any prevalent psychotic symptoms acknowledged by psychiatrists.[26] In the clinic of autism, we also encounter a variety of behavioral modalities, as well as varying quantitative degrees of symptomatic manifestations. These "different shades" of autism are designated today, in common psychiatric literature, under the scope of the "autism spectrum disorder" (ASD) (APA, 2013). This *spectrum* is delimited by two poles, in relation to which an autistic subject can be diagnosed as "low-functioning" or "high-functioning." As meta-psychological diagnostic categories, the two poles of the autism spectrum are categorically indiscernible, meaning they have no definite qualitative distinction but are determined on the basis of a quantitative accumulation of behavioral traits.[27] These traits are commonly diagnosed today by autism-specific behavioral evaluations such as M-CHAT-R (Robins, Fein, & Barton 2009). These are questionnaires that asses the severity of autism on the basis of an individual's scores in several independent behavioral categories, such as the interaction with caretakers and peers, tasks revolving around sensual perception, and the implementation of motor skills. Nevertheless, because these tests are based on apparent behavioral criteria, in more severe cases, autism is commonly confused with childhood psychosis or, on the other side of the spectrum, either disregarded or confused with other disorders such as "social communication disorder" (SCD) (Bishop, 1989).

In the Lacanian clinic, as it has been developed and presented so far, autism is not designated as a physical or behavioral disorder, but, rather,

---

[26] As is the case in "ordinary psychosis." See Redmond (2014).

[27] A full list of these traits is presented in Chap. 1.

as a subjective structure constituted as a result of foreclosure. Accordingly, autism is not diagnosed on the basis of a set of accumulating behavioral traits but is determined by structural criteria that manifest in the subject's relationship with language and jouissance. In the last two decades, Maleval provided several perspectives through which the clinic of autism can be articulated in this way (Maleval, 2003, 2009, 2011, 2012, 2015, 2018a). The models Maleval presents in his different papers are somewhat independent and can be said to display a progression in the development of his understanding of the autistic mode of access to language and jouissance. It is in his paper "Extension du Spectre de l'Autisme" (2015) that Maleval seems to integrate these different models on the basis of his notion of the "development" of the rim. In the previous chapter, I have designated the rim as the object of autistic foreclosure. Correspondingly, the development of the rim will be described in this section as the construction of a "neo-rim" that does not put the functioning of the drive back in place but provides the autistic subject with a supplementary mode of access to language and jouissance (Laurent, 2012a, pp. 69–70; Maleval, 2012, pp. 54, 102).

In his book *La Bataille de l'Autisme* (2012a), Laurent designates the "rim" as one of the major factors in the constitution of the autistic structure.[28] However, it is Maleval that systematically determines the varying severities of autism in accordance with the development of the supplementary construction of the rim. Beginning from its *absence*, moving through its *protective* function, then on to its *dynamic* use, and finally leading to its *hollowing-out*, Maleval argues that, in the clinic of autism, "the construction or election of a rim is the best element of a differential clinic" (Maleval, 2015, p. 769). Providing a novel conceptual account of the rim at the different modes of its development, Maleval offers an analysis of the progression of the linguistic functionality of autistic subjects—leading them from a perceived muteness to the dynamic use of a "supplementary" or "synthetic" Other. The following section will provide an *integrative account* of Maleval's various interpretations of the development of the supplementary construction of the rim. By selectively extracting some of the essential

---

[28] Laurent's implementation of the concept of the "rim" can be traced back to the discussion chapter in *L'Autisme et la Psychanalyse* (1992).

characteristics of Maleval's various models, this section will provide a revised account of this development, a development rooted in the different modes of linguistic functionality that are enabled by the subject's recourse to the sign. This revised account will include several substantial alterations and, in this sense, should be regarded as an interpretation and development of Maleval's work. On the basis of this integrative account, a new model for the diagnosis of autism will be provided. This model will be based on four structurally discernible diagnostic criteria that are distributed on an open-ended "spectrum" of autistic linguistic functionality. Within this spectrum, each criterion corresponds to a different modality in the development of the rim. This section will progress in correspondence with these modalities and complement them with examples derived from clinical cases as well as examples from books written by autistic individuals on the subject of autism.

The Absence of the Rim

According to Maleval (2015), what is described as the most severe form of autism manifests in a level of functionality that is extremely hard to differentiate from childhood psychosis (p. 766). This level of functionality precedes that which is described by Kanner (1943) and Asperger (1991) and is widely deliberated in the works of Donald Meltzer, Frances Tustin, Bruno Bettelheim, and the Leforts.[29] On this level, immediately succeeding autistic foreclosure, the subject has not yet established access to the dimension of the rim in any mode of its supplementary construction (Maleval, 2015, p. 767). With no rim, autistic subjects suffer from the constant threat of a brutal invasion of jouissance—what Laurent and Maleval associate with the experience of the "void in the real," the "black hole," or the "pure presence of death" (Laurent, 2012a, p. 84). Prone to this constant threat, autistic subjects alternate between two extreme existential poles—destruction and self-destruction—either the world or the subject itself is at the risk of being destroyed by an all-engulfing limitless void (Lefort & Lefort, 2003, p. 15). In order to surmount this terrible anxiety,

---

[29] Particularly in the Leforts' work with the autistic girl Marie François, presented in their book *The Birth of the Other* (1994).

autistic subjects commit acts of extreme violence, self-aggressiveness, and self-mutilation (scratching, biting, hitting, murdering, and dismembering objects), all with the aim of demarcating a rim for the holes they encounter in their environment, in objects, and on their bodies (Maleval, 2015, pp. 767–768). The demarcation of this rim is aimed at protecting these subjects from brutal invasions of jouissance that appear to come from nowhere and disseminate everywhere.

Linguistic expressions for autistic subjects on this level are almost absent. They appear only at the height of anxiety, manifesting in spontaneous broken utterances expressing sudden aggression and accompanied by the breaking and throwing of objects. After the sudden expression of these holophrastic vocalizations, subjects immediately return to a state of mutism, sinking into an even deeper silence (Maleval, 2012, pp. 38–39).

The Protective Rim

According to Maleval, the next level of autistic functionality is initiated by the construction of a supplementary rim that enables a certain mode of protection from the invasion of jouissance. Maleval terms this mode of construction the "protective rim" and adds that it relies on the use of a unique type of object (Maleval, 2018a, p. 62).[30]

In *Seminar XI: The Four Fundamental Concepts of Psychoanalysis (1964)*, Lacan states that "man thinks with his object" (SXI, p. 62). In this statement, the "object" Lacan refers to is *objet petit a*. By associating *objet petit a* with the act of thinking, Lacan highlights its crucial role in the constitution of the subject and its relationship with language. According to Maleval (2009), autistic subjects also initiate their relationship with language with the help of their objects (p. 170). Nevertheless, he argues that

---

[30] Maleval (2015) initially uses the term "insulating rim" (*Le bord isolant*) to describe the rim in this mode of construction (p. 771). Nevertheless, in this book I call it the "protective rim," a term presented in Maleval's later publication (2018a). I believe that the attempt to protect oneself from invasions of jouissance does not necessarily aim for an insulation. The designation of the rim in this mode of its construction as "insulating" is very much akin to Tustin's description of the pathological "autistic shell" (1972). As will shortly be disclosed, Maleval agrees that the rim in this mode of construction is not pathological but, by providing a sense of protection, also functions as a gateway to the world in its further modes of development.

due to their refusal to inscribe the drive object in the Other, autistic subjects must select a different type of object than *objet petit a*. This unique type of object is termed the "autistic object," an object that enables a different mode of access to language than the one that *objet petit a* provides (p. 171).

In her book *Autism and Child Psychosis* (1972), Tustin inaugurates the notion of the "autistic object," highlighting both its protective and pathological nature (pp. 125–126). Tustin describes a certain relationship of attachment between her autistic patients and the objects they select, noting how they surround themselves with hard objects with which they feel equated. She emphasizes the way autistic children stick objects on their bodies, scarcely using them for their objective functions but only for the sensation of hardness they provide (p. 115).[31] She argues that autistic children conceive of these objects as parts of their body and thus gain a sense of protection from the anxiety provoked by their encounters with the precarious outside world. Following Tustin, Laurent and Maleval develop a framework that attests to the facilitative nature of such autistic objects. In agreement with Tustin, they note that one of the initial uses of such objects is the construction of a bodily "shield" serving as a protection from unpredictable invasions of unbridled jouissance (Maleval, 2009, pp. 105–106). Accordingly, Maleval states that, with recourse to the autistic object, "the autistic subject situates the jouissance of the drive in an object outside of the body" (Maleval, 2015, p. 772). In this way, the subject "creates a cut in the mode of jouissance" and establishes on the body "a rim between the body and the outside world" (Maleval, 2011, p. 80). In other words, the autistic subject infuses the object with unique vital properties and, by sticking the object to the body, creates a certain separation from jouissance that previously invaded the body (Maleval, 2015, p. 770). In congruence with Maleval, I suggest calling the autistic object that is solely used for its protective function in the protective rim the "simple autistic object" (Maleval, 2009, p. 132).

While Maleval argues that the simple autistic object mimics something of the functionality of the *objet petit a*, its implementation is not identical to the one accomplished in the symbolic inscription of the latter (p. 170).

---

[31] Tustin (1992) calls this "two-dimensional" identification (p. 17).

In the case of *objet petit a*, such a procedure would involve a subtraction of a sum of jouissance from the subject's body that would then be inscribed in the Other. Due to the subject's refusal to inscribe the object of jouissance in the Other, the simple autistic object is not separated from the body but remains attached to the body as a supplementary rim (Maleval, 2018a, p. 63). In this sense, Laurent and Maleval argue that "in autism jouissance returns on the rim" of the body (Maleval, 2009, pp. 97, 106, 145; 2012, p. 47; 2015, p. 765; Laurent, 2012a, p. 66).[32] Contrary to the *objet petit a*, it is not so much that the protective function of the autistic object is rooted in the function of the signifier. It is through a "body event" (*événement de corps*) that the jouissance of the drive is dynamically deposited in an autistic object that is attached to the body as a supplementary rim (Laurent, 2012a, p. 69).

This process can also be elaborated from a linguistic point of view—one that is focused on the use of the sign.[33] According to this interpretation, the subject gains a certain mastery over a loss of jouissance through a unique form of linguistic operation that is achieved via the simple autistic object. As already noted, Maleval and Laurent argue that simple autistic objects function as deposits of jouissance. Moreover, simple autistic objects also have the capacity of being associated with linguistic signs (Maleval, 2009, p. 144). In this sense, through the mediation of the simple autistic object, a transitive relationship between the subject's jouissance and a linguistic sign can be achieved.

Jouissance ⇒ Autistic Object ⇒ Sign

On the basis of this relationship, when a subject linguistically negates a sign that is involved in it, this warrants a supplementary form of signification of a loss of jouissance via the autistic object.

Maleval uses Freud's (1920) account of the *Fort-da* game in order to stress this point. He provides several examples of its autistic variation

---

[32] Laurent initially used the term "returns on the rim" in direct relation to Lacan's account of the return of jouissance—in the body or the Other—as a result of psychotic foreclosure. Laurent (2012b) argues that "in autism, the return of jouissance occurs neither in the locus of the Other, as it does in paranoia, nor in the body, as it does in schizophrenia, but rather on the rim" (pp. 52–54).

[33] It is important to note that Maleval associates the linguistic interpretation that will shortly be presented with the functioning of the complex autistic object. Nevertheless, I choose to present it as a modality of the simple autistic object and describe the complex autistic object as a psychic apparatus that is composed of a multiplicity of simple autistic objects.

used by subjects in their attempt to protect themselves from unbearable invasions of jouissance. As I have already explained in Chap. 5, in the *Fort-da* game, the 18-month-old child toys with the presence and absence of an object (SE XVIII, pp. 14–17). Freud goes on to argue that this game enables the child to deal with its mother's absence by becoming an active factor in the object's loss rather than a passive victim. The child does so by selecting an object that is detached from the mother but retains some of her dynamic qualities, even in the face of the mother's devastating lack. Lacan adds that: "To this object we will later give the name it bears in the Lacanian algebra—the *petit a*" (SXI, p. 62).

Correspondingly, Maleval argues that the Freudian *Fort-da* game can be compared to a distinct type of behavior prevalent among autistic subjects, a behavior that he terms the "on/off conduct" (Maleval, 2009, p. 144). Such a behavior entails the orderly affirmation and then negation of the presence of a selected object through the use of a sign. Maleval provides an example of such a conduct from a case study of an autistic child who repetitively points at images in a book, names them, and then designates them as lost: "Strawberries, goodbye strawberries, there's no more. Snowman, goodbye, there's no more snowman" (Guillas, 1999). He provides another example from the case of an autistic boy named Joey, presented by Bettelheim, who voluntarily chooses to connect and disconnect from various objects that he intimately associates with different functions of his body, thus turning them on and off by choice (Bettelheim, 1967, p. 257).

According to Maleval, while the *Fort-da* game and the on/off conduct are similar in the sense that they are used in the treatment of a loss of jouissance, their comparison "clearly illustrates two distinct modes of relation to the object of jouissance and attests to very specific manners of its treatment" (Maleval, 2009, p. 141). More specifically, they treat the dimension of loss in two distinctly opposite ways. In the *Fort-da* game the absence of the object (*fort*—gone) precedes its signifying presence (*da*—there) in the oppositional couple *Fort-da*. As Lacan explicitly argues: "For the game of the cotton-reel is the subject's answer to what the mother's absence has created" (SXI, p. 62). On the other hand, in the on/off conduct, the autistic subject aims to lose an already present object. In other words, in the first case (*Fort-da*), the child attempts to compensate for the real absence of the mother through the affirmative symbolic designation of a loss (SI, pp. 173, 178; SXII, 23.1.62); in the second case (on/off), the child attempts to enact a loss of jouissance, where there is only presence, because no initial symbolic designation of loss is established due to autistic foreclosure (Maleval, 2009, pp. 144–145).[34]

Maleval proceeds to argue that the distinction between the *Fort-da* game and the on/off conduct is also rooted in the fact that the former is applied at the level of the signifier, while the latter is achieved at the level of the sign: "On/off conduct and Fort-da game seem to be two ways of dealing with the … pain of the lost object; however, while first works with the sign, the second works with the signifier" (p. 144). In the *Fort-da* game, two signifiers are brought in opposition in order to engender some signification of the dimension of loss. In the on/off conduct, an object invested with jouissance is linked with a sign that is then effaced by the use of a linguistic negation. In other words, in the on/off conduct, the subject gains mastery over a sum of jouissance that is deposited in a simple autistic object by associating it with a sign that can be controlled by being linguistically negated.

This coping strategy brings many autistic subjects to develop a growing "vocabulary" of signs that are associated with different simple autistic objects that are coupled with bodily sensations. This vocabulary provides them with a way through which jouissance can be rendered tolerable. From a very basic coupling between sensations and objects associated with sounds, the subject can progress to their association with words, developing more intricate coping abilities, strengthening the protective rim and enriching its capacities (Maleval, 2015, p. 772). As long as the child is allowed to participate in the repetitive on/off conduct that inaugurates these immutable transitive relationships, anxiety can be warded off.[35] That is for their preservation enables a sense of order and predictability in the world. With the progressive construction of the protective rim and the preservation of its integrity, the relationship with jouissance

---

[34] In this sense, the on/off conduct provides an alternative to the subject's "castration in the real." See Chap. 6, section on the foreclosure of the void.

[35] This goes very much against clinical approaches, such as Applied Behavioral Analysis (ABA), that aim to condition and normalize the way autistic individuals behave, sanctioning the extinction of "non-adaptive" behaviors that might be useful for their protective function.

is moderated, and destructive behaviors—characteristic of the absence of the rim—become rare. It does not put drive functionality in place but allows a certain degree of subjective animation that brings the child out of the pre-Kanner state of autistic functionality associated with the absence of the rim (p. 779).

In her paper "Negativity: Rejection" (2004), Julia Kristeva classifies such proto-linguistic gestures as "concrete operations." These gestures involve the subject's practical relationship with the destruction and organization of objects. Kristeva argues that they include "sensorimotor actions," such as in the case of Freud's *Fort-da* game, that primordially signify loss through a linguistic negation. She explicitly argues that "This negativity—this expenditure—posits an object as separate from the body proper and, at the very moment of separation, fixes it in place as absent, as a sign" (pp. 122–124). She adds that the negation of this linguistic unit puts the subject in a position of mastery through which it gains a protective competence (pp. 124–125).

The protective rim can also be associated with Tustin's (1992) account of the "auto-generated shell," functioning as armor that completely blocks off the autistic subject from the external world (p. 44). This is the "autistic shell" that Tustin classifies as "pathological," for from within it the subject is unapproachable and does not respond to external stimuli (pp. 191–207). Nevertheless, as we can clearly see, the protective rim, which is created on the basis of a controlled loss, does not strictly function as a shell but functions as a boundary as well (Maleval, 2018a, pp. 64). Thus, it does not only protect the autistic subject from the invasion of jouissance, it also provides the means for a certain mediation of internal and external stimuli, evoking in the subject a fascination with language as a means to acquire mastery over the world. In early stages, this fascination manifests as the acquisition of knowledge of different bodily sensations and the predictability of the interaction between objects. As will shortly be presented, in later stages, this knowledge can manifest in a variety of specific interests that materialize in the laborious cultivation of information and a passion for mastery in practical fields of expertise.

The Dynamic Rim

Following the utilization of signs in the construction of the protective rim, there arise, among many autistic subjects, a subjective affinity and general curiosity in regard to language. In these cases, subjects sometimes seek to further the development of the rim from its "protective" function to its "dynamic" function—into what Maleval terms the "dynamic rim" (Maleval, 2015, pp. 772–774). The dynamic rim is a more complex and versatile modality of the autistic rim. First, in contrast to the passive adoptions of objects contingently encountered in the child's surroundings in the construction of the protective rim, it involves the subject's active investment in the selection of the objects constructing it. Second, it is open to change, for its characteristics develop over time and its functionality can be adapted to different contexts and voluntarily used in different situations. Finally, it enables the subject to use language for means other than a protection from jouissance such as the development of specific interests that can be established in different fields of expertise. Therefore, it seems that the dynamic rim introduces autistic subjects to the means necessary for becoming independent in a dynamic world (p. 772).

Maleval (2009) proposes that the rim, in its varying modalities, can be composed of three components: the autistic object, the double, and specific interests which give rise to the synthetic Other (p. 108). In the integrative model developed in this chapter, I suggest that: the protective rim is solely composed of simple autistic objects; the dynamic rim is composed of "complex autistic objects," the double, and specific interests; and all of the above are supported by the synthetic Other (p. 157). The combined use of these components enables the autistic subject to utilize the dynamic rim in achieving intricate goals, providing a more complex mode of access to language and a level of subjective animation that is "livelier" than the one described by Kanner (1943) in his case studies.

Maleval argues that the development of specific interests is the source of the formation of the "synthetic Other." However, in this chapter I offer a different interpretation as to the function of the synthetic Other. I argue that the synthetic Other is a supplementary locus that functions as the support for all the modalities of the construction of the rim. In other words, due to the lack of access to the Other, the synthetic Other functions as the support for the development of autistic linguistic functionality on all of its levels. While Maleval, Laurent, and the Leforts provide a thorough account of both the complex autistic object and the double in the construction of the dynamic rim, this section will only briefly describe their essential qualities and focus on the synthetic Other and its development.

The Complex Autistic Object

Briefly stated, the complex autistic object can be viewed as a construct composed of a collection of simple autistic objects. It combines the localized dynamic function of several simple autistic objects into a complex apparatus that enables the subject to apply more intricate treatments of jouissance in more complex circumstances. Its dynamic function is to provide a long-lasting supplement for the regulation of the subject's jouissance (Maleval, 2009, pp. 164–166). Accordingly, Maleval describes it as a "jouissance regulator" and a "libido sensor" (p. 154). The subject can plug in and out of the complex autistic object, like an auxiliary machine, assimilating its dynamic properties when it specifically needs them (p. 170). A good example for the use of a complex autistic object can be found in Bruno Bettelheim's account of the case of Joey in his book *The Empty Fortress* (1967) and his paper "Joey, a 'Mechanical Boy' " (1959). Joey is an autistic child, treated by Bettelheim, who builds a machine made out of different objects he collects from his surroundings. What is so intriguing about Joey's case is the fact that he explicitly refers to his body as an auxiliary machine composed of smaller machines, which regulates the electrical currents going through it. Bettelheim notes that in order to eat, Joey has to plug into an electric circuit; in order to drink, Joey has to come into contact with a complicated piping system built with straws. Later on, a machine made out of light bulbs assists Joey in controlling his bowel movements. Bettelheim describes a successive election of objects that allows Joey to develop other secondary skills such as speaking and regulating emotions. It even allows him to gain superior engineering skills that help him lead an independent life and embark on a career in electrical engineering. Another excellent example for the use of a complex autistic object is Grandin's "squeeze machine"—a contraption constructed by Grandin that is used to wrap her body, offering her great relief in what she terms as the "hyper-arousal" of her nervous system (Grandin, 2006, p. 60).

The Double

The autistic double, a phenomenon thoroughly elaborated by the Leforts, is described by Maleval as a distinct manifestation of the complex autistic object—an "object-double" (Maleval, 2009, pp. 111, 156, 162). However, unlike the cases presented above, instead of successively assembling different objects into a complex apparatus, the double embodies a ready-made dynamic apparatus that the subject can assimilate into its dynamic rim as a whole.

Autistic children do not always distinguish between living individuals and inanimate objects (p. 135). Accordingly, when assimilating the autistic double into the dynamic rim, this double can take the form of an object, an imaginary companion, as well as a real person. In this sense, it can be a puppet, a character on a television show, or even the television itself, as long it is identified as an animated being by the subject (pp. 111–116, 155–156). By assimilating the autistic double into the dynamic rim, the subject gains the dynamic properties already attributed to it (p. 167).[36] Whenever the subject has the capacity to plug into the autistic double, it provides it with a sense of liveliness, allowing the subject to speak through it "by proxy" and sometimes even open it up to social exchange. Such is the case of an autistic child named André who utilizes his puppet-doubles in order to converse with his peers—each one with its own personality traits—without which he cannot support his artificial enunciation (p. 115).

---

[36] This entails neither a symbolic nor an imaginary identification, as autistic subjects are not disposed to any of these modes of identification.

Specific Interests

Some autistic subjects choose to extend their use of signs from a localized treatment of jouissance, to the use of signs with the aim of achieving personal and solitary forms of satisfaction. These forms of satisfaction sometimes develop into specific interests in particular fields of knowledge or practices (Maleval, 2015, p. 766; 2018a, p. 62). These specific interests commonly find their origin in the subject's attempts to temper anxiety by turning it into an extensive knowledgeability in a specific field related to it. Thus, a fear of using toilets can turn into a fascination with plumbing and a fear of the sound of thunder can turn into a special interest in weather prediction (Maleval, 2015, p. 773).

Some autistic subjects go on to develop their specific interests into well-accomplished and socially valued skills (Laurent, 2012a, p. 108; Maleval, 2009, pp. 108, 193; 2015, pp. 778–779). Autistic individuals that develop these skills sometimes become recognized specialists in a specific field such as computer science, mathematics, astronomy, as well as music and art. It is the capacity of these socially valued skills to open the subject to the domain of social exchange that makes them so important. Accordingly, they are determined by Maleval (2009) as the pinnacle of the development of the dynamic rim (p. 157), preceding the last modality in the development of the rim—the "hollowing-out of the rim." One of the most noted autistic individuals attesting to the development of such socially valued skills is Temple Grandin. In her book *Thinking in Pictures* (2006), she describes how she developed her obsession with her farmhouse "squeeze machine" into an academic expertise as a professor of animal science at Colorado State University.

The Synthetic Other

This synthetic Other is the supplementary locus that functions as the support for all the different modes of autistic linguistic functionality. Due to the lack of access to the signifier, the synthetic Other is solely disposed to the logic of the sign. Accordingly, it can be regarded as a two-dimensional matrix composed of a sequence of signs, in which signs and referents are rigidly linked. When reaching a certain level of complexity, the synthetic Other provides a basis for the coherence of the subject's reality and, in some cases, an access to the social bond up to the level of independence (Maleval, 2009, p. 198). Nevertheless, it is important to note that the synthetic Other cannot fully substitute the symbolic Other. It remains *synthetic*, in the sense of its being a fabricated supplement that can never fully replace the *organic* symbolic function of the signifier.[37]

Both the subject's specific interests and socially valued skills are manifestations of the most complex modes of linguistic functionality enabled by the synthetic Other. Accordingly, their development directs the construction of the synthetic Other in two distinct modalities through which the autistic subject can implement the use of language: (1) through a private language, in tune with the subject's feelings but opaque to others or (2) through an intellectualized language, appreciated by others but devoid of affect. The first, termed by Maleval the "closed synthetic Other," entails the subject being cut off from the intersubjective world and the social bond. The latter, termed the "open synthetic Other," entails the subject being cut off from itself—in the sense of the capacity of its language to interpret affect. It is in this sense that Maleval argues that "the autistic subject is necessarily split between his emotions and his intellect" (p. 105)—between the closed and open synthetic Other.

The Closed Synthetic Other

The synthetic Other, in both of its modalities, is composed of a matrix of signs. In the case of the closed synthetic Other, these signs encompass an organized system of knowledge in a specific field. The subject finds itself personally invested in this field but implements it only in essentially solitary activities of little practical utility that call for neither a partner nor an audience (p. 195). The signs composing the closed synthetic Other are

---

[37] It is interesting to think of the synthetic Other in relation to Lacan's definition of the sign. According to Lacan, the sign is not dependent on a subjectivized locus that carries with it an alterity (the Other). As I have previously mentioned, Lacan argues that "any center in which information is added up" can be taken as the locus of the sign (É, p. 269). In this sense, the synthetic Other can be described as a locus in which knowledge that is not subjectivized or endowed with alterity is systematically collected using signs.

voluntarily collected by the subject from pre-existing orderly formations in the world that can be adapted into an organized system of knowledge. These may include stable visual forms like icons, drawings, and matching objects. The same goes for auditory forms such as rhythms, beats, music, and songs. Other great sources of signs are organized systems composed of written words like calendars, dictionaries, train schedules, and other esoteric classifications of many kinds (pp. 197–198).

The closed synthetic Other can be viewed as the locus of a closed-off "private language." Firstly, because the closed synthetic Other is not utilized with the aim of communicating with others but is solely used with the aim of tempering with anxiety and achieving a solitary form of satisfaction (Maleval, 2011, p. 79). Secondly, because the signs composing the closed synthetic Other are not adopted from the symbolic Other, they are completely unique in their phonic form, comprised of neologisms (uniquely invented words), or words that convey a personal meaning only for the subject (Maleval, 2009, p. 100). Autistic subjects who are strongly disposed to the use of neologisms can get to a point where they invent a completely original language with its own grammar and vocabulary, composed of thousands of words (Maleval, 2011, p. 84). A good example for such a language can be found in the case of Daniel Tammet (2007), an autistic subject who invented a comprehensive new language called Mänti (p. 303). Some autistic subjects who are disposed to the use of the closed synthetic Other but do adopt comprehensible words do so by imitating internet videos, television shows, and overheard conversations. Nevertheless, they go on to associate these words with referents that usually have nothing to do with their accepted meaning. A good example for such conduct can be found in the case of Eric, an autistic child who uses the phrase "the trains are leaving" in order to express a difficult situation (Maleval, 2011, p. 83).

What is most distinct about the functionality of the closed synthetic Other is its capacity to enable the subject to implement its private language with the aim of developing a unique and personal mode of expression providing access to inner emotional experience (Maleval, 2009, p. 195). In other words, it provides the subject with the capacity to mobilize and localize jouissance in the body, giving rise to a non-threatening and enjoyable affective experience. However, this experience still remains a pervasive and immediate one, resisting its full appropriation or integration in language (p. 200). Because the closed synthetic Other is solely based on the sign, it is only able to provide the subject with the means to "delimit" jouissance but not to "cipher" it in a way that would be communicable to others or to itself (p. 214). Maleval clearly differentiates between these two modes of mediation of jouissance, naming the first the "delimitation" (*cadrer*) of jouissance and the latter the "ciphering" (*chiffrer*) of jouissance.[38] The "ciphering" of jouissance (SXXI, 20.11.73) is dependent on the recourse to the signifier that provides the means for its "interpretation" and transformation into a consistent affective vocabulary. With no access to the signifier, the closed synthetic Other can only allow the autistic subject to "delimit" jouissance. This highlights the major disadvantage of the autistic subject's sole reliance on the closed synthetic Other—the fact that it is not open to social exchange. Without socially profiting from the richness of their invented private sign language, autistic subjects, solely disposed to the closed synthetic Other, gain access to neither the social bond nor the skills enabling them to live an independent life. An inspiring account of this form of solitary satisfaction can be found in Amanda Bagg's video testimony called "In My Language" (2007).

The Open Synthetic Other

Directly basing himself on Lacan's brief commentaries on autism, Maleval (2009) argues that, while the closed synthetic Other enables the subject to construct a language, there is something about this language that remains "frozen" and thus limited in its adaptive capacities (p. 199). This is where the open synthetic Other is primarily distinguished, as it entails a certain dynamic quality that opens up the subject's accumulated knowledge to be used in changing circumstances and different social contexts and situations.

---

[38] Maleval uses the term *cedrer* which can also be translated as "framing." Nevertheless, in English, the act of "framing" can also be understood as a contextual procedure. Therefore, because autistic subjects do not contextualize jouissance, but can only mark its boundaries, I have chosen to translate it as "delimiting."

A common way the open synthetic Other initially materializes is in the formation of an imaginary world adopted or fabricated by the autistic child. These are complex universes, with robust histories and a multiplicity of rules and players that captivate the child up to the point where nothing else interests him or her (p. 202). The complexity of these imaginary worlds, as well as the subject's capacity to freely govern their development, provides the subject with a sense of mastery that can be—in some cases—implemented outside of these worlds as well. Moreover, when these imaginary worlds interest other people and they are willing to participate in their fabrication (while carefully abiding by their strict rules), the child is able to achieve some level of social bonding. A good example is the case of the B. family, reported by Oliver Sacks (1996), in which the two parents of an autistic child participate in the creation of the "Leutherian" universe and in this way gain access to their child's imaginary world (p. 648). Be that as it may, what is most compelling about the adoption or fabrication of such imaginary worlds—in the sense of the development of autistic linguistic functionality—is the fact that they create an appetite for the acquisition of knowledge in a variety of other fields, as well as the confidence to engage in new situations while relying on rules previously invented in these closed and stabilized domains (Maleval, 2009, p. 205). Accordingly, some autistic individuals choose to invest themselves in the investigation of the rules of the physical or intersubjective world. These rules offer them orderly and controllable intellectual models for the understanding of these worlds. Some autistic individuals use these intellectual models in order to understand human behavior; others go as far as making their expertise into a profession in a variety of fields (pp. 206–208).

Nevertheless, the open synthetic Other can only be considered to elevate the subject's linguistic functionality by relying on the logic of the sign, while never reaching the level of the signifier. In this sense, it can be compared to the level of the "symbol" in Peirce's account of the sign (Peirce, 1982, pp. 53–56). Like the signifier, Peirce's symbol relies on the intersubjective cultural domain for its meaning but, unlike the signifier, it conveys meaning through its rigid relationship with a semiotic-object. In other words, it lacks the fluidity and flexibility of the signifier and its capacity to signify different things when it is associated with different signifiers under different contexts. Similarly, while being able to comply with accepted cultural norms—ranging from basic norms, such as the use of a toilet, to more complex ones, such as giving an academic speech—autistic individuals still mostly behave incongruently and even artificially (Maleval, 2009, pp. 76, 85, 119). As will be shortly elaborated, even in the case of Grandin—whom Maleval views as an individual demonstrating one of the most developed implementations of the open synthetic Other—her use of language is still attested (by herself and others) to be endowed with a certain "rigidity," singling out its "synthetic" origin (pp. 207–209).

As I have already demonstrated in the previous chapter, one of the major ramifications of autistic foreclosure takes place in relation to the invocatory drive. These remifications are conditioned by the subject's radical refusal to inscribe the voice object in the Other. As result of this refusal the open synthetic Other is not engendered as the bearer of the subject's enunciative being (pp. 81, 198). This causes autistic subjects great difficulty in taking the position of the enunciator in their speech. This difficulty leads to the erasure of the subjective factor from speech, culminating in what Maleval terms as a "factual language" (Maleval, 2009, pp. 84–91). Autistic factual language firstly manifests on the level of the content of speech. Thus, when asked about his or her day, an autistic individual might recount a long list of accumulating facts, without providing any clue as to his or her own interpretation of these facts (Maleval, 2011, p. 84; 2012, p. 40). Secondly, this manifests on the level of an individual's intonation and the delivery of language. Accordingly, by resorting to a factual language, autistic individuals are disposed to the use of a "striking monochord tone," flat and devoid of affect (Maleval, 2012, pp. 38–40). In his book *Rencontrer l'Autiste et le Psychotique* (2015), François Hébert describes this form of speech as a dull, mechanical voice that attests to a dissociation between the musical aspect of language and the meaning it conveys (p. 208). Finally, this manifests in a difficulty to comprehend the subjective factor in the speech of others. Maleval argues that "The more the subjective variable is introduced into the denotative function of language, the more difficult it becomes for the autistic to understand" (Maleval, 2009, p. 210). Accordingly, autistic subjects have a hard time interpreting intonation and sometimes remain unaffected by humor and irony (pp. 171–172). It is in this sense that Grandin (2006) stresses that she prefers the technical language of science that appreciates clarity and precision at the price of erasing the subjective factor from language. She even goes as far as to equate her linguistic capacity to that of a computer (pp. 12, 159).

The erasure of the subjective factor from the domain of the open synthetic Other also entails the incapacity of language to interpret emotions (Maleval, 2009, p. 94). Accordingly, autistic subjects disposed to the open synthetic Other are estranged from affective knowledge (pp. 188, 218). As has already been discussed, Maleval associates the autistic sole recourse to the sign with a "failure of the knot between jouissance and language" (p. 216). At this point, we see that this failure also characterizes the open synthetic Other. Unable to "cipher" the subject's jouissance, the open synthetic Other is limited in its capacity to accurately express its feelings (p. 205). Accordingly, Donna Williams (2015), a famous autistic writer, reports that she cannot express emotions and words simultaneously. She attests to several tactics through which such a feat can be accomplished indirectly, such as imitation of memorized scenes. Regarding the understanding of emotions, she argues that she can mentally memorize the emotional meanings of certain gestures and, in some cases, extract them in order to interpret a situation. This is not linked to her actually comprehending the emotions represented but to a tactic based on an intellectual comparison of memorized social cues (p. 72). Accordingly, we see that the open synthetic Other enables the autistic subject to acquire knowledge about the world but knowledge that develops in an "emotional vacuum" (Maleval, 2009, p. 216).[39]

Finally, the open synthetic Other is also greatly affected by the strict linguistic limitations imposed on it by the structure of the sign. As I have already described, the sign entails a rigid and permanent relationship to its referent. Accordingly, the language enabled by the open synthetic Other is sometimes described as a rigid "code language" (p. 180; 2011, p. 85). For, as in a simple substitution cipher, each encrypted sign in the

---

[39] It is important to stress that while the open synthetic Other does not support the development of knowledge about emotions, autistic individuals disposed to its use do necessarily feel emotions and can learn to act according to their emotions.

open synthetic Other has only one term to which it refers. That is why autistic subjects describe the ideal of language as "a code that would connect words in a constant and rigid way to clearly determined objects or situations" (Maleval, 2012, p. 40). According to this ideal, autistic language, being utterly assimilated under the logic of the sign, is a language in which one word has one meaning (Maleval, 2009, p. 172). The more complex a language is, the more words with distinct referents and the more rules and structures, the less autistic subjects must rely on intuition and context (Maleval, 2011, p. 85).

Due to the rigidness of the open synthetic Other, a problem arises when autistic subjects attempt to discern general concepts in language that entail a certain level of ambiguity (p. 87). For example, a particular dog, like Lassie, would be easy to encode, but the general concept, "dog," would be difficult to insert into the matrix of the open synthetic Other. For the signification of the concept "dog" cannot be achieved in relation to a concrete referent in reality but only through the differential relationships between signifiers. Accordingly, autistic mnemonist Solomon Cherechevski reports that he cannot truly grasp the fact that the terms "pig" and "pork" denote the same animal (Maleval, 2015, p. 777) or, on the same note, Williams testifies that a "cow" stops being a cow for her when it is addressed as a part of a "flock" (Williams, 1998, p. 43).

Another linguistic aspect that forgoes the open synthetic Other due to its ambiguous nature is personal pronouns or "shifters."[40] Because words like "I" or "it" as well as "big," "small," or "after" have different referents in different circumstances and lack a referent when considered in isolation, autistic subjects find them to be very hard to comprehend without a concrete association with a specific noun (Maleval, 2009, pp. 79, 171–172; 2011, pp. 79, 87). A similar phenomena manifests in the autistic tendency to use proper names instead of common names. Instead of referring to "a television" an autistic child will usually address "the television," always using the definite article to designate objects in the world. Accordingly, each object is endowed with a proper name and not included

---

[40] On the role of shifters in the distinction between the subject of the statement and the subject of enunciation, see Chap. 6.

under a general common name—expanding the lexicon of the open synthetic Other to infinity (Maleval, 2009, p. 181).

The use of the sign in the construction of the open synthetic Other also entails problems with abstraction. Accordingly, autistic subjects report a difficulty in internalizing abstract concepts that have no concrete referent in reality (Maleval, 2012, p. 41). For example, Birger Sellin, an autistic subject with an inclination for mathematics, experiences great anxiety when faced with the abstract mathematical concept of the "empty set" (Laurent, 2012a, p. 68). In the case of Cherechevski, he claims that abstract terms like "infinity" and "negation of a negation" are almost inaccessible to him. The same problem will occur when dealing with non-mathematical abstract concepts lacking a distinct referent in reality, such as "peace" or "disease" as well as metaphorical phrases like "the weight of words" or "heart clenching" (Maleval, 2015, p. 777).

Nevertheless, Maleval (2012) insists that autistic subjects are not utterly divorced from the capacity to express and understand general concepts and abstractions. He suggests that they can establish an indirect access to general concepts and abstractions by resorting to their inventive capacity and the manipulation of iconic signs included in the open synthetic Other (pp. 41–42). According to Maleval, "the autistic child particularly appreciates icons … which schematically represent the entity, person, event or attribute" (p. 40). Images like a "U" on a road sign or the image of a man and a woman on the door of a public toilet convey a rigid connection between the sign and the image of its referent. Accordingly, when faced with concepts that are too general or abstract, Grandin (2006) transforms them into iconic signs and embeds them into the open synthetic Other, in association with other iconic signs: "I thought of peace as a dove, an Indian peace pipe … Honesty was represented by an image of placing ones hand on the Bible in court" (p. 17). Cherechevski links the concept "disease" to the image of "a fog that emanates from a person and envelopes him" (Maleval, 2015, p. 777). Similarly, when faced with a general concept such as "dog," Grandin (2006) uses her extraordinary visual memory in order to link together the images of each and every dog she has ever known in her life (p. 12). These tactics, enabled by the open synthetic Other, are described by Maleval as the fabrication of "pseudo-concepts" (Maleval, 2009, pp. 210–211). These pseudo-concepts are based on the exceptional memorization capacities of autistic subjects, their rich imagination, and sense of inventiveness. Nevertheless, while their use provides the autistic subject with some access to general concepts and abstractions, there is no doubt that it is limited in its capacity—especially in comparison to the Other of the signifier.

The Hollowing-Out of the Rim

In cases where autistic subjects become strongly disposed to the use of the open synthetic Other, the double and the autistic object lose their importance over time (Maleval, 2003, p. 206). In these cases, subjects rely more on their developed linguistic capacities and less on the objects used for the mediation of jouissance. The growing reliance on the open synthetic Other opens up access to the last mode of the development of the rim— the "hollowing-out" (*évidement*) of the rim (Maleval, 2015, p. 774). This mode entails the progressive libidinal disinvestment from autistic objects that are involved in the development of the rim. Accordingly, simple and complex autistic objects as well as doubles participate in an imaginary staging of their loss and are thus disinvested from the rim. Through this imaginary staging, the subject lets go of the immediate presence of the autistic object but keeps intact its dynamic capacities (in terms of the mediation of jouissance) by inscribing its loss in the open synthetic Other. In this sense, the autistic subject reaches the highest level of dynamism enabled by the development of the rim; it is a level on which the subject becomes independent from the autistic object and solely relies on its acquired skills and linguistic functionality. According to Maleval, this transformation produces in the subject "a remarkable change in the subjective position ... [that] produces changes in the autistic subjective economy that are felt as a significant progress" (Maleval, 2018a, p. 66; brackets added). For example, in her book *Nobody Nowhere* (1998), Williams attests to a funerary ceremony she conducted with the aim of killing her double—Willie. She wraps a doll in fabric, places it in a cardboard box painted black, and then goes on to immerse this box in a fishpond, after which she makes sure to erase all traces of the funeral (pp. 64–65). On the same note, Grandin allows her squeeze machine to deteriorate to a point beyond repair. Two years after it breaks down, she remarks in an interview that she does not feel the need to fix it, as she is "into hugging people now" (Wallis, 2010). It is important to note that, in such cases, the hollowing-out of the rim can also be accompanied by an act through which something of the dynamic qualities of the autistic object is invested in a domain that exceeds that of the subject's inner world. For Williams, this act was initiated by painting her self-portrait, amid tall grass, colorful roses, and a burning sun, on a mirror that was hanging in her living room. Williams becomes so invested in this image until she decides to incorporate it in her book (Maleval, 2009, p. 269). Thus, she extends this imaginary projection of her inner world into the social domain. In this way she accomplishes a supplementary inscription of a loss of jouissance in a place outside of herself, a supplementary inscription that functions as a singular solution to the structural refusal to inscribe the drive object in the Other.

The hollowing-out of the rim opens up a distinct level of functionality in autism that surpasses the one described by Asperger and associated today with Asperger's syndrome (APA, 2013). This is a level in which autistic subjects become independent, even to the point where a psychiatric diagnosis of autism can sometimes be disregarded (Maleval, 2015, p. 766). Maleval terms this level of functioning the "invisible pole" of autism. He adds that this pole is not only invisible to observers and clinicians but, in a lot of cases, is also invisible to the subject itself and, as a result, can be diagnosed only late in adulthood (p. 778). On this level, the resources accumulated in the different modes of the development of the rim, supported by the open synthetic Other, are utilized in what might be called a "normal" lifestyle—what under psychoanalytic terms could be determined as a seemingly neurotic conduct of a structured autistic. Interestingly enough, the Leforts (2003) devoted their last book on the subject of autism to the analysis of the autistic traits of such notable figures in the history of humanity that might be associated with the invisible pole, such as: Edgar Allan Poe, Fyodor Dostoevsky, Comte de Lautréamont, American President Woodrow Wilson, Blaise Pascal, and Marcel Proust.

The Autistic Linguistic Spectrum

One of the crucial aspects in the structuration of the subject involves the exact way in which its relationship with the language is constructed and used in the affirmation of psychic reality. Accordingly, Laurent (2012a) argues that:

> In neuroses, this space is that of "equivocations" as Lacan calls them in *L'étourdit*. In psychosis, it is the construction of a personal language that may include some ambiguities and, in autism, as we mentioned, it is the construction and displacement of a rim. (p. 103)

In this chapter, I have demonstrated that autistic foreclosure, while hindering access to the dimension of the signifier, enables the progressive acquisition of linguistic functionality based on the sign—going hand in hand with the progressive development of the rim. I have illustrated that, by utilizing the different components of the rim—the autistic object, the double, and specific interests, all of which are supported by the development of the synthetic Other—a mobilization of the subject's position in relation to jouissance and language can be achieved. At the end of this development, the rim is "hollowed-out," but the subject remains structurally autistic, open to the social bond but solely disposed to the logic of the sign with its numerous setbacks.

It is my contention that the model presented in this chapter is a viable alternative to the framework of the "autism spectrum disorder" (ASD) presented in the DSM-5 (APA, 2013). It is based on the subject's dynamic relationship with language and jouissance and always assumes that an underlying structure dictates the modalities and different severities of symptoms. Thus, this model provides the means through which the diagnosis of autism can surpass the level of behavioral criteria presented in the framework of the ASD, which is limited to two distinct diagnostic categories (low-functioning and high-functioning autism) and confounds autism with other psychical phenomena which give rise to similar behaviors. This model divides the autistic "linguistic spectrum" into four qualitatively distinct diagnostic categories based on the development of the rim: (1) the absence of the rim, (2) the protective rim, (3) the dynamic rim, and (4) the hollowing-out of the rim. It also accounts for the varying degrees of quantitative implementation internal to each diagnostic category: (1) simple vs. complex autistic object, (2) specific interests vs. socially valued skills, (3) open vs. closed synthetic Other, and (4) imaginary staging of loss vs. incorporation of loss in social domain. In this sense, this model calls for the establishment of several distinct clinical strategies corresponding with each of the aforementioned diagnostic categories. In each of these, clinicians are expected to facilitate and support autistic subjects in the development of the particular dynamic qualities of the rim as well as assist them in the transition between its different modalities: from the absence of the rim to a protective rim, from the protective rim to the dynamic rim, and from the dynamic rim to the hollowing-out of the rim. Accordingly, clinical work with autistic subjects diagnosed on the lower (pre-Kanner) pole of the linguistic spectrum would involve an environment rich with objects that can be adopted and incorporated in an on/off conduct, thus constructing a protective rim. Comparatively, clinical work with autistic subjects that aim to develop the dynamic rim would entail a content-rich environment and the involvement of the clinician in directing the subject's unique modes of satisfaction to more complex apparatuses that are based on the acquisition of knowledge. Finally, work with autistic subjects aiming to hollow-out the rim would be more similar to clinical work we see in the cognitive and psychoanalytic clinic. Respectively, on the one hand, a more pedagogical approach can be adopted in which knowledge about intersubjective relationships and integration in the social bond can be directedly provided to subjects. On the other hand, a more dynamic approach can be adopted, progressing an imaginary staging of the loss of the components of the rim as well as work oriented at incorporating something of the subject's inner world in the social bond.

These are mere suggestions, but they come to demonstrate the diversified potential of the meta-psychological perspective developed in this book. This perspective is rooted in the Lacanian psychoanalytic framework but can be implemented in different fields and developed by different practitioners, that is, under the condition that autism is designated as a unique *mode of being* that should not be cured or eradicated, and that

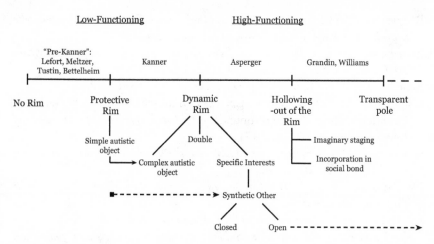

Fig. 7.2 Newly proposed schema of the Lacanian approach to the *Autistic Linguistic Spectrum*

the inventiveness and singularity of each autistic subject are taken as a decisive factor in the direction of the treatment.

Compiling the conclusions derived in this chapter, I summarize the newly proposed Lacanian approach to the clinic of autism in the following schema of the *Autistic Linguistic Spectrum*—see Fig. 7.2.

Works Cited

American Psychiatric Association. (2013). *DSM 5. American Journal of Psychiatry* (5th ed.). Washington, DC: American Psychiatric Publishing.

Asperger, H. (1991). "Autistic Psychopathy" in Childhood. In U. Frith (Ed.), *Autism and Asperger Syndrome* (pp. 37–92). Cambridge, UK: Cambridge University Press.

Atkin, A. (2013). *Peirce's Theory of Signs*. Retrieved from https://plato.stanford.edu/archives/sum2013/entries/peirce-semiotics/

Baggs, A. [silentmiaow] (2007, January 15). *In My Language*. [Video File]. Retrieved from https://youtu.be/JnylM1hI2jc

Benoist, V. (2011). L'Autre dans L'Autisme. *International Psychology, Practice and Research, 2*, 1–13.

Berquez, G. (1983). *L'autisme Infantile: Introduction à une Clinique Relationnelle selon Kanner*. Paris: Presses Universitaires de France.

Bettelheim, B. (1959). Joey, a 'Mechanical Boy'. *Scientific American, 200*(3), 116–130.

Bettelheim, B. (1967). *The Empty Fortress*. New York: The Free Press.

Bishop, D. V. M. (1989). Autism, Asperger's Syndrome and Semantic-Pragmatic Disorder: Where Are the Boundaries? *British Journal of Disorders of Communication, 24*(2), 107–121.

Chiesa, L. (2007). *Subjectivity and Otherness: A Philosophical Reading of Lacan*. Cambridge, MA: MIT Press.

De Saussure, F. (1959). *Course in General Linguistics*. New York: Philosophical Library.

Defoe, D. (1994). *Robinson Crusoe [1719]*. London: Warne.

Fink, B. (1997). *The Lacanian Subject: Between Language and Jouissance*. Princeton, NJ: Princeton University Press.

Freud, S. (1894). The Neuro-Psychoses of Defence. In *The Standard Edition of the Complete Psychological Works of Sigmund Freud, Volume III (1893–1899): Early Psycho- Analytic Publications* (pp. 41–61).

Freud, S. (1920). Beyond the Pleasure Principle. In *The Standard Edition of the Complete Psychological Works of Sigmund Freud, Volume XVIII (1920–1922): Beyond the Pleasure Principle, Group Psychology and Other Works* (pp. 1–64).

Freud, S. (1925). Negation. In *The Standard Edition of the Complete Psychological Works of Sigmund Freud, Volume XIX (1923–1925): The Ego and the Id and Other Works* (pp. 233–240).

Grandin, T. (2006). *Thinking in Pictures, Expanded Edition: My Life with Autism*. New York: Vintage.

Guillas, G. (1999). Que l'Autre Soit. *Du Changement Dans l'autisme? Journée de l'ACF/VLB*, 197–199.

Hébert, F. (2015). *Rencontrer l'Autiste et le Psychotique: Jeux et Détours*. Paris: Dunod.

Hook, D., & Vanheule, S. (2016). Revisiting the Master-Signifier, or, Mandela and Repression. *Frontiers in Psychology, 6*, 2028.

Kanner, L. (1943). Autistic Disturbances of Affective Contact. *Nervous Child, 2*(3), 217–250.

Klein, M. (1930). The Importance of Symbol-Formation in the Development of the Ego. *The International Journal of Psycho-Analysis, 11*, 24–39.

Kristeva, J. (2004). Negativity: Rejection. In D. K. Keenan (Ed.), *Hegel and Contemporary Continental Philosophy* (pp. 108–164). Albany, NY: SUNY Press.

Lacan, J. (1975). Conferences and Conversations at North American Universities. In *Yale University, Kanzer Seminar* (Vol. 4, pp. 5–66).

Lacan, J. (1977). *Ecrits: A Selection*. (A. Sheridan, Ed.), Trans. Alan Sheridan. New York: Norton & Company.

Lacan, J. (1988). *The Seminar of Jacques Lacan, Book I, Freud's Papers on Technique (1953–1954)*. (J.-A. Miller, Ed.). New York: Norton & Company.

Lacan, J. (1989). Geneva Lecture on the Symptom. *Analysis*, (1), 7–26.

Lacan, J. (1997). *The Seminar of Jacques Lacan, Book III, The Psychoses (1955–1956)*. (J.-A. Miller, Ed.). New York: Norton & Company.

Lacan, J. (2001). *The Seminar, Book XI, The Four Fundamental Concepts of Psychoanalysis (1964)*. (J.-A. Miller, Ed.). New York: Norton & Company.

Lacan, J. (2006). *Écrits*. (B. Fink, Ed.). New York: Norton & Company.

Lacan, J. (2016). *The Seminar of Jacques Lacan, Book XXIII, The Sinthome (1975–1976)*. (J.-A. Miller, Ed.). Cambridge, UK: Polity.

Lacan, J. (2019). *The Seminar of Jacques Lacan, Book VI, Desire and Its Interpretation (1958–1959)*. Cambridge, UK: Polity.

Lacan, J. (n.d.-a). *The Seminar of Jacques Lacan, Book IX, Identification (1961–1962)*. Trans. Gallagher, C. Unpublished.

Lacan, J. (n.d.-b). *The Seminar, Book XII, Crucial Problems for Psychoanalysis (1964–1965)*. Trans. Gallagher, C. Unpublished.

Lacan, J. (n.d.-c). *The Seminar, Book XIV, The Logic of Phantasy (1966–1967)*. Trans. Gallagher, C. Unpublished.

Lacan, J. (n.d.-d). *The Seminar, Book XXI, The Names-of-the-Father (1973–1974)*. Trans. Gallagher, C. Unpublished.

Laurent, E. (1992). Discusion. In *L'Autisme et la Psychanalyse*. Toulouse, France: Presses Universitaires du Mirail.

Laurent, É. (2012a). *La Bataille de l'Autisme*. Paris: Navarin.

Laurent, É. (2012b). Autism and Psychosis: Further Dialogue with Robert and Rosine Lefort. *Psychoanalytical Notebooks*, *25*, 11–26.

Lefort, R., & Lefort, R. (1994). *Birth of the Other*. Oxfort, UK: University of Illinois Press.

Lefort, R., & Lefort, R. (2003). *La Distinction de L'Autisme*. Paris: Seuil.

Lefort, R., & Lefort, R. (2010). L'Enfant au Loup et le Président. In J. Miller (Ed.), *L'Avenir de L'Autisme Avec Rosine et Robert Lefort* (pp. 143–151). Paris: Navarin.

Maleval, J.-C. (2003). L'Objet Autistique à la Machine: Les Suppléances du Signe. *Fabienne Hulak, Pensée Psychotique et Création de Systèmes, ERES « Hors Collection »*, 197–217.

Maleval, J.-C. (2009). *L'Autiste et sa Voix*. Paris: Seuil.

Maleval, J.-C. (2011). Langue Verbeuse, Langue Factuelle et Phrases Spontanées chez l'Autiste. *La Cause Freudienne, 2*, 77–92.

Maleval, J.-C. (2012). Why the Hypothesis of an Autistic Structure? *Psychoanalytical Notebooks, 25*, 27–49.

Maleval, J.-C. (2015). Extension du Spectre de l'Autisme. *L'évolution Psychiatrique, 90*, 764–781.

Maleval, J.-C. (2018a). Nourrir l'Intelligence de l'Autiste ou Mobiliser sa Jouissance. *La Cause Du Désir, 98*(1), 59–66.

Maleval, J.-C. (2018b). Da Estrutura Autista. *Revista ASEPHallus de Orientação Lacaniana, 13*(26), 4–38.

Miller, J. (2010). *L'Avenir de L'Autisme*. Paris: Navarin.

Peirce, C. S. (1977). *Semiotic and Significs*. Bloomington, IN: Indiana University Press.

Peirce, C. S. (1982). On a New List of Categories. In *Writings of Charles S. Peirce: A Chronological Edition, Volume 2 (1867–1871)* (Vol. 2, pp. 49–58). Bloomington, IN: Indiana University Press.

Pickett, E., Pullara, O., O'grady, J., & Gordon, B. (2009). Speech Acquisition in Older Nonverbal Individuals with Autism: A Review of Features, Methods, and Prognosis. *Cognitive and Behavioral Neurology, 22*(1), 1–21.

Redmond, J. (2014). *Ordinary Psychosis and the Body: A Contemporary Lacanian Approach*. London: Palgrave Macmillan.

Robins, D. L., Fein, D., & Barton, M. (2009). *Modified Checklist for Autism in Toddlers: Revised with Follow-Up*. Retrieved from http://www.mchatscreen.com

Sacks, O. (1996). *An Anthropologist on Mars: Seven Paradoxical Tales*. New York: Vintage.

Tammet, D. (2007). *Born on a Blue Day: Inside the Extraordinary Mind of an Autistic Savant*. London: Hodder & Stoughton.

Tustin, F. (1972). *Autism and Child Psychosis*. London: Hogarth Press.

Tustin, F. (1992). *The Protective Shell in Children and Adults*. London: Karnac Books.

Wallis, C. (2010, February 6). Temple Grandin on Temple Grandin. *Time Magazine*.

Williams, D. (1998). *Nobody Nowhere: The Remarkable Autobiography of an Autistic Girl*. London: Jessica Kingsley Publishers.

Williams, D. (2015). *Somebody Somewhere: Breaking Free from the World of Autism*. Portland, OR: Broadway Books.

8

Autism as a Singular Subjective Structure

The first to call for a re-articulation of the psychoanalytic clinic of autism on the basis of the hypothesis of a singular autistic subjective structure were Robert and Rosine Lefort. Beginning their concentrated work with autistic subjects in 1969, in their newly founded *École Expérimentale de Bonneuil-sur-Marne*, the Leforts assembled a body of knowledge that inspired many future Lacanian psychoanalysts to develop the clinic of autism independently from that of neurosis and psychosis. Prompted by the Leforts' intuition, this book has been devoted to further developing this body of knowledge. More specifically, it aimed to substantiate the hypothesis that autism is a unique *mode of being* or, in other words, a singular subjective structure, in line with the three major subjective structures elaborated in psychoanalysis by Freud and Lacan: neurosis, perversion, and psychosis.

In order to substantiate this hypothesis, the unique structural features of autistic subjectivity have been conceptually elaborated and developed. These features were compared to those of the neurotic and the psychotic structures in order to provide sufficient evidence attesting to the singularity of autism. The aforementioned elaboration found its point of departure in the notion of a unique *constitutive exclusion* and was developed in

© The Author(s) 2020
L. S. Brenner, *The Autistic Subject*, The Palgrave Lacan Series,
https://doi.org/10.1007/978-3-030-50715-2_8

relation to the psychoanalytic understanding of the subject. Accordingly, the most defining characteristics of a subjective structure were attributed to the constitutive psychic mechanism of exclusion at its origin. In particular, three psychic mechanisms of *constitutive exclusion*, elaborated by Freud and Lacan, were designated as the underlying cause determining the singularity of three corresponding subjective structures—repression (*Verdrängung*) for neurosis, disavowal (*Verleugnung*) for perversion, and foreclosure (*Verwerfung*) for psychosis. In the same manner, in order to distinguish the defining characteristics of autism, the constitutive psychic mechanism at its origin (*Autistic foreclosure*) was thoroughly analyzed, and three decisive factors of its characterization and distinction were emphasized. These factors were (1) its position in the original model of repression presented by Freud, (2) the exact nature of its object of exclusion, and (3) the unique mode of linguistic functionality that it enables. Let us then summarize the conclusions of these inquiries in the following section with the aim of underlining the singularity and irreducibility of the mechanism of *autistic foreclosure* and, as a result, of the *autistic subjective structure* itself.

Conclusions

Singular Position in the Model of Repression

In Chap. 3, I explicated the model of repression as comprised of a *primordial constitutive repression* ("primal repression") that is sequentially followed by *repression as a defense mechanism* ("secondary repression"). I also argued that while secondary repression is attributed solely to the constitution of the neurotic subjective structure (i.e., *neurotic repression*), primal repression is a psychic mechanism that takes part in the constitution of all subjective structures. In accordance with Freud, I identified two corresponding procedures internal to primal repression—an *expulsion* (*Ausstoßung*) and an *affirmation* (*Bejahung*). Based on this distinction, in Chap. 4, I classified both *neurotic repression* and *psychotic foreclosure* as mechanisms relying on the inscription of the signifier of the

Name-of-the-Father. In this sense, I situated both mechanisms in the model of repression sequentially following the instatement of the minimal relationship to the symbolic by the signifier of the Name-of-the-Father.

In Chap. 5, I demonstrated that *Ausstoßung* is a mechanism that can also be divided into a negative and an affirmative aspect—a primordial "expulsion" and an affirmative signifying function. Based on this distinction, I described *psychotic foreclosure* as a mechanism that sequentially follows *Bejahung*, radically excludes the signifier of the Name-of-the-Father, and thus prevents the level of signification necessary for the structuration of the neurotic subjective structure, and brings about the structuration of psychosis.

- *Ausstoßung* ⇒ *Bejahung* ⇒ *psychotic foreclosure* ⇒ psychosis

Correspondingly, I described *autistic foreclosure* as a mechanism that sequentially follows the affirmative aspect of *Ausstoßung*, hinders the functioning of *Bejahung*, and thus prevents the level of minimal relationship to the symbolic necessary for the structuration of both the neurotic and psychotic subjective structures, and brings about the structuration of autism.

- *Ausstoßung* ⇒ *autistic foreclosure* ⇒ autism

Accordingly, parallel to Lacan's definition of *psychotic foreclosure* as a mechanism that opposes *Bejahung* in the model of repression (É, p. 323), I have described *autistic foreclosure* as a mechanism that opposes *Ausstoßung*. It is this decisive distinction of the level on which *autistic foreclosure* functions that strongly attests to *autistic foreclosure* being a singular constitutive mechanism irreducible to the purview of *neurotic repression* or *psychotic foreclosure* (see Fig. 5.3 in Chap. 5).

Singular Object of Exclusion

In Chap. 3, I explicated the exact nature of the psychic object excluded in *neurotic repression*. In Freudian terms, I illustrated how, in *neurotic repression*, an idea that comes into distressing opposition to the ego is detached from its corresponding quota of affect, expelled from consciousness and confined to the unconscious. In Lacanian terms, these "ideas" correspond to the signifiers that compose the signifying material of the symbolic order itself. In this sense, according to Lacan's interpretation of *neurotic repression*, a signifier that comes into "conflict" with the ego is excluded from consciousness into the unconscious. This signifier then goes on to form new relationships with other repressed signifiers in the unconscious. In Chap. 4, I also indicated the exact nature of the psychic object excluded in *psychotic foreclosure*. In Freudian terms, it gained two designations: first, as an idea alongside its corresponding affect and any other aspect of reality to which they are related; second, as all libidinal cathexes invested in objects in the exterior world (object-libido). Ultimately, in Lacanian terms, it was designated solely as the primordial signifier of the Name-of-the-Father.

In Chap. 5, I demonstrated that the psychic object radically excluded in *autistic foreclosure* cannot be reduced to any of the objects mentioned above. Specifically, I argued that while *autistic foreclosure* does hinder the functioning of *Bejahung* and, as a result, hinders the inscription of the signifier of the Name-of-the-Father, this signifier cannot be regarded as its direct object of exclusion. Accordingly, in Chap. 6, I proposed three different psychic objects that can be designated as the object radically excluded in *autistic foreclosure*: (1) the unary trait as the precursor of pure difference, (2) the rim as the symbolic designator of the hole, and (3) the rim as the symbolic marker of the circuit of the invocatory drive. All these psychic objects are engendered on a level that precedes the minimal relationship to the symbolic that is enabled by the inscription of the signifier of the Name-of-the-Father. Accordingly, they cannot be reduced to or identified with this signifier. It is this strong distinction of the object radically excluded in *autistic foreclosure* that provides further conceptual support for *autistic foreclosure* being a singular constitutive mechanism irreducible to the purview of *neurotic repression* or *psychotic foreclosure*.

Singular Mode of Linguistic Functionality

In Chap. 3, I presented a structural analysis of the exact mode of linguistic functionality enabled by *neurotic repression*. I associated this mode with a closed semantic network that is constituted on the basis of an exclusion of an element from the network. The exclusion of this element instates it as an external limit point in relation to which all other elements internal to the network are designated. This form of *external* limitation enables this semantic network to consistently and coherently convey meaning *internal* to its domain. Correspondingly, I noted that, in Lacan's account of neurosis, it is the signifier of the Name-of-the-Father that marks this *extimate* limit point and enables the consistent and coherent functioning of the symbolic order (SVII, p. 139). By doing so, it authorizes the following linguistic features: it preserves the consistency of the relationship between the signifier and the signified; it functions as an anchoring point for the subject in the symbolic order; it allows the subject to "inhabit" language and make it one's own; finally, it enables language to mediate the subject's jouissance.

In Chap. 4, I described the mode of linguistic functionality enabled by *psychotic foreclosure*. According to Lacan, when the signifier of the Name-of-the-Father is radically excluded, many of the symbolic features presented above are altered, putting the consistency and coherence of the symbolic order at risk. It withholds the authoritative function of the symbolic law and renders the symbolic order as a confused sentimental mass of discourse, a mass in which signifier and signified present themselves in a completely divided form. Finally, it prevents the subject from "inhabiting" language and interferes with its capacity to mediate the subject's jouissance.

In Chap. 7, I demonstrated that the mode of linguistic functionality enabled by *autistic foreclosure* is radically divorced from the domain of the signifier. This entails the subject's refusal of alienation in the signifier and impedes the most initial forms of identification enabling access to the symbolic order. Therefore, I argued that autistic linguistic functionality is dependent on the functioning of the sign. Unlike the signifier, which engenders meaning through its differential relationships with other

signifiers and has no exterior referent, the sign entails a permanent relationship with a single referent (semiotic object) and has no relationship
with other signs. Accordingly, when acquiring the linguistic capacities
rooted in the functioning of the sign (i.e., when constructing the "supplementary" or "synthetic" Other) the autistic subject is disposed to a unique
mode of linguistic functionality, a functionality fundamentally distinct
from the one that neurotic and psychotic subjects are disposed to. This
unique form of autistic "sign language" lacks the dynamic nature of the
symbolic order due to its dependence on the rigid and permanent relationship between a sign and its referent. In this sense, it is akin to a "code
language" in which one word has only one meaning. This is why it is a
poor vehicle for the signification of ambiguities, general concepts, and
abstractions. Moreover, it lacks the capacity to mediate jouissance and is
thus rendered as a "factual language," delivered through a "striking monochord tone," flat and devoid of affect, in which the enunciative presence
of the subject is erased. It is this clear distinction of the mode of linguistic
functionality enabled by *autistic foreclosure* that provides final conceptual
support for *autistic foreclosure* being a singular constitutive mechanism
irreducible to the purview of *neurotic repression* or *psychotic foreclosure*.

Summary of the Line of Argument

Taking into account (1) the unique level of its functioning in the model
of repression, (2) the distinct nature of the psychic object it excludes, and
(3) the singular mode of linguistic functionality enabled by it, I come to
the final conclusion: *autistic foreclosure is a singular psychic mechanism of
constitutive exclusion irreducible to any of the other constitutive mechanisms
elaborated by Freud and Lacan.* On the basis of this conclusion and
because, in psychoanalysis, the singularity of a subjective structure is
determined by the singularity of the constitutive psychic mechanism at
its origin, I necessarily infer that *autism is a singular subjective structure,
irreducible to any of the other subjective structures elaborated by Freud and
Lacan—neurosis, perversion, and psychosis.*

Contributions to the Field of Autism Research

In this book I have attempted to provide a detailed and accurate account of the Lacanian psychoanalytic understanding of autism. However, this book also aims to contribute to the understanding of autism by progressing beyond the conceptual confines Lacan and his followers had provided. As to Lacan himself, he had only presented a few explicit remarks on the subject of autism, basically arguing that autistic subjects are in fact subjects of language. In this book, the unique mode of autistic linguistic functionality has been developed and explicated beyond its initial designation by Lacan, primarily relying on the notion of the primacy of the sign. Rosine and Robert Lefort were the first to hypothesize that autism is a singular subjective structure. This contention was based on their work with autistic subjects from which they deduced a multiplicity of autistic subjective features that could not be reduced to the scope of a theory on psychosis. Nevertheless, the Leforts mostly concentrated on more severe cases of autism and did not provide a comprehensive account of autistic subjective features that characterize subjects that are rigorously invested in language. In this book, the singularity of the autistic subjective structure was not strictly substantiated on the basis of the symptoms and behaviors of autistic subjects but on the basis of the structural elaboration of the constitutive psychic mechanism that is their underlying cause—*autistic foreclosure*. This endeavor provided a framework that can account for the full "spectrum" of autistic symptomatology. Being closest in form to Maleval's account of autism, the framework presented in this book provided several augmentations to his work. Firstly, by articulating it in structural terms associated with the functioning of autistic foreclosure. Second, by developing an integrative account that offers several alterations in its conceptual dictum putting an emphasis on the autistic recourse to the sign. In regard to Laurent's work on the subject of autism, this book has provided further conceptual foundations that reinforce its explanatory depth, especially by focusing the discussion of the foreclosure of the hole on the figure of the rim. Finally, this book has provided an original designation of autistic foreclosure in terms of its positioning in the model of primal repression and an original interpretation of the

Freudian account of *Ausstoßung*. All of the above enabled this book to provide a stronger case for the designation of autism as a singular subjective structure.

The designation of autism as a singular subjective structure can contribute to the field of autism research on several levels. Firstly, it prescribes a *realist* approach to autism, addressing it as a knowledge-independent phenomenon that underlies and conditions both its behavioral manifestations and its symptomatic categorization. In this sense, it goes against constructivist perspectives that would designate autism as a signifier that haphazardly groups together independently existing and treatable conditions (physiological or psychic). It bestows on autism an intrinsic quality, manifest in an underlying *subjective structure* through which the whole of autistic psychic reality is constructed.

Secondly, this designation ascribes the singularity of the *autistic subjective structure* to the defining characteristics of the constitutive psychic mechanism at its origin—*autistic foreclosure*. Through this ascription, it avoids reducing the essence of autism to autistic symptoms which are diverse, multifaceted, manifest in varied degrees and hard to essentially demarcate. In contrast, the essence of autism is identified with the structural conditions that enable autistic symptoms to manifest in the first place. Accordingly, a framework is provided in which the singularity of autism can be recognized and not conflated with other underlying conditions that have similar overlapping symptoms.

Thirdly, the designation of autism as a subjective structure provides an alternative to its determination as a mental or physical disorder. In psychoanalysis, all subjective structures are, in a sense, pathological and entail some form of suffering. One must admit that autistic subjects endure a great deal of suffering when they face the demands of the internal and external world. Nevertheless, there are many other inherent aspects defining autistic subjectivity that are not contained in the relationship between a pathology and the suffering it produces. The approach proposed in this book provides the means to address the singularity of autism without reducing it to a disorder that strictly engenders suffering. It addresses autism as a singular *mode of being*, fundamentally linked to one's identity and most basic practices of existence, a mode through which—in a singular way—human suffering also manifests.

Not reducing autism to a disorder goes hand in hand with not defining it in terms of a *negation* of a different category—for example, *non*-adaptivity or *dis*-function. This warrants an *affirmative* designation of autism according to features that are *not* subordinated to other clinical categories. In other words, it necessitates the apprehension of autism in affirmative terms singular to its own domain. Autism is commonly studied today mainly with a focus on the disabilities and handicaps it gives rise to. Accordingly, some of the most widespread theories of autism determine it in terms of a *deficit* of empathy (Baron-Cohen & Wheelwright, 2004), *impairment* of executive cognitive capabilities (Pennington & Ozonoff, 1996), *weak* central coherence or *deficit* in central processing of sensory data (Happé & Frith, 2006), and even as *mind-blindness* (Baron-Cohen, 1997; Frith, 2001). Designating autism on the basis of its affirmative features problematizes the way it is addressed in these scientific studies. It calls for scientists to implement their research with an aim toward explaining what autism *is*—to provide empirical evidence for the singularity of its internal functioning and not its dependence on the failure of other mental or physiological faculties. Correspondingly, scientists should aim to explicate the unique emotional states autistic individuals experience, their distinctive sensory processing abilities, and the power of the autistic *mind* to *see* some things that others just cannot see.

On the same note, the designation of autism in this book problematizes some conventional clinical approaches. Initially, by attesting to four distinct levels of linguistic functionality available to autistic subjects, it supplies the clinic of autism with four different trajectories on the "autistic linguistic spectrum"; each trajectory necessitates a different clinical approach that is oriented toward a distinct level of linguistic facilitation. As I have explained in Chap. 7, clinicians are expected to facilitate and support autistic individuals in the transition between these four levels in the following ways: to develop their linguistic capacities enabling them to cope with and inhabit their world; to use language in the mediation of jouissance; and to find a unique form of satisfaction that can enable their incorporation into the social bond. Moreover, by designating autism as a legitimate *mode of being*—that is, something that someone *is* in every respect and not something that someone contingently *has*—the clinic of autism is re-oriented toward supporting individuals in *being* autistic and not "curing" them of autism. Accordingly, this designation adheres to a *normative* perspective promoted by many outspoken autistic individuals who explicitly argue that autism is part of who they are and, thus, would never wish to be non-autistic, even if they could (Grandin, 2006; Shapiro, 2006; Sinclair, 1993). Addressing autism as a singular subjective structure necessitates the acceptance of autistic individuals' singularity as the gateway to the alleviation of their suffering and their entry into the social bond. Accordingly, it runs counter to such approaches that aim to condition and normalize the behavior of autistic individuals such as Applied Behavioral Analysis (ABA). This popular approach aims to train autistic individuals to adopt pre-determined normalized behaviors and neglect non-adaptive behaviors in order to temper their anxiety and help them cope with the demands of everyday life (Bailey & Burch, 2017; Martin & Pear, 2015). Unlike the ABA approach, the framework presented in this book dictates that clinicians acknowledge the capacity of autistic subjects to voluntarily utilize language in the alleviation of their suffering, be attentive to their inventiveness, and understand that therapeutic progress entails the adoption of singular solutions spontaneously developed by each individual. Such an approach can be seen in the case of Joey, where Bettelheim (1959) supports the construction of his unique machine out of objects he spontaneously elects from his environment.

Fourthly, the designation of autism as a singular subjective structure impacts the psychoanalytic understanding of autism. It is important to remember that even in contemporary Lacanian psychoanalytic circles, autism and psychosis are thought to share a number of common symptomatic features. Firstly, both subjective structures entail alterations in the use of language, including the use of neologisms and the application of speech in a non-coherent or non-communicative way. These linguistic alterations bring about crucial transformations in the capacity to mediate jouissance (Declercq, 2002, p. 102; Maleval, 2009, pp. 215–216). Moreover, both structures demonstrate problems with the internalization of the body image in early forms of identification that give rise to the phenomenon of the double (SIII, pp. 145, 194, 209, 240, 277; Laurent, 2012, p. 82; Lefort & Lefort, 2003, pp. 27–34; Maleval, 2009, pp. 109–127, 223). All of the above are related in one way or another to the clinic of the foreclosure of the Name-of-the-Father, which is the clinic of psychosis. Designating autism as a singular subjective structure markedly differentiates autism from psychosis. It situates the psychoanalytic clinic of autism outside its confines—not revolving around an opposition to *Bejahung* but an opposition to *Ausstoßung*. As I will shortly demonstrate, it warrants re-thinking Lacan's definition of the subject of language, the common definition of the unconscious, and the subject's identification in the mirror stage. Otherwise, one of the most pressing polemics against the implementation of psychoanalysis in cases of autism emphasizes that psychoanalysts always "blame the mother." This view is promoted in a variety of media articles that argue that the psychoanalysis of autism is confined to the notion of the "cold mother" (Sauret, Askofaré, & Macary-Garipuy, 2016; Yudell, 2012). It is true that in the history of psychoanalysis some have gone on that route, flirting with this idea. However, I venture to argue that limiting the theoretical richness of psychoanalytic texts having to do with autism—especially in the Lacanian field—to this scope is crudely reductive.[1] Be that as it may, this book presents a rigorous psychoanalytic framework that does not adhere to this motif in any way.

Finally, regarding the significance of the technical work achieved in this book, one has to acknowledge the fact that it is based almost entirely on texts written in French with no English translation. And indeed, the Anglophone academic world, which conducts the lion's share of current research on autism, is utterly oblivious to the conceptual progress achieved in this field by French psychoanalysts. This book articulates and develops some of the contemporary French psychoanalytic notions on the subject of autism in a way that makes it approachable to an English-speaking audience. Therefore, it comes to demonstrate to the Anglophone world that psychoanalysis has much more to say about autism than what is

---

[1] Such reductive readings are many times associated with Bettelheim's book *The Empty Fortress* (1967). In this book he argues that all mothers and fathers display both destructive and loving intentions that affect children at an early stage. The idea that the mother is to blame for the onset of autism is explicitly debased by Bettelheim in the same book when he argues that "it is not the maternal attitude that produces autism, but the child's spontaneous reaction to it" (p. 69).

commonly acknowledged. This way, it opens up the possibility for the dissemination of some of this knowledge in other paradigms in the field of autism research.

More to Develop

The conceptual development of psychoanalytic notions in this book provides many prospects for further research in the field of *psychoanalysis*. Firstly, describing autistic subjects as lacking access to the locus of the signifier problematizes the conventional Lacanian definition of the subject as being represented by a signifier for another signifier (SIX, 27.2.67). While still being subjects of language, autistic subjects do not comply with the above-mentioned definition but only with what Lacan defines as the "most elementary form of subjectivity": "someone who is accessible to a sign" (SIX, 6.12.61). Nevertheless, in this book, autistic subjectivity was not defined as "elementary" but as a singular modality of the structuration of the subject in relation to language. Therefore, an opportunity arises to further question the conventional Lacanian definition of the subject and to consolidate it with the unique mode of linguistic functionality enabled by the recourse to the sign in autism. The incorporation of the sign in the definition of a non-elementary form of subjectivity might extend its explanatory scope.

A second topic that may be fruitful for further research in the field of psychoanalysis involves the common definition of the unconscious. Freud (1915) argues that the constitution of the division between consciousness and the unconscious is established in primal repression (SE XIV, p. 147). Nevertheless, in this book I have argued that, in autism, repression does not function on any level. Accordingly, some questions are posed: what impact does the absence of repression have on the Freudian definition of the unconscious? And, correspondingly, can an unconscious without repression be related to Lacan's description of the psychotic unconscious as that which is brought "out into the open" like an open sky (*à ciel ouvert*) (SIII, p. 59)? Moreover, Lacan argues that the unconscious is structured like a language and is essentially composed of signifiers. Nevertheless, in this book, autism was characterized by a lack of access to the domain of signifiers. While this characterization of autism does not dictate a complete revision of Lacan's definition of the unconscious as being structured like a language, it may warrant some alterations in its definition as functioning according to the laws that govern the interplay between signifiers. Therefore, another interesting question is posed: how does the unconscious function when it is composed of signs?

A third prospect for further research in the field of psychoanalysis concerns the unique mode of autistic identification that Lacan describes as "a single and unique primary identification, with the following names—the void, the dark" (SI, p. 69). The radical failure in the two conventional modes of identification in autism—imaginary and symbolic—necessitates the articulation of the primary identification with the "void" in other terms. Accordingly, the following questions arise: What form of identification does the logic of the sign entail? Is this an identification that can be described as having to do with the register of the real? How can autistic identification with the "void" be situated in the schema of the mirror stage? What kind of mirror is enabled by the "synthetic Other"? And, what kind of image is reflected from it? Furthermore, the "autistic double" is a unique psychic phenomenon that is rooted in the autistic subject's unique mode of identification. It is distinct from the "persecutory double" described by psychotic subjects, as it brings comfort and mobilizes the subject instead of tormenting it. Accordingly, some other questions are raised: What is the function of the autistic double in the subject's identification? What warrants its facilitative nature instead of its persecutory nature? Can the autistic double be considered as a supplement to a body image in the mirror stage? Interestingly enough, in *Seminar I: Freud's Papers on Technique (1953–1954)*, Lacan provides an analysis of the coordinates of the mirror stage on the basis of the case of Little Dick. He discusses the inclination of the mirror as well as the fact that, in the case of Dick, some of the original elements in the schema find no inscription (SI, pp. 140–150). The conclusions reached in this book, as well as Lacan's formulation of the coordinates of the mirror stage in the case of Little Dick, provide good ground for further elaboration of the aforementioned questions regarding identification.[2]

A fourth prospect for further research in the field of psychoanalysis is the notion of autistic spatial perception. Laurent (2012) goes to great length to attest to the fact that autistic subjects only *seem* to suffer from a sensory deficiency. He provides an example of an autistic child who becomes extremely anxious when he sees an airplane flying in the sky, reacting as if it was just beside him (p. 76). Laurent suggests that this example does not demonstrate that the child is suffering from sensory deficiency but rather from a setback in the capacity of the symbolic to mediate spatial perception, a setback that causes a cancelation of distance. In Chap. 6, I have briefly mentioned the association between autistic foreclosure and a theory of spatial separation provided by Burgoyne (2000). Burgoyne argues that the development of autistic linguistic functionality can be associated with a progression between several forms of symbolic separation culminating in "metric space"—a form of spatial construction that is characteristic of neurotic spatial perception. Based on the conclusions reached in relation to the four levels of autistic linguistic functionality, this theory can be developed and thus provide new prospects for the understanding of autistic spatial perception.

Finally, the subject of autistic art is not included in the scope of this book. Nevertheless, many autistic individuals partake in artistic activities and also manage to find satisfaction in them. This leads many practitioners to agree that artistic activities can be a useful tool in the therapy offered to autistic individuals (Schweizer, Knorth, & Spreen, 2014). But what is art without access to the signifier? What is the effect of the primacy of the sign on the materialization of the imaginary in the image? What is the relationship between the artistic object and the autistic object? And, what is the therapeutic factor of the artistic work that autistic individuals partake in? All of these, and more, provide viable prospects for the further investigation of autism in the field of psychoanalysis.

Prospects for further *empirical research* based on the conclusions of this book are vast. These would entail the simplification and translation of

---

[2] This topic, already presented at an international conference (Brenner, 2019), will be tackled in a future publication.

structural and linguistic models presented in this book in a way that would generate new hypotheses that could be empirically studied and tested.[3] For instance, Lacan's distinction between language and speech can provide a good basis for empirical research that could help better understand the radical form of autistic selective mutism and the autistic aversion to the use of the voice. Many autistic subjects find using their voice for the sake of communication to be traumatic. They argue that the experience of their enunciation is unbearable. Nevertheless, we do see many high-functioning autistic individuals who do find ways to use language for their own advantage. In these cases, autistic individuals implement a variety of coping strategies that are employed in an attempt to speak without actively engaging in the "phatic function" (SX, pp. 275–276). Some autistic individuals use a very monotonic voice, devoid of affect; some use a very high-pitched voice; some use dolls, portraying them as the actual enunciator when they speak through them "in-proxy"; and some repeat sentences and words in the exact intonation and order in which they first heard them. All of these are implemented in an attempt to engage the voice in a unique form of speech that solely conveys information and is utterly devoid of the inter-subjective dimension of language (Grandin, 2006). On the basis of the distinction between language and speech, and through the investigation of the diverse coping strategies employed by autistic individuals, an opportunity arises to single out the exact factor that inhibits the incorporation of the subject's thoughts and ideas in its spoken voice.

The split between emotions and the intellect, associated in this book with autistic linguistic functionality, can have an impact on accepted methods through which emotions and thoughts are extracted and measured in empirical studies of autistic individuals. For instance, one common method to score an individual's capacity to understand and relate to other people's states of mind ("theory of mind") is through verbal questionnaires or tasks that require the assembly of a story or a narrative (Baron-Cohen, 2000; Happé, 1995; Ozonoff et al., 1991). These entail

---

[3] This is not a task undertaken in this book. Therefore, the following remarks should be taken as suggestions for further development and should not be taken as detailed engagements with the theoretical frameworks presented.

complex contextual and semantic tasks that necessitate the use of one's intellectual and linguistic capacities in order to convey one's emotions or the understanding of the emotions of others. Low scores on these questioners have brought several major scholars in the field of autism research to argue that autistic subjects have a deficit of empathy (Baron-Cohen & Wheelwright, 2004) and even lack empathy (Barnbaum, 2008). However, many autistic individuals testify to having a strong sense of compassion and a sympathy toward people and animals (Grandin, 2006; Laznik, 2014; Maleval, 2009, p. 125; Stubblefield, 2013). These autistic individuals contend that they do have feelings but find it hard to verbally convey them through a vocalized coherent narrative. The framework developed in this book suggests that the split between emotions and the intellect is an outcome of the autistic recourse to the sign and lack of access to the locus of the signifier. Without the use of signifiers, emotions cannot be "interpreted" and comprehensively transmitted to others or to oneself. The split between emotions and the intellect warrants the development of new methods through which emotions and thoughts are extracted and measured in empirical studies; these would be methods that either (1) take into account the limited capacity of signs to convey emotional states, that is, due to the rigid relationship between sign and referent and the fact that specific signs may only designate a specific emotion in a specific context, or (2) will not attempt to measure emotional states through an intellectual understanding but through alternative means that might convey one's emotions in their immediacy (Black, Barzy, Williams, & Ferguson, 2018).[4]

Finally, one of the leading theories in the field of cognitive psychology, aiming to explain the underlying cause of autism, associates it with a general disintegration of sensory experience (Jolliffe & Baron-Cohen, 1999). In this book, I have argued that the autistic disorganized sensory experience is one of the effects autistic foreclosure has on the subject's mode of access to language. I have claimed that without recourse to the signifier and the Other, sensory experience is not symbolically mediated and the subject experiences it as a constant invasion. I have proposed that the linguistic access to the sign can be used in the treatment of such

---

[4] See Amanda Baggs' video testimony titled "In My Language" (2007).

sensory disorganization. I have argued that by associating between sensations, objects, and linguistic signs, the autistic subject can gain some mastery over jouissance through what is termed the on/off conduct.[5] Accordingly, empirical studies implementing methods of "sensory integration," in which specific experimental apparatuses produce a decrease in sensory arousal, can be used in order to selectively target specific sensations treatable by the on/off conduct. These could entail, for instance, apparatuses of sensory deprivation, implemented in a virtual reality environment. The effects of the on/off conduct can be studied in accordance with its implementation on selected objects that are approached by the subject on separate sensory levels. A unique gesture or sound could be used by the subject to negate a specific sensation; it could then be generalized and associated with different terms or behaviors that the subject can adopt and use outside of the experimental setting.

On a Final Note…

On a final note, I would like to quote Lacan's last recorded words on the subject of autism. While attending a seminar in Geneva in 1975, Lacan responds to a curious practitioner who inquires about the meaning of autism in the context of the *talking cure* (*Redekur*) and wonders if psychoanalysts have anything to say to autistic subjects at all. To this practitioner, Lacan (1989) answers:

> As the name indicates, autistics hear themselves. They hear lots of things. Normally this even leads to hallucination, and hallucinations have always a more or less vocal character. Not all autistics hear voices, but they articulate lots of things … That you have trouble hearing, grasping the point of what they say, doesn't prevent these people from being rather verbose. (pp. 19–20)

With these words, Lacan emphasizes that despite all the challenges autistic subjects face in their relationship with language, they are still *speaking beings*—that is, subjects of language. The goal of this book was

---

[5] On the on/off conduct, see Chap. 7.

to substantiate the singularity of the autistic subjective position in relation to language. In this way, it also aspired to substantiate Lacan's contention presented above that, whether it is in the context of the *talking cure* or social exchange, autistic subjects say lots of things in a singular way and, accordingly, in the end, surely one should listen to what they say—*on the threshold of language.*

Works Cited

Baggs, A. [silentmiaow] (2007, January 15). *In My Language*. [Video File]. Retrieved from https://youtu.be/JnylM1hI2jc

Bailey, J. S., & Burch, M. R. (2017). *Research Methods in Applied Behavior Analysis*. London: Routledge.

Barnbaum, D. R. (2008). *The Ethics of Autism: Among Them, but Not of Them*. Bloomington, IN: Indiana University Press.

Baron-Cohen, S. (1997). *Mindblindness: An Essay on Autism and Theory of Mind*. Cambridge, MA: MIT Press.

Baron-Cohen, S. (2000). Theory of Mind and Autism: A Fifteen Year Review. *Understanding Other Minds: Perspectives from Developmental Cognitive Neuroscience, 2*, 3–20.

Baron-Cohen, S., & Wheelwright, S. (2004). The Empathy Quotient: An Investigation of Adults with Asperger Syndrome or High Functioning Autism, and Normal Sex Differences. *Journal of Autism and Developmental Disorders, 34*(2), 163–175.

Benoist, V. (2011). L'Autre dans L'Autisme. *International Psychology, Practice and Research*, (2), 1–13.

Bettelheim, B. (1959). Joey, A 'Mechanical Boy'. *Scientific American, 200*(3), 116–130.

Bettelheim, B. (1967). *The Empty Fortress*. New York: The Free Press.

Black, J., Barzy, M., Williams, D., & Ferguson, H. (2018). Intact Counterfactual Emotion Processing in Autism Spectrum Disorder: Evidence from Eye-Tracking. *Autism Research*, 1–23.

Brenner, L. S. (2019). *The Mirror in the Real: Autistic Identification in the Mirror Stage, Écrits International Conference*. Pittsburg.

Burgoyne, B. (2000). Autism and Topology. *Drawing the Soul: Schemas and Models in Psychoanalysis, 1*, 190–217.

Declercq, F. (2002). The Real of the Body in Lacanian Theory. *Analysis*, (11), 99–114.

Freud, S. (1915). Repression. In *The Standard Edition of the Complete Psychological Works of Sigmund Freud, Volume XIV (1914–1916): On the History of the Psycho-Analytic Movement, Papers on Metapsychology and Other Works* (pp. 141–158).

Frith, U. (2001). Mind Blindness and the Brain in Autism. *Neuron*, *32*(6), 969–979.

Grandin, T. (2006). *Thinking in Pictures, Expanded Edition: My Life with Autism*. New York: Vintage.

Happé, F., & Frith, U. (2006). The Weak Coherence Account: Detail-Focused Cognitive Style in Autism Spectrum Disorders. *Journal of Autism and Developmental Disorders, 36*(1), 5–25.

Happé, F. G. E. (1995). The Role of Age and Verbal Ability in the Theory of Mind Task Performance of Subjects with Autism. *Child Development, 66*(3), 843–855.

Hyppolite, J. (2006). A Spoken Commentary on Freud's Verneinung. In *Écrits* (pp. 746–754). New York: Norton & Company.

Jolliffe, T., & Baron-Cohen, S. (1999). A Test of Central Coherence Theory: Linguistic Processing in High-Functioning Adults with Autism or Asperger Syndrome: Is Local Coherence Impaired? *Cognition, 71*(2), 149–185.

Lacan, J. (1988). In J.-A. Miller (Ed.), *The Seminar of Jacques Lacan, Book I, Freud's Papers on Technique (1953–1954)*. New-York: Norton & Company.

Lacan, J. (1989). Geneva Lecture on the Symptom. *Analysis*, (1), 7–26.

Lacan, J. (1992). In J.-A. Miller (Ed.), *The Seminar, Book VII, The Ethics of Psychoanalysis (1959–1960)*. New York: Norton & Company.

Lacan, J. (1997). In J.-A. Miller (Ed.), *The Seminar of Jacques Lacan, Book III, The Psychoses (1955–1956)*. New York: Norton & Company.

Lacan, J. (2006). In B. Fink (Ed.), *Écrits*. New York: Norton & Company.

Lacan, J. (2014). In J. Miller (Ed.), *The Seminar of Jacques Lacan, Book X, Anxiety (1962–1963)*. Cambridge, UK: Polity.

Lacan, J. (n.d.). *The Seminar of Jacques Lacan, Book IX, Identification (1961-1962)*. Trans. Gallagher, C. Unpublished.

Laplanche, J., & Leclaire, S. (1972). The Unconscious: A Psychoanalytic Study. *Yale French Studies*, (48), 118–175.

Laurent, É. (2012). La bataille de l'autisme. Paris: Navarin.

Laznik, M. C. (2014). Empathie Émotionnelle et Autisme. In *Autismes et psychanalyses* (pp. 367–393). Toulouse, France: ERES.

Lefort, R., & Lefort, R. (2003). *La Distinction de L'Autisme*. Paris: Seuil.

Maleval, J.-C. (2009). *L'Autiste et sa Voix*. Paris: Seuil.

Maleval, J.-C. (2012). Why the Hypothesis of an Autistic Structure? *Psychoanalytical Notebooks*, (25), 27–49.

Martin, G., & Pear, J. J. (2015). *Behavior Modification: What It Is and How to Do It*. London: Psychology Press.

Ozonoff, S. et al. (1991). Executive Function Deficits in High-Functioning Autistic Individuals. *Journal of Child Psychology and Psychiatry, 32*(7), 1081–1105. Retrieved from http://prism.talis.com/greenwich-ac/items/357735

Pennington, B. F., & Ozonoff, S. (1996). Executive Functions and Developmental Psychopathology. *Journal of Child Psychology and Psychiatry, 37*(1), 51–87.

Sauret, M.-J., Askofaré, S., & Macary-Garipuy, P. (2016). Current Controversies in the Treatment of Autism in France. *Journal of the Circle for Lacanian Ideology Critique, 5*, 127–144.

Schweizer, C., Knorth, E. J., & Spreen, M. (2014). Art Therapy with Children with Autism Spectrum Disorders: A Review of Clinical Case Descriptions on 'What Works'. *The Arts in Psychotherapy, 41*(5), 577–593.

Shapiro, J. (2006). Autism Movement Seeks Acceptance, Not Cures. *Disabilityscoop: The Premier Source for Developmental Disability News*. Retrieved from http://www.npr.org/ templates/story/story.php

Sinclair, J. (1993). Don't Mourn for Us. Our Voice. *Autism Network International*. Retrieved from http://www.autreat.com/dont_mourn.html

Stubblefield, A. (2013). Knowing Other Minds: Ethics and Autism. In J. L. Anderson & S. Cushing (Eds.), *The Philosophy of Autism* (pp. 143–166). Lanham, MD: Rowman & Littlefield Publishers.

Yudell, M. (2012). *Why Are the French Still Blaming Mothers for Autism?* Retrieved November 28, 2018, from http://www.philly.com/philly/blogs/public_health/Why-are-the-French-still-blaming-mothers-for-autism-.html?arc404=true

Index[1]

---

[1] Note: Page numbers followed by 'n' refer to notes.

© The Author(s) 2020
L. S. Brenner, *The Autistic Subject*, The Palgrave Lacan Series,
https://doi.org/10.1007/978-3-030-50715-2